ASSESSMENT AND EVALUATION OF HEALTH AND MEDICAL CARE

ASSESSMENT AND EVALUATION OF HEALTH AND MEDICAL CARE
A methods text

Edited by
Crispin Jenkinson

Open University Press
Buckingham • Philadelphia

Open University Press
Celtic Court
22 Ballmoor
Buckingham
MK18 1XW

and
1900 Frost Road, Suite 101
Bristol, PA 19007, USA

First Published 1997

A catalogue record of this book is available from the British Library

ISBN   0 335 19705 1 (pb)   0 335 19706 X (hb)

Library of Congress Cataloging-in-Publication Data
Assessment and evaluation of health and medical care : a methods text
/ edited by Crispin Jenkinson.
    p. cm.
    Includes bibliographical references and index.
    ISBN 0–335–19705–1 (pbk.). — ISBN 0–335–19706–X (hardback)
    1. Medical care—Evaluation—Methodology. I. Jenkinson, Crispin.
1962– .
    [DNLM: 1. Outcome Assessment (Health Care). 2. Health Services
Research—methods. 3. Epidemiologic Methods. W 84.1 A845 1997]
RA399.A1A88   1997
362.1′068′4—dc21
DNLM/DLC
for Library of Congress   97–2673
                                                                      CIP

Typeset by Graphicraft Typesetters Ltd, Hong Kong
Printed in Great Britain by Biddles Ltd, Guildford and King's Lynn

Contents

Notes on contributors

Helen Doll, BSc, DipStat, MSc, Statistician, Health Services Research Unit, Department of Public Health, University of Oxford.

Ray Fitzpatrick, MA, MSc, PhD, HonMFPHM, Professor, Department of Public Health, University of Oxford, and Fellow, Nuffield College, Oxford.

Crispin Jenkinson, BA, MSc, DPhil, HonMFPHM, Deputy Director, Health Services Research Unit, Department of Public Health, University of Oxford and Fellow, Green College, Oxford.

Tim Lancaster, BA, MSc, MRCP, MRCGP, Senior Clinical Lecturer, ICRF General Practice Research Group, Department of Primary Health Care, University of Oxford.

Richard Layte, BA, MSc, DPhil, Research Officer, Nuffield College, Oxford.

Jonathan Mant, MA, MSc, MFPHM, Clinical Lecturer, Department of Public Health, University of Oxford.

Hannah McGee, BA, PhD, CPsychol, Senior Lecturer, Department of Psychology, Royal College of Surgeons in Ireland, Dublin, Ireland.

Sasha Shepperd, BSc, MSc, Research Officer, Health Services Research Unit, Department of Public Health, University of Oxford.

Chris Silagy, FRACGP, FAFPHM (RACP), PhD, Professor, Department of General Practice, Flinders University of South Australia School of Medicine, Adelaide, Australia.

Sarah Stewart-Brown, MA, PhD, FRCP, FFPHM, Director, Health Services Research Unit, Department of Public Health, University of Oxford.

Katherine Watson, BScEcon, MA, DPhil, Lecturer, School of Social Sciences, University of Birmingham.

Lucie Wright, SRN, BA, MSc, Lecturer in Medical Sociology, School of Life Sciences, Roehampton Institute, London.

Sue Ziebland, BA, MSc, Senior Research Fellow, ICRF General Practice Research Group, Department of Primary Health Care, University of Oxford.

1

Assessment and evaluation of health and medical care: an introduction and overview

Crispin Jenkinson

Introduction

The twentieth century has seen a phenomenal growth in research into health and health care. New medical treatments have been developed at a rate that was inconceivable in previous centuries, and the number and availability of medical facilities, physicians and professionals allied to medicine has grown exponentially. However, despite all of this, evaluation of the efficacy of treatments remains an area of considerable debate. Historically, evaluation relied for the most part upon the intuition and subjective assessments of health professionals who, it was assumed, were capable of assessing the intended objectives and success of treatment. Often such assessments were based on personal experience and clinical anecdotes (Holland 1983). This traditional, and rather unscientific, manner of evaluation has fallen from favour with many who believe that rigorous research is required to ascertain the effectiveness of treatments. Important factors that have stimulated the move towards such evaluation have been the fear that many procedures are of no benefit, and may even be harmful, and the growing awareness that resources are limited and that provision of health care must be made within financial constraints. Consequently, evaluation should determine which treatments work and which should be provided. However, there is no one simple way to evaluate health and medical treatments. The purpose of this book is to provide a critical introduction to the most commonly used forms of evaluation used by health services researchers and epidemiologists. It documents a number of quite distinct research methodologies, providing examples of their application, and is intended to give the reader a sense of the variety of methods at the disposal of researchers and the pros and cons of these different approaches.

The need to evaluate medical care is not new. Indeed, the method of evaluation often seen as the 'gold standard' in terms of scientific rigour, the clinical trial, dates back to the eighteenth century when Lind, in his classic study aboard the *Salisbury*, evaluated six treatments for scurvy on 12 patients (Bull 1959). He found that patients in the group that were given oranges and lemons recovered quickly. However, while the need for evaluation has always been present the adoption of a scientifically rigorous basis for this evaluation has been slow to gain universal recognition. Perhaps the most famous attempt to stir up interest in providing a scientific basis to health services evaluation was made by Cochrane in his monograph *Effectiveness and Efficiency* (Cochrane 1972). Cochrane argued that the 'development of effective and efficient health services needs hard evidence, preferably based upon randomized trials, that the application of each procedure either alters the natural history of disease in an appreciable proportion of patients or otherwise benefits them at reasonable cost (Cochrane 1972). Cochrane devoted his monograph to developing this position. However, as Ian Russell recently remarked, powerful though his argument is for rigorous health services evaluation, it does leave responsibility for defining the task precisely and for developing appropriate research methods to those who seek to follow Cochrane (Russell 1996).

Evaluation

It has been suggested that decisions about groups of patients are made by some combination of personal values, available resources and evidence (Gray 1997). At present much of the weight of decision making tends to be placed upon values and resources which leads to little more than opinion-based decision making. However, increasingly attention is being paid to evidence derived from research. This evaluation must be both critical and as objective as possible. The purpose of health services research is not simply to determine whether a given treatment works, but to estimate the benefits and costs of implementing the policy or procedure of interest. Benefits and costs in this instance refer to the clinical, social, economic and system-wide impact of the policy or procedure. Consequently, for medical evaluation to be meaningful it requires expertise from a wide variety of fields; medicine, statistics, economics, sociology and psychology. From this point of view a treatment assessed by trial that is found to be successful can, for example, only be regarded as such if it produces an outcome that is beneficial to quality of life (and possibly also extends it), and patient satisfaction and yet does so without being prohibitively expensive. Evidence-based health care requires that the best information is available and this will come not only from trials but also from non-experimental 'observational' data.

The breadth of methods

One thing that those engaged in health services research and epidemiology do not lack is a variety of methods, but the dominant methodology tends to be the randomized controlled trial. Chapter 2 by Shepperd and colleagues documents the principles of trial design, highlighting the benefits as well as the potential pitfalls in this area. Insufficient attention to sample size and appropriate outcomes can lead to results of trials being at best meaningless and at worst actively harmful. The chapter also explores the use of trial designs to assess new ways of providing care in the community. Many have argued, both from positions in government and within the health services, that placing care into the community can reduce costs without adversely affecting the quality of treatment or the outcomes of treatment. One such initiative is the notion of 'hospital at home', in which patients may receive all their care in the home, or are discharged to home early and receive some of their care in the home setting. Health professionals visit the home and provide treatment and, some believe, this leads to cost savings. However, despite the introduction of such schemes throughout the world precious little evidence exists to support the claim that they are likely to lead to the same outcomes as hospital care at a cost saving.

While undertaking a trial of such an intervention poses considerable logistical and practical difficulties such an undertaking is necessary due to the widespread, yet unfounded belief, that hospital at home schemes will be an important aspect of medical care in the future. The chapter discusses the problems of setting up such an evaluation. However, the dominance of the trial, with a 'hard' end-point such as death, has tended to place other methods and outcomes into a rather second class position. This is unfortunate given that many questions posed in health care and medicine are largely unconcerned with death, or even with selecting between treatments. For example, the randomized controlled trial cannot easily be used to evaluate long-term outcomes or rare events.

In Chapter 3, Mant and Jenkinson document the use of observational techniques (the case control study and cohort study). These methodologies have been used to explore, for example, the relationship between smoking and lung cancer and the pill and breast cancer. Furthermore, to fully understand the impact of health promotion messages and to gain data on the general health and well being of the population it is necessary to undertake social surveys.

While the social survey can rarely provide a means of assessing therapies it is an invaluable tool for providing a description of a population and consequently providing important information as to the factors that influence health and well-being. In Chapter 4, Layte and Jenkinson outline the principles of survey design and take a practical example to show the potential limitations of this method.

The two following chapters, 5 and 6, discuss important aspects of health care that, traditionally, have not been systematically measured in the health care system; Jenkinson and McGee discuss the part played by health status measures in the assessment of health and medical interventions. Chapter 5 places emphasis on the manner by which measures are validated and then selected for inclusion in studies. While there seems to be general agreement on the importance of measuring health related quality of life there is considerable debate as to the best measures to use; it is important that research carefully considers the basis on which outcome measures of this form are chosen. It is imperative that researchers understand the operating characteristics of any given measure and consider the possible impact these may have upon their use with any specific patient group; simply selecting a measure without due consideration could mean that it taps areas inappropriate for a selected group or is insufficiently sensitive to change for use with specific patient groups.

Methodological problems and limitations are also discussed in Chapter 6 by Fitzpatrick on patient satisfaction. He argues that an important role exists for standardized measures of patient satisfaction, but that this should not be explored at the expense of more in-depth qualitative methods for assessing satisfaction.

The potential value of such qualitative methods is discussed by Ziebland and Wright in Chapter 7. Taking observational techniques and in-depth interviewing as examples of qualitative design, they highlight the potential benefits that this method of research can have over what are sometimes seen as more 'scientific' approaches. Qualitative methods, they argue, can help to minimize the disparity between what people say they do and what they actually do. However, qualitative research must, like all forms of research, be undertaken rigorously for the results to be meaningful. The authors document some of the procedures that should be followed to ensure that qualitative data can withstand critical scrutiny.

An important aspect of health care evaluation relates to costs and benefits. Issues of rationing, prioritization and cost containment are now fundamental issues in the provision of health care throughout the world. There is a greater demand for health care services than available resources can meet, and with the introduction of new therapies, drugs and technology the demand for health care continues to rise. A central part of evaluation, therefore, should consider the costs of treatment and the opportunity costs of selecting one form of treatment over another, or, perhaps more controversially, one patient group over another.

The issues of economic assessment of health care are considered by Watson who, in Chapter 8 outlines the different methods of economic assessment and considers attempts to put economic principles into practice in the arena of health care. Issues concerning the costs and benefits of a health service activity are also considered in Chapter 9 by Stewart-Brown, who discusses the distinct problems surrounding screening programmes. While screening programmes are obviously not a research methodology in themselves they highlight some of the practical, ethical and financial difficulties that face health care providers and purchasers.

The final chapter by Lancaster and colleagues discusses the principles of overviews and meta-analysis. It is striking to think that had the technique of meta-analysis been adopted to assess the value of thrombolysis for myocardial infarction in the 1960s and 1970s life-saving treatment could have been given to thousands of patients. The importance of systematic reviews and meta-analysis cannot be underestimated and they are important methodologies for the assessment of treatment regimes in health and medical care. They are perhaps the most recent addition to a comprehensive tool-kit of methods available to health researchers.

This textbook is intended to introduce students and health professionals to the wide variety of methodologies available: to their benefits and limitations, and to some of the products of their application. It is a textbook that draws on a very wide range of knowledge and expertise, with contributions from those trained in medicine, public health, statistics, psychology, economics and sociology. For evaluation of health and medical care to be successful this wide range of expertise is necessary. It is hoped that this book highlights the breadth of the field of health and medical evaluation, and provides some insight into the difficulties and challenges of this important area of research.

References

Bull, J.P. (1959) The historical development of clinical therapeutic trials, *Journal of Chronic Diseases*, 10: 218–48.

Cochrane, A. (1972) *Effectiveness and Efficiency: Random Reflections on Health Services*. London: Nuffield Provincial Hospitals Trust.

Gray, J.A.M. (1997) *Evidence Based Health Care. How to Make Health Policy and Management Decisions*. London: Churchill Livingstone.

Holland, W. (1983) Introduction, in W. Holland (ed.) *Evaluation of Health Care.* Oxford: Oxford University Press.

Russell, I. (1996) Methods of health services evaluation: the gospel of Archie Cochrane after 25 years, *Journal of Health Services Research and Policy*, 1: 114–15.

2

Randomized controlled trials

**Sasha Shepperd, Helen Doll and
Crispin Jenkinson**

Introduction

The randomized controlled trial (RCT) is generally regarded as the most
scientifically rigorous method of testing hypotheses available in epidemiology and health services research. The basic principles of this study design
are simple. An RCT is a longitudinal study in which the participants are
randomly allocated into groups, usually called 'study' and 'control' groups.
In its simplest form, patients in the study group will receive a therapeutic
procedure while those in the control group will not, or alternatively those
in the study group will receive a new medication and those in the control
group an established medication. The strength of randomization is that
both known and unknown confounders are likely to be distributed equally
among the groups. The two main reasons for using randomization are to
minimize bias, and to produce a sample that is representative of the population from which the patient group is drawn.

RCTs are increasingly seen as the most precise and informative method
of resolving uncertainties regarding the merit of health care interventions
(Chalmers *et al.* 1992). Small or moderate differences can be difficult to
establish reliably from observational studies such as cohort studies or case
control studies (see Chapter 3), since the magnitude of the observed effect
of the treatment or procedure may be about the same as the amount of
uncontrolled confounding. Most often the effects of therapeutic or preventive measures are small to moderate in size. However, such effects can be
extremely important when viewed in terms of a population.

Principles of randomized controlled trials

The distinguishing feature of the RCT is that individuals, or units, are randomly allocated to groups. Randomization should ensure that each participant has the same chance of receiving each of the possible treatments, whether they be active treatments or placebo. Neither the individual allocating the treatment, nor the participant, can determine in advance which treatment the subject will receive (Pocock 1983). Providing the sample size is large enough to reduce sampling error, randomization can prevent confounding with the independent variables by ensuring they are evenly distributed between the two groups.

Two different approaches, described as explanatory and pragmatic, can be applied to RCTs (Schwartz and Lellouch 1967). In general an explanatory trial will seek to determine whether a given treatment is *efficacious*, i.e. whether it works under ideal laboratory conditions. The outcome measures used to evaluate treatment in such trials are generally physiological measures. On the other hand, pragmatic trials attempt to determine the *effectiveness* of a treatment in clinical practice (Russell 1996). The approach adopted is determined by the aim of the trial. Patients recruited to explanatory trials differ from one another only in terms of the treatment they receive. For example, they may receive either active treatment in the form of a new drug, or inactive treatment in the form of a placebo (i.e. an inert substance that, while appearing similar to the active treatment, is intended to have no therapeutic effect). Contextual factors such as the timing of the treatment, diet, and additional care are controlled or fixed to obtain optimal conditions. In pragmatic trials, these contextual factors are not fixed and ordinary current practice may be adhered to. Approaches to selection criteria also differ, with explanatory trials recruiting a more homogeneous population than pragmatic trials. However, care must be taken in pragmatic trials not to recruit a study population that is too heterogeneous, as the population then becomes difficult to define and thus limiting the usefulness of the results.

The need for a control group

A control group allows the comparison of treatments. Without a comparison group it is often impossible to judge if the effects of a treatment should be ascribed to the characteristics of the patients or the treatment. A control group provides a point of reference to which the treatment can be compared. However, the control group is of little use if it does not resemble the treatment group in all ways, other than the treatment itself. Dissimilar groups can occur if patients are selected in different ways for each of the groups to be compared. Providing that a sufficient number of subjects are recruited, randomization can ensure that the characteristics of patients in the comparison group or groups are similar.

Random allocation

The key to successful randomization is that each patient has a known chance of being given each treatment, but the treatment groups into which they are allocated cannot be predicted. If this is breached then the validity of the study design is lost as patients in the treatment groups may vary in systematic ways. This may result in treatment groups that are not comparable and distort the association between the intervention and the outcome, leading to an incorrect estimation of effect. Many experiments fail because random assignment is not adhered to, or because patients are assigned to treatment groups using a predetermined systematic method (Pocock 1983). Examples of these non-random methods include assigning patients to a treatment group by their date of birth, or their date of admission to hospital, the month of the year, or hospital ID number. The main problem with these predetermined methods is that it can be known in advance into which group patients will be allocated, and this may affect the willingness of certain medical staff to enter people for the trial. Consequently, randomization should be undertaken using a set of random numbers. One option is to use a random number generator on a computer, or alternatively tables of random numbers which are often found in the appendices of statistics books.

There are other methods of assigning treatment groups if randomization is unacceptable to the patient or clinician (Bradley 1993; Silverman and Altman 1996), such as preference trials, where patients select between, for example, competing treatments. However, these modified approaches are non-randomized, and should therefore be treated with caution because of the potential influence of uncontrolled confounders. Brewin and Bradley (1989) argue that in instances where psychological or motivational factors are prominent and influence outcome, randomization may lead to the effect of certain treatment regimes being underestimated. They recommend an alternative design in which patients are allocated to groups according to their preferred treatment choice. This design, they argue, will provide information about the effects of a treatment under optimal motivational conditions. This method may have the advantage of increasing the number of patients recruited to a trial, and reducing the number of drop outs (Bradley 1993), but its use is limited, as results may, for example, reflect the expectations of patients rather than a true treatment effect. Furthermore, comparisons between self-selected groups are likely to be biased, limiting the extent to which results can be applied to the target population. Indeed, for interventions where patient's have a strong preference it is likely that these motivational factors will have a role to play in the outcome. If groups are weighted by these attributes the estimates of the outcomes will reflect this. If the intervention is only to be offered to patients with a strong preference this is not a problem. However, a more likely scenario is that the results of a trial are to be extrapolated to a population with mixed preferences.

Small trials and randomization

If the trial is not very large then it is possible that the trial groups, even after random allocation, may be unbalanced with regard to factors known to influence treatment response. Thus any difference in outcome between the groups could be attributable to these confounding factors rather than any differential effect of treatment. Although there are statistical methods that can adjust for these confounding factors in the analysis, this may well not be possible if the trial is small: after such adjustment there may not be enough variability left in the data to allow the effects of treatment to be determined with sufficient precision.

Stratified randomization

Stratified randomization is a method which ensures that the treatment groups are balanced with regard to pre-determined potential confounding factors. Thus any difference between the treatments cannot be attributable to treatment group differences in these factors. Randomization takes place within each factor grouping. For example, if it is clear that age will influence the response to treatment then randomization would take place within certain pre-determined age groupings, or strata, such as <30, 30–40, 40+ years. Similarly, if it is also known that the sex of the patient is also likely to influence treatment response then more strata can be created to include this factor: <30 and male, <30 and female, 30–40 and male, 30–40 and female, and so on. In practice, a separate randomization list would be prepared for each stratum before the trial began. This list should be balanced in that after a certain number of patients (referred to as the block size) have been randomized within each stratum, an equal number of patients have been allocated to each treatment. This is called restricted randomization and, provided the trial is large enough in relation to the block size, it ensures balance of the different patient factors across the treatments. The method is often referred to as random permuted blocks within strata.

Minimization

Minimization is another method of randomization adopted when a trial is small and the number of patient strata large. Minimization allocates individuals to a treatment group in a way that ensures that the percentage of subjects in each overall factor grouping, rather than in each particular stratum, is similar in each of the treatment groups. For instance, in the example given above, the groups would be similar with regard to the percentage male and female, and the percentage in each age group, but not with regard to particular combinations of these factors. In practice, this is often the sort of balance across the treatment groups that is most relevant. The first patient is randomized using simple randomization. Subsequent patients are allocated to the group that has the smallest number of individuals with the particular features of the patient to be randomized. Thus, if a male patient aged between 30 and 40 years is to be randomized, then the number of male patients plus the number of all patients aged 30–40 would be calculated for each group (note that this will give a combined total larger than the number of patients in the trial). If the treatment groups have the same number of such individuals, then simple randomization is used. (Further details of this and other randomization methods can be found in Pocock 1983.)

Avoiding bias

Bias occurs in a study if there is a systematic error in collecting or inter-preting data. Bias can be categorized as selection bias or information bias. Selection bias refers to the process of identifying the study population. Information, or observation, bias includes any systematic error in the meas-urement of information on exposure or outcome.

Selection bias is unlikely to occur in a randomized controlled trial at the point of recruitment as each patient has an equal chance of being allocated to one of the treatment groups, providing the randomization schedule is adhered to. However, bias may occur due to non-response or loss to follow -up if patients drop out of the study. Information, or observation, bias can occur if the investigator assessing the outcome is not blinded to the group the patient has been allocated to, or if the patient is aware of the treatment they received. This is a problem for some pragmatic trials where there is no placebo equivalent for the control group, and therefore it is unlikely the investigator assessing the outcome will be blind to the assigned treatment. Knowing the participant's treatment group may result in the assessor sys-tematically soliciting, recording, or interpreting information from study participants in a biased manner.

Blinding

Blinding is the most effective way of minimizing the likelihood of any systematic difference in the ascertainment of outcomes between study groups. The observer's judgement may be affected by knowing the treatment that a subject is getting, or by knowledge of previous measurements for that subject. For example, clinicians enthusiasm for a new treatment may well influence their judgement, and the judgement of patients, and lead to over optimistic results. Trials are referred to as double blind if neither the per-son assessing the patient, nor the patient, are aware of the treatment group the patient was allocated to. In some instances even the data analysis is undertaken by someone who is not told into which group patients have been allocated: the person undertaking the analysis will be aware that groups exist but not which are, for example, under active treatment or a placebo. In such instances the trial is 'triple blinded' (i.e. patient, doctor

and researcher do not know, until after the data has been
which group patients are allocated). If only the patient is ui
allocated treatment this is referred to as a single blind trial. Foi
it is impossible for the person assessing the outcomes, or th
to be blind to the allocated treatment (for example, in trials e
effect of different ways of organizing care).

In instances where it is not possible to incorporate blinding of the subject or investigator into the study design it is especially important that other approaches known to minimize observation bias be utilized to increase the degree of objectivity in the measurement of the outcome. This is a particular concern if the outcomes of interest include subjective outcomes such as functional ability, health status or psychological well-being. Methods to minimize observation bias include employing research staff who are independent of the intervention to assess the outcomes. Training research staff using mock interviews and role play, and providing them with clearly written instructions on how to administer questionnaires, or conduct interviews, may help to prevent a researcher unwittingly influencing participant responses. These instructions should include standardized responses to questions about the study; methods for helping participants understand the questions; and, making explicit standard techniques for dealing with errors or missing information. Practical methods for minimizing losses to follow-up and missing data should be included in the study design. For example, simple strategies may include telephone calls and written reminders to non-responders and drop outs. These procedures must be applied equally to all participants to minimize bias effectively.

Intention to treat analysis

Patients entering a trial can go down a number of different routes during the process of the study. They can either adhere to the trial protocol and comply with the treatment to which they have been allocated; they can withdraw from the trial; or, they can cross over to another treatment group. Patients may deviate in less major ways such as lapses with compliance. If trial deviations are a major occurrence then the protocol and trial administration need to be re-examined. A pilot phase of the trial can help to identify these problems and minimize their occurrence when the full trial is being run.

The only safe way to deal with such deviations when analysing trial data is to keep all randomized patients in the trial data set, and analyse groups according to the randomization schedule (Altman 1991; Pocock 1983). Any other approaches to the analysis will potentially introduce bias. Analysing all patients according to the groups to which they were assigned is known as an 'intention to treat analysis'. This approach more closely approximates actual practice: it is unlikely, whatever the practice situation, that all patients will remain on a treatment or care schedule with no changes. For example, a patient experiencing side-effects from a medication may skip doses or discontinue treatment. Likewise the type of care being provided for a patient may change. For example a patient requiring palliative care may begin their course of care at home and then switch to hospital care, or vice-versa.

Sample size and power calculations

One of the most important questions the organizers of an RCT need to answer is the number of patients that should be included in the trial. This is because the trial should be large enough so that it has sufficient probability (or 'power') of declaring a difference of pre-defined magnitude, if one exists, statistically significant. All other factors remaining equal, the smaller the trial, the smaller its power (and consequently the greater its Type II error, β; i.e. the probability of declaring a difference not significant if such a difference exists; power $= 1 - \beta$). Indeed, one of the most common errors in RCTs, and in medical research in general, is for trial organizers to conclude that the lack of any statistically significant difference between the treatments implies that no difference exists (Freiman et al. 1978), whereas the lack of a statistically significant difference could simply be because the trial was not large enough to be able to declare such a difference significant. Thus it is clearly a misuse of resources to conduct a trial that is not large enough have enough power to declare a difference significant at some specified level. It is also, of course, a waste of resources to conduct a trial that includes many more patients than would have been necessary. Moreover, there is an ethical need to prevent more patients than necessary receiving an inferior treatment.

There are statistical formulae available for calculating the size of a trial. These require the trial organizers to select a main outcome measure and specify the minimum difference (a difference that is believed to be of clinical significance) between the treatments that the study should have enough power to be able to detect at a particular significance level, α, say $p < 0.05$. Most statistical textbooks give details of how to calculate sample size, and these calculations can also be performed within particular statistical packages such as Epi-Info and Power.[1]

It should be stressed that in most instances treatment effects are not large and consequently there is often a requirement for large-scale trials (Gray et al. 1995). There has been an unreal expectation among many trialists that treatment effects will be large and consequently relatively small trials have been embarked upon which have had little chance of detecting moderate levels of improvement, which one would realistically assume would be the real outcome of treatment. For example, cancer trials have often included only a few hundred patients and would be unlikely to detect a 10 per cent reduction in mortality (Gray *et al.* 1995). Relatively small differences in a trial can translate into huge effects at the population level. Large 'simple' trials (known as 'mega-trials') are characterized by a large sample size and an easily measured outcome (e.g. death). For example, the ISIS (International Study of Infarct Survival) trials included many thousands of patients. In ISIS-1 16,027 patients were studied and a 15 per cent reduction in hospital deaths was recorded for those patients who received intravenous beta-blockers in the acute phase of a myocardial infarction (MI) (ISIS-1 Collaborative Group, 1986). Such a large sample size is necessary to be certain the effect is not a product of random chance. Consequently, this finding has influenced practice and saves thousands of lives a year around the globe. ISIS trials have also demonstrated the value of streptokinase and aspirin in reducing the likelihood of death after suspected MI, (ISIS-2 Collaborative Group 1988) and the small improvement in mortality gained by administering ACE inhibitor drugs post myocardial infarction in ISIS-4 has led to the suggestion that all eligible MI patients should receive such treatment (Sleight 1994).

Selection of subjects and problems of recruitment

The main aim of recruiting a sample of patients is that they provide an accurate representation of the population from which they were taken. There are five steps to achieving a study population for a trial. These are:

1 defining the study population of interest, i.e. the type of patient to be recruited;
2 developing a set of inclusion criteria;
3 developing a set of exclusion criteria;
4 identifying the setting where patients will be recruited from;
5 designing and establishing a recruitment process whereby eligible patients can be easily identified and referred to the trial.

A balance must be reached in the pursuit of a representative sample of patients. If the requirements are too narrow, creating a homogeneous group, it may not be possible to recruit a sufficient number of patients. If, however, the entry criteria are too wide the results may prove difficult to interpret, as it will not be known to which patients the results apply.

Recruitment procedures can be fraught with difficulties which adversely affect the number of patients recruited to a trial. Conducting a pilot study can help to identify potential barriers to recruitment, and give the investigators an opportunity to put strategies in place to ensure eligible patients are not being missed. A pilot will also help investigators set realistic recruitment targets. Poor recruitment can be due to a number of factors, these include a lack of support for the trial and study collaborators simply forgetting to refer patients to the trial (Peto *et al.* 1993). A lack of support can seriously jeopardize a trial, and if this is identified as a problem it may be that the investigators should opt for another setting. Strategies can be employed to deal with forgetting to refer eligible patients. These include holding seminars for relevant staff; advertising the study in the trial centre(s); providing clear information packs with simple recruitment instructions for people referring patients to the trial; setting recruitment targets; sending out reminders; developing a simple randomization procedure; and, being in regular contact with local collaborators in the trial centre who refer patients to the trial, providing them with regular updates with the trial progress.

Stopping rules

Guidelines should be developed as part of the trial protocol to aid decisions about stopping the trial early, or making modifications. It is usual for a trial to have a monitoring group, independent of the trial investigators, to review interim data. The role of the monitoring group is to protect the welfare of the trial participants. If the data indicates a clear beneficial effect for one treatment over another then early termination of the trial must be considered. However, this is a decision not to be taken lightly as a number of factors need to be considered in advance. These include the strength of the statistical association, the known or postulated mechanisms for the data, and the results available from other studies. Caution must be exercised to avoid prematurely stopping a trial based on emerging trends which may well be transient.

Ethical issues surrounding trial design

Trials are based upon a 'utilitarian' notion of benefit: that is a belief that the results of a trial may indicate the value and efficacy of a treatment, and consequently all those treated should be placed on it. Utilitarianism assumes that the greatest benefit should accrue to the greatest number of people. Consequently, during the trial itself there is a chance that some people may be given treatment that will, once the results of the trial is known, be withdrawn. Alternatively, they may be placed on a placebo treatment but after the trial active treatment may be encouraged. Thus, some people, who are included in trials, may receive less than ideal care. Given a 'reasonable' level of uncertainty many argue that this approach is justified, although a 'deontological' view states that doctors should give the best treatment that they currently believe to be available, and hence entering patients into trials is rarely something they could ethically justify.

The concept of randomization can arouse strong opposition, chiefly because it implies a loss of freedom for both the patient and the doctor.

This is not the case if people are treated as autonomous agents, and are given the opportunity to decide if they wish to become participants in research. If it is agreed a priori that the patients recruited to a trial are capable of being placed in the treatment or control group then randomization is justified on the grounds of uncertainty. If a doctor believes that a patient will benefit from a particular treatment, or type of care, even in the absence of any evidence of benefit, then the doctor should not enter the patient into the trial. Doctors should ideally, therefore, be in a position of 'equipoise' (i.e. they should not believe treatment in one arm of the trial is more likely to be more efficacious than the other(s)). However, trials are usually designed to answer questions where uncertainty exists, and consequently researchers and clinicians may agree to take part in a trial despite the fact they have a hunch about the efficacy of a certain intervention. A particularly striking case is that of the MRC Vitamin Trial designed to evaluate whether vitamin supplements can act to prevent neural tube defects (NTDs), associated with conditions such as spina bifida, in the developing foetus (MRC Vitamin Study Research Group 1991). The trial confirmed the belief that increases in folic acid consumption prior to and during pregnancies can reduce the likelihood of NTDs. Many researchers had argued, however, that the trial was unnecessary, and potentially unethical, because data available from existing cohort studies indicated the value of folic acid (Smithells et al. 1980, 1981; Smithells 1982). Such a view was not universally held, some claiming that without a randomized trial the results were biased and unreliable (Stone 1980). The MRC trial provided evidence of the value of folic acid supplementation, and recruitment was in fact terminated earlier than originally planned due to the size of the beneficial effect. However, in some instances researchers who are uncomfortable with the principle of randomization may take part in a trial and attempt to influence the randomization procedure. Oakley found that midwives participating in a study providing extra social support to pregnant women attempted to influence the group their patients were randomized into. The midwives tried to identify patterns in the allocations, and also tried to persuade the secretary randomizing patients to disclose the randomization code (Oakley 1990). Obviously, such behaviour is contrary to the spirit of randomization and can have deleterious effects on results. Technically, people with such strong views should not agree to take part in the study as they are not in any way in a situation of equipoise between the treatment options.

In some situations, randomization can provide a fair way of allocating treatment; for example when a type of therapy, or form of care, is in short supply. In this situation randomization gives each patient an equal chance of receiving the scarce treatment. A classical example is the trial of streptomycin to treat pulmonary tuberculosis conducted by the Medical Research Council in 1946 (Medical Research Council 1948; Hill 1963). At the time of the trial only small amounts of streptomycin were available, providing an opportunity to conduct a controlled trial to test the value of the treatment. This trial is described as the first clinical trial with a properly randomized control group (Pocock 1983).

The design and conduct of clinical trials should reflect the special circumstances of each study. Ethical considerations should be carefully considered throughout to ensure the patient's well-being is not compromised. The general ethical requirements of clinical research world wide are outlined in the Declaration of Helsinki issued by the World Medical Association in 1960, and revised in 1975, which states that research must conform to accepted scientific principles, must follow a protocol that has been assessed by an independent committee and be undertaken by suitably qualified investigators (the full text of the document is reproduced in Mason and McCall-Smith 1994). All patients entered into trials should consent to taking part and be informed of the purpose of the trial. Patients have the right to refuse being entered into a trial or to provide informed consent and consequently take part.

Informed consent

Informed consent of patients eligible for a given trial is universally needed both to protect the patient's right to self-determination, and to protect investigators in case of litigation. Patients consenting to participate in an RCT consent to receiving any one of the treatment options planned in the study, and to random allocation. They therefore require both information and understanding. However, there is disagreement about the degree of disclosure necessary. Arguments against providing patients with detailed information focus on the emotional distress the patient may experience with full disclosure; the difficulty of the task; and, the loss of confidence in their doctor the patient may experience with the revelation of the uncertainty about the best treatment (Hellman and Hellman 1991; Silverman and Altman 1996). This, it is argued may harm the doctor–patient relationship.

Variations to the standard RCT

Crossover designs

A crossover design is a design in which each patient receives two or more treatments in sequence and outcomes in the same patient are compared; the comparisons are 'within-patient' (Senn 1993). Thus, in a two-treatment, or two-period, crossover study, each patient's response under treatment A is compared with the same patient's response under treatment B, the order of treatments being decided randomly (Senn 1994). In a multi-period crossover design more than two treatments are administered to each patient.

A crossover design is, of course, only applicable when it is possible to treat a patient in more than one way, when the treatment effect is short term, and when the long-term condition of the patient remains fairly stable. For example, a crossover design could be used in evaluating hypertensive therapy and the use of anti-inflammatory drugs for arthritis. A crossover design would clearly not be applicable in the comparison of different surgical procedures.

The advantage of a crossover design is that it can produce results that reach a given level of statistical significance with fewer patients. The reason for this is that crossover designs eliminate between-patient variability. However, so as to avoid bias, it is important in the conduct of a crossover design that certain principles are adhered to. These include random allocation of treatment order to each patient (i.e. whether treatment A is administered first or second), consideration of any possible residual effect of the initial treatment on subsequent treatment (carry-over effect), and any possible period effect. A period effect is when the patients tend to respond preferentially to either the first or a subsequent treatment irrespective of what this treatment actually is. For example, the tendency of patients to naturally improve over time (patients tend to present for treatment when their symptoms are most severe) may be reflected in subsequent treatments appearing more effective. A possible carry-over effect can be overcome by the use of a 'wash-out period', an interval between cessation of one treatment and the starting of another. Carry-over effects are residual effects of previous treatments that may influence the participant's response to the current treatment. Wash-out periods are intended to allow sufficient time between successive treatments for the treatment effects to disappear.

n of I trials

An n of 1 trial is a randomized double blind crossover comparison of an active drug against placebo in a single patient. This study design can be used by a practitioner to evaluate the effect of a treatment on an individual patient in an unbiased manner (Guyatt et al. 1986). A recent study reported the use of n of 1 trials in a general practice setting to evaluate individual treatment regimes for osteoarthritis. The main objective was to evaluate individual patient responses to paracetamol and a non-steroidal anti-inflammatory drug in terms of pain relief and general well-being. The study indicated that paracetamol provided adequate control of symptoms for many of the patients (March et al. 1994). Large-scale trials tend to indicate the benefit of treatments 'on average' whereas n of 1 trials indicate the efficacy (or otherwise) of treatments at the level of the individual patient (Campbell 1994).

Guyatt and colleagues (1986) report using an n of 1 study, using a series of pairs of treatments, to evaluate the effectiveness of a treatment regimen

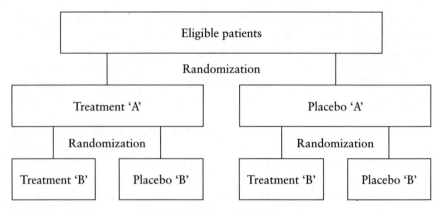

Figure 2.1   An example of factorial trial design

of a patient with uncontrolled asthma. Neither the clinician nor the patient were certain of the effect of two out of the four medications, theophylline and ipratropium, that were part of the patient's treatment regime (although they favoured the theophylline over the ipratropium). The patient agreed to participate in a double blind *n* of 1 trial to evaluate the effectiveness of the two treatments. The patient was first randomized to theophylline or a placebo for a series of 10-day treatment periods, rating his symptoms at the end of each period. After two treatment periods the patient reported feeling much worse at the beginning of each period, the *n* of 1 trial was discontinued and the code broken to reveal that the patient was receiving theophylline at the beginning of each treatment period. This drug was discontinued. The patient then took part in an *n* of 1 trial of ipratropium. A similar procedure was followed and the patient rated his symptoms using an identical scale but on three occasions during a seven-day period. Again after two treatment periods the patient wished the trial to end, reporting an improvement of symptoms at the end of the first treatment period and at the beginning of the second treatment period. When the code was broken it was revealed that the patient was taking ipratropium during these periods. This drug was therefore continued.

Factorial designs

In a factorial design subjects are first randomized to one of the possible treatment groups, and then within each treatment group are further randomized to a different treatment to evaluate a second question (Pocock 1983). The advantage of this design is that more than one question can be answered in a single trial, without necessarily substantially increasing the costs of the trial (see Figure 2.1).

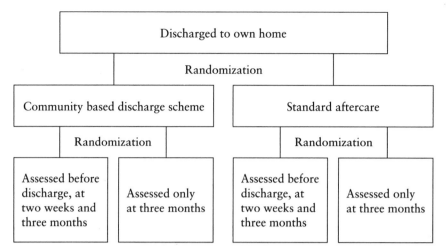

Figure 2.2 Factorial design to overcome interaction effects caused by assessment

Possible interaction effects between the different treatments should be considered when planning a factorial design. Although it is more likely that a factorial design will identify interaction effects. A factorial design was used for this purpose by (Townsend *et al.* 1988) to evaluate a hospital discharge scheme. Patients were randomly allocated to standard care or a community-based hospital discharge scheme. The hospital discharge scheme provided elderly patients with the support of a care attendant in their home after discharge from hospital. The care attendants visited the patients before they were discharged, on their first day at home, and for up to 12 hours a week for two weeks. All patients recruited to the study were formally assessed for physical independence and psychological well-being. The study investigators were concerned that the assessment itself would have an effect, perhaps by discovering care needs that would otherwise not be brought to attention. Therefore both the standard aftercare group and the community based hospital discharge scheme were randomly allocated into a further two groups, one group which was assessed at discharge, two weeks and three months and the other group assessed at only three months (see Figure 2.2).

Sequential designs

A sequential trial design is a design in which the sample size is not fixed beforehand. Instead, the data are assessed on a large number of occasions, even as frequently as after every new observation, and if any difference between the treatments being compared reaches statistical significance the trial is stopped. The set of criteria for stopping the trial is called the 'stopping rule' (see above). A group sequential design is a particular type of sequential design in which only a few interim analyses are performed. This type of design allows the trial investigators to monitor the progress of the trial while keeping the number of inspections low (see Armitage and Berry 1987 and Pocock 1983). The advantage of a sequential design is that a statistically significant result may, in principle, be obtained with the minimum number of patients. This clearly is of particular relevance when the condition being treated is life-threatening and ethical issues mean that no more than the minimum number of patients be given an inferior treatment.

There are various factors that need to be taken into account in the conduct and analysis of a sequential design. The 'stopping rule' should ideally relate to only one outcome variable, with other comparisons acting either to confirm or question the results of this one comparison. The main outcome variable should be of sufficiently short time scale, since long-term measures such as mortality would usually not provide information quick enough to prevent any unnecessary entries of patients into the trial. Another factor in devising the stopping rule is that the difference between the treatments must be of clinical significance: statistical significance does not imply clinical significance. It is important that the results of any interim analyses be kept entirely confidential. This is because any trend for one treatment to appear more effective than the other, even if not reaching statistical significance, can make it ethically difficult for those entering patients into the trial to randomize any subsequent patients if they are aware of this fact.

Zelen's design

It is argued that randomization can deter patients from entering trials (Gallo et al. 1995). Zelen (1979) has proposed an alternative design to overcome some of these potential difficulties. In this design informed consent is obtained after randomization, and only from those patients randomly allocated to the experimental treatment or intervention. Patients who decline the intervention receive the control treatment. In the analysis these patients are grouped with the patients receiving the intervention, and compared with the patients allocated to the control group. If a large number of patients allocated to the intervention cross over to the control group, the study design is compromised, reducing the statistical power. While this type of design may offer an alternative for some trials, it is difficult to implement in many health service research trials where patient outcomes are measured by administering questionnaires, or conducting interviews. In these circumstances patients provide the investigator with a level of information that can not be collected routinely, but requires active participation from each individual patient. Therefore, when patients consent to participate in a trial they are also consenting to provide detailed information during the follow-up times.

Randomized controlled trials and surgery

The principles of the RCT can be applied to surgical interventions in much the same way as drug interventions. The patients are randomized to two or more groups who receive either the standard treatment or the new treatment(s). RCTs were, however, adopted more slowly in surgery than in other medical disciplines. One of the first RCTs undertaken in surgery was conducted by Goligher and colleagues in 1964 investigating surgical treatment for peptic ulcer disease. Although this trial gave credibility to the role of RCTs in the assessment of surgical practice there has been a greater reliance in surgery on the results from observational studies (see Chapter 3) than in any other medical discipline (Solomon and McLeod 1993).

The historical development of surgery mirrored developments in other branches of medicine in that during the nineteenth century numerous advances were made and quickly became practice. Many developments were so clear in their effectiveness that the lack of formal evaluations of their efficacy using large numbers and control groups of patients did not hinder progress. Consequently, the RCT was adopted less frequently as a method of assessing surgical interventions than medical ones. Furthermore, surgery presents certain difficulties for the conduct of successful RCTs. These include both methodological as well as feasibility issues (Stirrat *et al.* 1992).

Methodological issues

In an RCT the interventions the patients receive need to be standardized so that it is possible to generalize the results from the trial to future patients with the same condition. In an RCT evaluating a pharmaceutical treatment this can clearly be achieved by administering the same quantity of drug to each patient. In a surgical RCT, however, it is difficult to standardize the procedure(s) the patients will receive since surgeons vary both in their ability and expertise, and in their preference for performing a particular technique. Moreover, characteristics of the technique itself might alter during the course of a trial. This illustrates the two philosophies for conducting an RCT in surgery which are based either on 'idealistic' or 'pragmatic' approaches. The idealistic approach assumes that surgeon-related factors are excluded and it is possible to compare particular procedures undertaken by surgeons who are performing with equal (and optimal) effectiveness. Clearly, this is difficult to achieve in practice, and the more usual approach is the pragmatic approach in which the comparison assumes that surgeons vary in terms of competence and expertise, and may vary in the exact manner by which they undertake any given procedure. This approach more closely mirrors practice outside the trial and thus the generalizability of the trial results under this model (particularly if the study was conducted in more than one centre) is that much greater. In particular, such a model allows for the different learning curves (the pattern of improvement over time) of the procedures being evaluated, as well as each surgeon's different points on the learning curve. It is generally preferable for each surgeon to offer all interventions under study so that any surgeon related factors are distributed equally among the groups, and also for there to be agreed criteria for the performance of the main aspects of the procedure.

Another methodological issue which can interfere with setting up a surgical RCT is the placebo effect of surgery and the related difficulty of blinding patients to the treatment received. Since it is not ethically acceptable to perform sham operations, although one such has been reported (Dimond et al. 1958), it is difficult to disentangle the placebo effect of the surgery from the true effect, and difficult to blind the patient to the actual procedure he/she has received. These concerns are particularly relevant when the outcome is measured in terms of quality of life measures rather than 'hard' measures such as reoperation or death. It is possible, however, for independent assessors of outcome to be blind to the procedure received.

The choice of an appropriate control group can also be difficult since different surgeons may have different views about the 'gold standard' technique. In situations in which there is no such clinical consensus it is possible for the control group to be the individual surgeon's preferred technique. This is a particularly flexible and pragmatic approach and one which may well encourage surgeon participation in the trial and thus the representativeness of the trial results.

Feasibility issues

It is often not possible to undertake a particular RCT in surgery because for one reason or another it is not feasible. This may be because the disease is so rare that the trial could not be large enough to have adequate 'power' to declare a clinically significant difference statistically significant (see above), because of patient or surgeon preferences, or because of specific consequences of the surgical procedure(s). Surgical procedures are usually permanent and thus it is often not possible to reverse the treatment and give the patient the more effective one. In such situations patients usually have a preference regarding therapy and may not wish to enter into a standard RCT. Indeed, in such circumstances it would be inappropriate to decide treatment modality solely by random allocation (Taylor et al. 1984). A design which may overcome this problem is the randomized consent design, otherwise called Zelen's design (see above), or alternatively some form of non-randomized comparison. It is possible, however, for such feasibility issues to be overcome. For example, a trial comparing lumpectomy (removal of a cancerous tumour from the breast) and mastectomy (removal of both the breast and the cancer) has been completed successfully, even though it was slow in recruiting patients (Fisher et al. 1989).

Another feasibility issue (which is not solely confined to RCTs in surgery – see the section below on RCTs in health services research) is the timing of the RCT in relation to the development of a new procedure. Although it has been argued that even the first patient undergoing a new procedure should be randomized (Chalmers 1975), it is generally regarded that the learning curve associated with any new procedure will put early patients at a disadvantage, biasing the results against the new treatment. Conversely, it is difficult to initiate a new trial when the procedure is established and surgeons perceive it as being optimal. Thus there is a fairly small window of opportunity in which to undertake an evaluation. There have been many instances of the uptake of new procedures before their formal assessment, under the assumption that these new techniques would be advantageous, for example the rapid introduction of laparoscopic techniques in cholecystectomy, and the use of transurethral resection of the prostate in the treatment of benign prostatic hypertrophy. However, in a review of 46 RCTs in surgery and anaesthesia, Gilbert et al. (1977) found that in only half the trials was the new procedure found to be preferable.

An illustration of the possible consequences of the uncontrolled adoption of a new technique is the treatment of benign prostatic hyperplasia, or BPH. Until the 1960s, prostatectomy for BPH was undertaken by open surgery, this requiring open incision in order to remove the enlarged prostate. Transurethral resection of the prostate (TURP) was adopted without formal evaluation since it was assumed that the lack of requirement for an incision could only be beneficial, especially when performed on a small gland; moreover, early results from the new technique were encouraging. Thus, by the mid-1980s TURP was performed in 95 per cent of men referred to specialist units. However, a retrospective study of 54,000 prostatectomies in the 1980s found an increased risk of death, compared with open surgery, 90 days, one five and eight years after TURP (Roos et al. 1989). However, since these data were not obtained from a randomized trial it is possible that this difference could be attributed to differences in case mix. Thus a prospective trial of open versus transurethral resection of the prostate has been proposed (Holtgrewe 1990; Jenkins et al. 1992).

The RCT has been historically more prevalent in assessing medical interventions than surgical ones but their use is increasing in this area of medicine. While RCTs in surgery present particular problems these are not insurmountable and consequently the RCT in surgery can be a powerful tool in addressing important clinical issues.

Randomized controlled trials and health services research

The formal logic of RCTs is universal to nearly all health care questions, and is increasingly used as a method in health services research (Balas

- Lengthy consultation with health service personnel
- Disputes between interested parties
- Difficulties obtaining a precise definition of the intervention
- Lack of data on which to base sample size calculations
- Complex process of randomization
- Collecting data from multiple sources
- Inappropriate financial data for economic evaluation
- Pressure to produce results before the trial ends

due to limited funds

Figure 2.3   Problems that may arise in health services research trials

et al. 1995). A number of areas need to be considered when RCTs are applied to health service research. The example of an RCT of a 'hospital at home' scheme is used here to illustrate some of these problems, and to show that it is feasible to conduct RCTs of service innovations such as hospital at home (see Figure 2.3).

An example: comparing hospital care with home care

Interest has grown in new ways of delivering care in the community, in order to reduce hospital length of stay and avoid admissions. In the UK this trend towards home care is in line with a broad background of policy which has given primary care an increasing role in meeting the health needs of the population since the 1980s (Hughes and Gordon 1992). In addition, changes in medical technology, such as day case surgery, have shown that some of the post-operative care traditionally carried out in hospital can be carried out at home (Kessels-Buickhuisen 1994; Stoker *et al.* 1994). There is, however, considerable uncertainty about the costs and effectiveness of this type of service in comparison to hospital care. A controlled trial, with prospective specification of outcomes, and random allocation to traditional or the new form of care, offers, in theory, a powerful method for resolving some of these uncertainties. Consequently, a randomized controlled trial was designed to test if hospital at home leads to cost savings, a reduction in the use of secondary care, and an improvement in quality of life compared with hospital care (Shepperd *et al.* 1994). This section will briefly describe some of the areas that need to be considered when designing an RCT of a service innovation.

Consultation

A central problem of health service research RCTs is that they usually concern a variety of occupational groups who may view the question (or possible results) of the trial as threatening to their role. The trial may also be perceived as a source of unsustainable additional work, or be seen as an opportunity to obtain resources or rewards. Although adherence to a trial protocol is a problem that is not unique to health services research RCTs, comparisons between settings have specific problems linked to the intervention. The people who are at the very centre of these trials are not like the inert substances in a standard clinical trial. Instead they have a voice in shaping, resisting and confusing the very design and conduct of the trial. Consequently a lengthy consultation exercise was undertaken to learn about the different groups' interests.

The timing of the evaluation

Another distinctive feature of health service research RCTs is that they often seek to evaluate service innovations that are still taking shape. This means that political problems surrounding the acceptance of a new way of delivering care are encountered. But perhaps more serious is the potential disadvantage of starting a trial at the same time a service is introduced, as the evaluation is then of an immature service. However, it is not clear at what point in its development a service should be evaluated. If a service is allowed to develop unchecked then it is unlikely an evaluation will be supported. Furthermore, the continued evolution of a service such as hospital at home, driven by technological advances and local resources, means that it is difficult to know which model is the most relevant in the future. This difficulty in standardizing a service, compared to a technical intervention, is a problem common to this type of health service evaluation.

Randomization

Previous studies have described the difficulties of random allocation of service provision (McWhinney *et al.* 1995). Randomization would be impossible to implement if professionals *routinely* admitted patients to hospital at home (Knowelden *et al.* 1985). Furthermore, if hospital at home care were routinely available it would be difficult to justify to the patient the principle of randomization on the grounds of uncertainty, as the patient would have the option of choosing their preferred form of care. The preferred option is for the service and the evaluation to commence simultaneously and for eligible patients to be only admitted to hospital at home if they were randomly allocated to this form of care.

Outcomes

Although outcomes such as morbidity and mortality are an important clinical concern with hospital at home, their rarity makes them impractical as primary end-points in a trial such as this. Health service research is often in practice concerned with outcomes focused on well-being. There is usually a need to conduct a cost benefit or cost utility analysis which requires some measure of quality of life. Advocates of subjective health status measurement suggest that both disease specific and generic measures of health status should be included (Pound *et al.* 1994; Pound *et al.* 1995;

Maloney 1995; Lawton 1991; Kraus 1991; SF-36 User's Manual 1989). Although there is a growing body of research on the responsiveness of these instruments (Lydick and Epstein 1993; Fitzpatrick *et al.* 1992) few have been used to evaluate health services in controlled trials (Fletcher *et al.* 1992). For many measures the data on which to base sample size calculations do not exist. Even when data exists it is not always known what level of change in an instrument score is important (Guyatt *et al.* 1991). Furthermore, when information does exist it may be based on follow-up times that are not applicable to the planned study.

Economic data

The main practical problem in collecting economic data in the UK is that providers have only recently begun to attach costs to services. Even when available, data are not standardized between trusts, and may reflect variation in methods used to calculate costs rather than true differences. This has implications for the generalizability of the cost data beyond the trial setting.

Methodological issues surrounding prospective economic analysis as part of a trial have been discussed elsewhere (Drummond *et al.* 1987; Drummond 1994; O'Brien *et al.* 1994). These include general problems such as the absence of data on the distribution of resource variables, and therefore the sampling variation for costs. A more specific problem concerns estimating the point at which a new service reaches technical efficiency. For example, in the case of hospital at home, the organization of the scheme will change in the light of experience. These changes will be reflected in the costs of the service (Mowat and Morgan 1982).

Conclusions

The RCT has become the 'gold standard' for the evaluation of medical treatment. Ever since Archie Cochrane's now famous monograph on the need for RCTs to evaluate the effectiveness of treatments (Cochrane 1972) the acceptance and application of this methodology has grown exponentially. However, despite its widespread acceptance, one should not underestimate the complexities of undertaking such a seemingly simple experimental design. Many trials have been conducted that were flawed in terms of randomization, sample size calculations, and selection of appropriate outcome measures: for the most part all these trials have done is wasted time and resources; at worst, however, they can lead to the retention or adoption of worthless, or even dangerous, treatments. However, when properly conducted they can lead to changes in practice that both reduce mortality and morbidity and improve quality of life.

Note

1 Epi Info is a product of the Division of Surveillance and Epidemiology, Center for Disease Control and Prevention, Atlanta, Georgia. Power is a product of Epicenter Software, Pasedena, California.

References

Altman, D.G. (1991) *Practical Statistics for Medical Research.* London: Chapman and Hall.
Armitage, P. and Berry, G. (1987) *Statistical Methods in Medical Research.* Oxford: Blackwell, 442–54.
Balas, E.A., Austin, S.M., Ewigman, B.G., Brown, G.D. and Mitchell, J.A. (1995) Methods of randomized controlled clinical trials in health services research, *Medical Care*, 33: 687–99.
Bradley, C. (1993) A review of some alternatives to conventional randomized controlled trials, *Diabetes Care*, 16: 509–18.
Brewin, C.R. and Bradley, C. (1989) Patient preferences and randomized controlled trials, *British Medical Journal*, 299, 313–15.
Bull, J.P. (1959) The historical development of clinical therapeutic trials, *Journal of Chronic Disease*, 10, 218–48.
Campbell, M.J. (1994) Commentary: *n* of 1 trials may be useful for informed decision making, *British Medical Journal*, 309: 1044–5.
Chalmers, I., Dickersin, K. and Chalmers, T.C. (1992) Getting to grips with Archie Cochrane's agenda, *British Medical Journal*, 305: 786–8.
Cochrane, A. (1972) *Effectiveness and Efficiency.* London: The Nuffield Provincial Hospitals Trust.
Drummond, M.F., Stoddart, G.L. and Torrance, G.W. (1987) *Methods for the Economic Evaluation of Health Care Programmes.* Oxford: Oxford University Press.
Drummond, M.F. (1994) *Economic Analysis Alongside Controlled Trials.* Leeds: Department of Health.
Fisher, B., Redmond C., Poisson, R., Margolese, R., Wolmark, N., Wickerham, L., Fisher, E., Deutsch, M., Caplan, R., Pilch, Y. (1989) Eight year results of a randomized clinical trial comparing total mastectomy and lumpectomy with or without irradiation in the treatment of breast cancer, *New England Journal of Medicine*, 320: 822–8.
Fitzpatrick, R., Ziebland, S., Jenkinson, C. and Mowat, A. (1992) The importance of sensitivity to change as a criterion for selection of health status measures, *Quality in Health Care*, 1: 89–93.
Fletcher, A.E., Dickinson, E.J. and Philp, I. (1992) Review: Audit measures: quality of life instruments for everyday use with elderly patients, *Age and Ageing*, 21: 142–50.
Freiman, J.A., Chalmers, T.C., Smith, H., *et al.* (1978) The importance of beta, the type II error and sample size in the design and interpretation of the randomized controlled trial, *New England Journal of Medicine*, 290: 690–4.

Gallo, C., Perrone, F., De Placido, S. and Glusti, C. (1995) Informed versus randomized consent to clinical trials, *Lancet*, 346: 1060–64.

Gilbert, J.P., McPeek, B. and Mosteller, F. (1977) Statistics and ethics in surgery and anaesthesia, *Science*, 198: 684–9.

Goligher, J.C., Pulvertaft, C.N. and Watkinson, G. (1964) Controlled clinical trial of vagotomy and gastroenterostomy, vagotomy and antrectomy, and subtotal gastrectomy in elective treatment of duodenal ulcer: interim report, *British Medical Journal*, 1: 455–60.

Gray, R., Clarke, M., Collins, R. and Peto, R. (1995) Making randomised trials larger: a simple solution?, *European Journal of Surgical Oncology*, 21: 137–9.

Guyatt, G., Sackett, D., Taylor, W.D., Chong, J., Roberts, R. and Pugsley, S. (1986) Determining optimal therapy – randomized trials in individual patients, *The New Journal of Medicine*, 314: 889–92.

Guyatt, G., Feeny, D. and Patrick, D. (1991) Issues in quality of life measurement in clinical trials, *Controlled Clinical Trials*, 12: 79S–90S.

Hellman, S. and Hellman, D.S. (1991) Of mice but not men: problems of the randomized controlled trial, *The New England Journal of Medicine*, 324: 1585–92.

Hill, A.B. (1963) Medical ethics and controlled trials, *British Medical Journal*, 1: 1043–9.

Holtgrewe, H.L. (1990) Prospective BPH study. *AUA today*, p. 24.

Hughes, J. and Gordon, P. (1992) *Hospitals and Primary Care*. London: King's Fund Centre.

ISIS-1 Collaborative Group (1986) Randomised trial of intravenous atenolol among 16,027 cases of suspected acute myocardial infarction: ISIS-1, *Lancet*, ii: 57–66.

ISIS-2 Collaborative Group (1988) Randomised trial of intravenous streptokinase, oral aspirin, both or neither among 17,187 cases of suspected acute myocardial infarction, *Lancet*, ii: 349–60.

Jenkins, B.J., Sharma, P., Badenoch, D.F., Fowler, C.G. and Blandy, J.P. (1992) Ethics, logistics and a trial of transurethral versus open prostatectomy, *British Journal of Urology*, 69: 372–74.

Kessels-Buickhuisen, M. (1994) Home comforts. *Health Services Journal*, 3 March, 24–7.

Kraus, N. (1991) *The Interstudy Quality Edge*. Minneapolis: Interstudy.

Lawton, M.P. (1991) The Philadelphia Geriatric Centre Morale Scale: a revision, *Journal of Gerontology*, 30: 85–9.

Lydick, E. and Epstein, R.S. (1993) Interpretation of quality of life changes, *Quality of Life Research*, 2: 221–6.

Maloney, F.C. (1995) Functional evaluation: the Barthel Index, *Maryland State Medical Journal*, 14: 61–5.

March, L., Irwig, L., Schwartz, J., Simpson, J., Chock, C. and Brooks, P. (1994) *n* of 1 trials comparing a non-steroidal anti-inflammatory drug with paracetamol in osteoarthritis, *British Medical Journal*, 309: 1041–4.

Mason, J.K. and McCall-Smith, A. (1994) *Law and Medical Ethics* (4th edn). London: Butterworth.

McWhinney, I.R., Bass, M.J. and Donner, A. (1995) Evaluation of a palliative care service: problems and pitfalls, *British Medical Journal*, 309: 1340–42.

Medical Research Council (1948) Streptomycin treatment of pulmonary tuberculosis, *British Medical Journal*, ii: 769–82.

MRC Vitamin Study Research Group (1991) Prevention of neural tube defects: results from the MRC Vitamin Study, *Lancet*, 338: 132–7.

Mowat, W.G. and Morgan, R.T. (1982) Peterborough hospital at home scheme, *British Medical Journal*, 307: 641–43.

Oakley, A. (1990) Who's afraid of the randomised control trial?, in H. Roberts (ed.) *Women's Health Counts*. London: Routledge.

O'Brien, B.J., Drummond, M.F., Labelle, R.J. and Willan, A. (1994) In search of power and significance: issues in the design and analysis of stochastic cost-effectiveness studies in health care, *Medical Care*, 32: 150–63.

Peto, V., Coulter, A. and Bond, A. (1993) Factors affecting general practitioners' recruitment of patients into a prospective study, *Family Practice*, 10: 207–11.

Pocock, S.J. (1983) *Clinical Trials: A Practical Approach*. New York: John Wiley.

Pound, P., Gompertz, P. and Ebrahim, S. (1994) Patient satisfaction with stroke services, *Clinical Rehabilitation*, 8: 7–17.

Pound, P., Gompertz, P. and Ebrahim, S. (1995) Development and results of a questionnaire to measure carer satisfaction after stroke, *Journal of Epidemiology and Community Health*, 47: 500–5.

Roos, N.P., Wennberg, J.E., Malenka, D.J. *et al.* (1989) Mortality and reoperation after open and transurethral resection of the prostate for benign prostatic hyperplasia, *New England Journal of Medicine*, 320: 1120–4.

Russell, I. (1996) Methods of health services evaluation: the gospel of Archie Cochrane after 25 years, *Journal of Health Services Research and Policy*, 1: 114–15.

Schwartz, D. and Lellouch, J. (1967) Explanatory and pragmatic attitudes in therapeutical trials, *Journal of Chronic Diseases*, 20: 637–48.

Senn, S.J. (1993) *Cross-over Trials in Clinical Research*. Chichester: John Wiley.

Senn, S. (1994) The AB/BA crossover: past, present and future?, *Statistical Methods in Medical Research*, 3: 303–24.

SF-36 User's Manual (1989) *SF-36 Health Status Questionnaire User's Manual*. Minneapolis: Quality Quest.

Shepperd, S., Gray, A., Jenkinson, C. and Vessey, M. (1994) *Protocol for a Randomised Controlled Trial of a Hospital at Home Scheme*. Oxford: Health Services Research Unit.

Silverman, W.A. and Altman, D.G. (1996) Patients' preferences and randomized trials, *Lancet*, 347: 171–4.

Sleight, P. (1994) Vasodilators after acute myocardial infarction: ISIS IV, *American Journal of Hypertension*, 7 (9, part 2): 102S–105S.

Smithells, R.W. (1982) Neural tube defects: prevention by vitamin supplements, *Paediatrics*, 69: 498–9.

Smithells, R.W., Sheppard, S., Schorah, C.J., Seller, M.J., Nevin, N.C., Harris, R., Read, A.P. and Fielding, D.W. (1980) Possible prevention of neural tube defects by periconceptional vitamin supplementation, *Lancet*, i: 339–40.

Smithells, R.W., Sheppard, S., Schorah, C.J., Seller, M.J., Nevin, N.C., Harris, R., Read, A.P., Fielding, D.W. and Walker, S. (1981) Vitamin supplementation and neural tube defects, *Lancet*, 2: 1425.

Solomon, M.J. and McLeod, R.S. (1993) Clinical studies in surgical journals. Have we improved?, *Diseases of the Colon and Rectum*, 36: 43–48.

Stirrat, G.M., Farndon, J., Farrow, S.C. and Dwyer, N. (1992) The challenge of evaluating surgical procedures, *Annals of the Royal College of Surgeons of England*, 74: 80–4.

Stoker, D.L., Spiegelhalter, D.J., Singh, R. and Wellwood, J.M. (1994) Laparoscopic versus open inguinal hernia repair: randomized prospective trial, *Lancet*, 343: 1243–5.

Stone, D.H. (1980) Possible prevention of neural tube defects by periconceptional vitamin supplementation, *Lancet*, i: 647.

Taylor, K., Margolese, R.G. and Soskolne, C.L. (1984) Physicians' reasons for not entering eligible patients in a randomized clinical trial of adjuvant surgery for breast cancer, *New England Journal of Medicine*, 310: 1363–7.

Townsend, J., Piper, M., Frank, A.O., Dyer, S., North, W.R. and Meade, T.W. (1988) Reduction in hospital readmission stay of elderly patients by a community based hospital discharge scheme: a randomized controlled trial, *British Medical Journal*, 297: 544–7.

Winsor, C.P. (1948) Probability and Listerism, *Human Biology*, 169: 161–9.

Zelen, M. (1979) A new design for randomized clinical trials, *New England Journal of Medicine*, 300: 1242–5.

3

Case control and cohort studies

Jonathan Mant and Crispin Jenkinson

Introduction

A common question in health care is whether exposure to something will
increase the risk of (or perhaps protect against) a disease. The 'something',
usually referred to in this context as a possible *risk factor*, might be an
environmental factor such as air pollution, an aspect of lifestyle such as
smoking, a medical treatment such as a drug, or characteristics of an individual, such as genetic make-up. For example, does exposure to car exhaust
fumes increase the risk of asthma? Or, does taking the oral contraceptive
pill protect against ovarian cancer? There are two complementary ways to
address this sort of question: laboratory-based experimental studies, which
are outside the scope of this book, and population-based epidemiological
studies. This chapter describes the two principal types of epidemiological
study in this context: case control and cohort studies.

Case control studies

In essence, the design of a case control study is simple. Two groups of
people are identified: people who have the disease that is being studied
('cases'), and people who do not have the disease ('controls'). The extent
to which both groups have been exposed to the risk factor (or factors) of
interest is measured, and the exposure of one group is compared to the
other. For example, in a study exploring what factors contribute to sudden
infant death syndrome – 'cot death' (i.e. when an apparently healthy baby
dies in their cot without any obvious cause), cases were babies who had
died of this syndrome, and controls were babies who were still alive (Fleming

Table 3.1 Derivation of an odds ratio from the results of a case control study

	Cases	Controls
Mother smoked after pregnancy	129	209
Mother did not smoke after pregnancy	66	571
Total	195	780

Notes:
Odds of death if mother smokes = 129/209 = 0.6172
Odds of death if mother does not smoke = 66/571 = 0.1156
Odds ratio = 0.6172/0.1156 = 5.34

et al. 1996; Blair *et al.* 1996). Interviews were carried out with the families of both sets of babies to find out about their exposure to different possible risk factors. The investigators found that parental smoking, bed sharing with parents, and sleeping prone or on the side were all more likely in babies who had died. The results are expressed as an odds ratio, which is the odds of death in the exposed group divided by the odds of death in the unexposed group. The derivation of an odds ratio is illustrated in Table 3.1, which shows that the odds ratio for sudden death in infants of mothers who smoke after pregnancy is just over 5. In other words, the odds of a child of a mother who smokes dying of sudden infant death syndrome is five times higher than the odds of a child of a mother who does not smoke.

A major difficulty with case control studies is trying to ascertain the extent to which alternative explanations might account for an observed association. For example, is it correct to conclude from Blair *et al.*'s study that smoking does increase the risk of sudden infant death syndrome (Blair *et al.* 1996)? Three types of alternative explanation need to be considered: confounding, bias and chance.

Confounding

A *confounding* factor is something that is associated both with the exposure and the disease being investigated. For example, there have been a number of case control studies looking at whether taking the oral contraceptive pill (ocp) might be linked to an increased risk of breast cancer. A meta-analysis (see Chapter 10) of these studies concluded that women who take the oral contraceptive pill are at increased risk of having breast cancer diagnosed (Collaborative Group on Hormonal Factors in Breast Cancer 1996). However, it has been suggested that the observed association may be due to confounding: Hemminki (1996) argues that women who take oral contraceptives are more likely to be fertile and be sexually active than women not on the pill. If either fertility or sexual activity was related to breast cancer risk, then an observed association between the ocp and breast cancer may have nothing to do with a harmful effect of the pill, but simply reflect the differing fertility or sexual activity of people who take the pill compared to non-users.

It has also been argued that another possible confounder of any relationship between the ocp and breast cancer might be cigarette smoking (Trichopoulos and Katsouyanni 1989). Commenting on one of the case control studies (UK National Case-Control Study Group 1989), Trichopoulos and Katsouyanni argue that women who use the ocp are advised not to smoke, and therefore smoking could be a confounder if it protects against breast cancer. In other words, if women give up smoking to be on the ocp, they may inadvertently be increasing their risk of breast cancer by losing the (postulated) protective effect of tobacco. In fact, recent evidence suggests that smoking increases rather than reduces the risk of breast cancer (Bennicke et al. 1995; Morabia et al. 1996). If this is the case, then confounding would still be occurring, but the effect of smoking would be to mask any link between the ocp and breast cancer, if indeed people who take the ocp are less likely to smoke. In other words, confounding can work in both directions: it may cause an apparent relationship between a risk factor and a disease that does not in fact exist, or it may cause a real association to disappear. The possibility of confounding can be taken into account in the design and in the analysis of a case control study.

In the design of the study one could *restrict* the selection of cases and controls in a way that would nullify the effects of the confounder. For example, one could remove the possibility of smoking confounding the effects of the ocp on risk of breast cancer by only selecting cases and controls who did not smoke. Alternatively, one could select the controls in such a way that they *matched* the cases with regard to the presence or absence of the risk factor. In this example, a case (of breast cancer) who was a smoker would need to be matched with a control (someone who does not have breast cancer) who also smokes. It is quite common for the controls in a case control study to be matched to the cases with regard to a couple of potential confounders, particularly age and sex. However, in a matched study one cannot look at the impact of the matched variable(s) on the risk of disease, and if one 'overmatches' then one may mask the true effect of the risk factor(s) that are being investigated. If one has used a matched design, it is important that the analysis takes acccount of the matching. In Blair et al.'s study of cot death, the controls were selected from the same neighbourhood and were the same age as the infants who had died. This matching necessitates a slightly more sophisticated derivation of the odds ratio than that shown in Table 3.1.

One can make adjustments for the effects of a confounder in the analysis of a case control study, provided that it was measured. Discussion of the mathematics of making such adjustments is beyond the scope of this book. Techniques include stratification and multiple logistic regression. For example, in Fleming *et al.*'s study of risk factors for sudden infant death, one of the risk factors looked at was use of a duvet. Ignoring confounding factors, the odds of death were 2.82 times higher if a duvet was used. However, if the results were adjusted to take account of factors such as maternal age and birthweight the odds ratio fell to 1.72 (Fleming *et al.* 1996).

Bias

There are two main sources of bias in case control studies: *selection bias* and *information bias*. *Selection bias* occurs if either the cases or the controls are selected in a way that is influenced by whether or not they were exposed to the risk factor(s) under study. In essence, it is a manifestation of confounding. For example, several case control studies have shown that hormone replacement therapy (HRT) reduces the risk of heart disease in women (Barrett-Connor and Bush 1991). Women who elect to take HRT are likely to be different from women who do not take HRT in several ways. Matthews *et al.* have shown that women who subsequently decide to take HRT tend to have lower blood pressure, take more exercise, weigh less, drink more alcohol, and to be better educated than women who do not take HRT (Matthews *et al.* 1996). These factors, because they lower risk of heart disease in their own right, will confound any relationship between HRT and heart disease. Therefore, a case control study looking at this issue will be prone to selection bias since the exposure of cases and controls to HRT may be different simply because of the different characteristics of the two groups and not because HRT changes an individual's risk of heart disease.

Information bias occurs in a case control study if there are differences in the way that information on exposure to the risk factor(s) under study has been obtained. This bias may be introduced by the subjects themselves or by the investigator. An example of an information bias that might be introduced by the subjects is *recall bias*. Recall bias occurs if (usually) the cases are more likely to remember exposure to the risk factor under study by virtue of their having the disease. For example, case control studies looking at risk factors for congenital abnormalities will often rely on mothers reporting exposure. It is likely that parents seeking to find a cause for their child's birth defect will be more likely to remember exposure to possible risk factors than parents of healthy children (Swan *et al.* 1992). To try to get round this problem, in a case control study looking for a possible link between spermicides and certain birth defects, controls were selected who had other birth defects that were not under investigation (Louik *et al.* 1987). An example of information bias that might be introduced by the investigator is *ascertainment bias*, which occurs if identification of exposure is more complete in cases than in controls (or vice versa). This is more likely if the investigator is aware of the status of the individual (i.e. case or control) on whom she or he is collecting information. For example, in an interview, the investigator may probe more deeply for exposure of cases than of controls. Sometimes it is possible to *blind* the researcher to the status of the interviewee, to minimize the risk of this occurring.

Chance

The possibility that observed differences between cases and controls might simply be due to chance is explored by carrying out statistical tests of significance, perhaps by calculating a *p value* or a *confidence interval*. The *p* value reflects the probability that the results would have occurred if in reality there was no difference between cases and controls. Thus, a *p* value of 0.01 means that if there was no difference between cases and controls, the chance of observing differences as big as those found in the study is 0.01, i.e. 1 in 100. By convention, if a *p* value is less than 0.05 (i.e. 1 in 20), it is usually stated that the differences are statistically significant – i.e. they are unlikely to have occurred as a result of chance. A confidence interval is a range of values within which the true value is likely to lie. For example, in Fleming *et al.*'s study of risk factors for sudden infant death, the adjusted (see above) odds ratio for using a duvet was 1.72, but the confidence interval around this result was from 0.90 to 3.30 (Fleming *et al.* 1996). In other words, it is likely that the true odds ratio for death if a duvet is used lies between 0.90 and 3.30. In this example, the confidence interval includes the value 1 (i.e. that using a duvet has no effect on risk of death), so it is possible that the increased risk that was observed was due to chance. Usually, authors will give 95 per cent confidence intervals. What this means is that 95 times out of 100 (or 19 times out of 20), the true value will lie within the range given by the confidence interval. Larger studies will have narrower confidence intervals.

Cohort studies

In a cohort study, a group or groups of individuals are classified by the extent to which they have been exposed to a possible risk factor, and then followed up over time to see if they develop the disease(s) under invest-igation. The rates of disease in the different groups are then compared, to see if they are higher in the group that had higher exposure to the possible risk factor. For example, in a classic study which investigated the health effects of smoking, all British doctors were classified according to whether they were current smokers, ex-smokers, or non-smokers (Doll and Hill 1954).

Table 3.2   Relative risk and attributable risk.

	Annual mortality per 100,000 men	
	Non-smokers	*Current smokers*
Lung cancer	14	209
Ischaemic heart disease	572	892

Source: Doll *et al.* 1994
Notes:
1 Relative risk of lung cancer in smokers (as compared to non-smokers):
  rate in exposed/rate in unexposed =
  209 per 100,000 per annum/14 per 100,000 per annum = 14.9
2 Relative risk of ischaemic heart disease in smokers (as compared to non-smokers):
  rate in exposed/rate in unexposed =
  892 per 100,000 per annum/572 per 100,000 per annum = 1.6
3 Attributable risk of lung cancer from smoking:
  rate in exposed/rate in unexposed = 209 − 14 = 195 per 100,000 per annum
4 Attributable risk of ischaemic heart disease from smoking:
  rate in exposed/rate in unexposed = 892 − 572 = 320 per 100,000 men per annum.
In other words, in a population of 100,000 smokers, one would expect 320 extra deaths per annum from ischaemic heart disease than would occur in a population of 100,000 non-smokers. In contrast, despite the much higher relative risk, one would expect 'only' 195 extra deaths from lung cancer.

This was done by sending a short questionnaire about smoking habits to everyone who was on the medical register and was resident in the United Kingdom in October 1951. Those doctors who returned questionnaires were then followed up for the next 40 years, to ascertain if and when they died, and if so, what was their cause of death (Doll *et al.* 1994). The annual mortality rate from lung cancer in non-smokers was found to be 14 per 100,000 as compared to 58 per 100,000 in ex-smokers and 209 per 100,000 in current smokers (Doll *et al.* 1994). In other words, a current smoker is 14.9 (209/14) times as likely to die of lung cancer as a non-smoker. Often, the results of a cohort study are expressed in terms of a rate ratio, or *relative risk*. In this example, the relative risk of a smoker dying of lung cancer as compared to a non-smoker is 14.9 (see Table 3.2).

In the Doll and Hill study, it was possible to look at the relationship between smoking and many diseases. One important association that was found was between smoking and death from ischaemic heart disease. The relative risk of smokers dying of ischaemic heart disease is 1.6 as compared to non-smokers. This sounds much less impressive than the relative risk of dying of lung cancer, but in fact, smoking kills more people through heart disease than it does through lung cancer. This is because heart disease is much more common than lung cancer, so a small increase in the relative risk has a much greater impact. In order to reflect this, sometimes in a cohort study the *attributable risk* is reported as well as the relative risk.

The attributable risk reflects the absolute change in the rate of a disease that occurs by being exposed to the risk factor. The derivation of attributable risk is shown in table two, using smoking, lung cancer and ischaemic heart disease as an example.

Type of comparison group

A cohort study involves comparing the rate at which different groups of individuals, defined in terms of their exposure to the risk factor under study, develop the disease(s) under investigation. Sometimes, it is possible to use a single group, and sub-divide them on the basis of their exposure history. The Doll and Hill study is an example of such an approach: a single group of people – British doctors – was identified and subdivided on the basis of their self-reported smoking habits.

Another example where such an *internal comparison* group was used was the Oxford-FPA study, which was a cohort study that looked at the long-term effects on health of the oral contraceptive pill (ocp) (Vessey *et al.* 1989). In this study, women who attended Family Planning Clinics between 1968 and 1974 were divided into groups on the basis of what form of contraception they were using. The subsequent mortality of women who were using the ocp was compared with the mortality of women who were using an intra-uterine device or a diaphragm. The groups had similar all-cause mortality rates after 20 years of follow up, providing some evidence for the safety of the oral contraceptive pill (Vessey *et al.* 1989). However, the mortality rates of women who were in the study are much lower than the mortality rates of the general female population of England and Wales (Vessey *et al.* 1977). This is because, in general, women who attend family planning clinics represent a healthy sub-set of the general population: they are sexually active, and are less likely to smoke or be grossly overweight, and more likely to be in the higher social classes (Vessey *et al.* 1977).

This atypical nature of the study cohort does not matter when the comparison group is internal, but it can be important when an *external comparison* group is used, as will often be the case when a study is looking at the effects of an occupational exposure. For example, in a cohort study looking at the health effects of occupational exposure to radiation, the study population comprised all employees of the United Kingdom Atomic Energy Authority (UKAEA) (Fraser *et al.* 1993). Part of the analysis involved comparing the mortality experience of the study cohort to an external comparison group: the whole population of England and Wales. The advantage of using such a comparison group is that the death rates are already published, so do not require any additional data gathering. The disadvantage is that people who are in employment are healthier than the population as a whole, which includes people who are unemployed for reasons of ill health. As a result, mortality rates in the study cohort will invariably be lower than mortality rates in the general population. This *healthy worker effect* was evident in Fraser *et al.*'s study, where the overall mortality rate of UKAEA employees was 20 per cent below the national average.

Retrospective cohort studies

A cohort study may be *prospective* or *retrospective*. The Doll and Hill Study and the Oxford-FPA study are both examples of prospective cohort studies, where groups of individuals are defined on the basis of their exposure to the risk factor under study and followed up *prospectively* for several years (40 in the case of the Doll and Hill study) to see whether they develop the outcome of interest. Fraser *et al.*'s study was partly a retrospective study, in that when the study was set up in the late 1970s, data was used to define exposure going back to 1946, and deaths that had occurred between 1946 and 1979 were determined *retrospectively*. In other words, in a retrospective cohort study, the outcomes of interest have already occurred when the study is initiated. A retrospective cohort study can be done more quickly and cheaply than a prospective study, but needs to rely on pre-existing records for data collection.

An area of research where retrospective cohort studies have come into their own is in exploring the link between foetal growth and adult coronary heart disease (Barker *et al.* 1993). Barker and colleagues have demonstrated that low growth rates *in utero* and infancy are associated with high death rates from cardiovascular disease in adulthood by retrospectively following up the mortality of people born in the early part of this century in places where, fortuitously, good maternity and/or infant health records were kept. Obtaining empirical evidence for such a link is impractical using a prospective design, but several studies have now been published which test the 'Barker Hypothesis' using a retrospective approach (Fall *et al.* 1995; Christensen *et al.* 1995).

Interpretation of a cohort study

The same alternative explanations (chance, bias and confounding) that were considered for a case control study when an association is observed between exposure to a risk factor and the development of a disease apply to the interpretation of a cohort study. A type of bias that is of particular relevance to cohort studies is that which can arise from *losses to follow-up*. Inevitably, not everyone who is entered into a study will be followed up successfully for the entire study period. Problems arise if loss to follow up is related to exposure to the risk factor under study and to development of the outcome of interest.

Prognosis

In addition to looking at questions of whether exposure to specific risk factors are associated with specific diseases, cohort studies can also be useful in determining prognosis. For example, Hutton *et al.* demonstrated that over 85 per cent of a cohort of children born with cerebral palsy survive to the age of 20 (Hutton *et al.* 1994); and extrapolation from following what happened to a cohort of haemophiliacs who are HIV positive suggests that there is roughly a 25 per cent chance of remaining free of AIDS 20 years after infection with HIV (Phillips *et al.* 1994).

Comparison of case control and cohort studies

In investigating whether a risk factor might be associated with a given disease, case control and cohort studies have different advantages and disadvantages (summarized in Table 3.3). In general, a case control study will 'give an answer' much more quickly than a cohort study, especially a prospective cohort study, and will be much cheaper to perform. In a case control study, the starting point is a comparison of exposure to risk factors of people with disease and people without disease. Therefore, it follows that it is possible to look at many different risk factors, and it will be an efficient way to investigate causes of rare diseases, but an inefficient way of investigating whether a rare risk factor is linked to a disease. Conversely, in a cohort study, the starting point is identifying exposed and unexposed individuals and following them up to determine whether or not they develop disease. A cohort study can thus look at the link between exposure and many diseases, and can be used to investigate the effect of rare exposures (e.g. occupational exposure); however, it is not an efficient way of investigating rare diseases. For example, there are a number of case control studies which suggest there is a link between use of the oral contraceptive pill and liver cancer (Mant and Vessey 1995), but a large cohort study of the health effects of the oral contraceptive pill, despite recruiting over 17,000 women, had only had one case of liver cancer after 20 years of follow up (Vessey *et al.* 1989).

When assessing whether a link between exposure to a risk factor and occurrence of disease might be causal (see below), it is important to know whether the exposure did in fact precede the onset of the disease. For example, is the association between smoking and lung cancer because smoking causes lung cancer, or because people with lung cancer find that smoking eases their symptoms? In a cohort study, where identification of exposure precedes onset of disease, this is not a problem. It can, however, be an issue in a case control study, where ascertainment of exposure is made after the disease has developed.

Table 3.3 Comparison of cohort and case control studies

	Cohort study	Case control study
Design	Measure exposure in groups of individuals, and then follow them up to see if they develop the disease(s) of interest	Identify individuals with disease and individuals without disease and measure exposure in the two groups
Analysis	Compare rates of disease in exposed and unexposed groups	Compare odds of exposure in diseased group to undiseased group
Particularly suited for	Investigating effect of rare exposures; looking at multiple effects of a single exposure	Investigating rare diseases; looking at many possible causes of a single disease
Advantages	Can reliably determine whether exposure preceded disease onset. Allows incidence rates and attributable risk to be calculated.	Cheap; quick to do; will involve many less patients than a cohort study
Disadvantages	Expensive May take many years (unless retrospective)	Generally prone to more types of bias than cohort studies. Greater reliance on retrospective data collection, which may be more unreliable and prone to bias. May be difficult to determine whether exposure preceded onset of disease. Cannot directly calculate incidence rates and attributable risk

The principal result of a case control study is usually an odds ratio (see Table 3.1), which many people find more difficult to understand than a relative risk or a rate ratio (see Table 3.2), which is one way in which the results of a cohort study can be presented. However, if the incidence of disease is low, then in fact the odds ratio is approximately the same as the relative risk. This is illustrated in Table 3.4. Analysis of a cohort study depends upon calculation of incidence rates in exposed and unexposed populations. This allows the results to be expressed in other ways, such as attributable risk (see Table 3.2). Such calculations are not possible in case control studies, since population rates cannot be directly obtained.

Table 3.4 Similarity between relative risk and odds ratio.

The results of a cohort study might be presented as the following 2 × 2 table:

	Disease present	Disease absent	Disease rate
Exposed	a	b	b/(a + b)
Unexposed	c	d	d(c + d)

Comparing the rates of disease in the two groups gives the rate ratio, or the relative risk, which is given by:

$$\frac{a/(a+b)}{c/(c+d)} \quad \text{or} \quad \frac{0.209\%}{0.014\%} = 14.93$$

In a cohort study, there is no need to calculate the odds ratio, but this would be given by:

$$\frac{a/b}{c/d} \quad \text{or} \quad \frac{209/99791}{14/99986} = 14.96$$

Thus, in this instance, the odds ratio and the relative risk are virtually the same. This is because the outcome of interest, lung cancer, is rare, so $(a + b) \approx b$, and $(c + d) \approx d$, with the result that:

$$\frac{a/(a+b)}{c/(c+d)} \approx \frac{a/b}{c/d}$$

This approximation of the odds ratio to the relative risk does not hold true if the outcome of interest is common in the population under study.

Source: Doll *et al.* 1994

British doctors study

	Lung cancer	No lung cancer	Lung cancer rate
Smoker	209	99,791	209/(209 + 99791) = 0.209%
Non-smoker	14	99,986	14/(14 + 99986) = 0.014%

Other types of epidemiological evidence

While case control and cohort studies are the principal epidemiological approaches to assessing the relationship between a risk factor and disease, there are other possible designs.

The simplest approach is the *case report*, which describes a single case of disease which is noteworthy because of some particular feature or features. Thus, in October 1995, two case reports were published concerning Creutzfeldt-Jakob Disease (CJD) in teenagers in the UK (Britton *et al.* 1995; Bateman *et al.* 1995). These were the first cases of CJD to be reported in this age group in the UK. Neither case had been exposed to any of the established risk factors for CJD, but both had some exposure to beef products. This type of report can really do no more than raise the possibility of a link between the disease and the exposure in question – in this case, beef contaminated with bovine spongiform encephalopathy (BSE).

The logical extension of a case report is a *case series*, which describes a group of cases with common features. In March 1996, information was released concerning 10 cases of a new variant of CJD in the UK. This new type of CJD affected young people (average age 27), and was characterized by clinical features that were substantially different from the 'traditional' form of the disease (Will *et al.* 1996). The expert committee advising the UK government concluded that 'the most likely explanation for the 10 new cases is exposure to the agent that causes bovine spongiform encephalopathy in cattle that occurred before the ban on the use of cow offal was introduced in 1989' (Dillner 1996). While evidence from a case series is stronger than that from a single case report, it is nevertheless weak, and can do no more than raise a hypothesis. The principal problems with a case series are that there is no proper comparison group, and any apparent link may be no more than coincidence.

A third type of study is an *ecological study*, where exposure to the risk factor is correlated to disease incidence in different populations. For example, Hofman and Wientjens looked at the incidence of CJD disease in different countries in Europe in 1993 and 1994, and found that the UK, with a much higher risk of exposure to BSE than other European countries, did not have a higher incidence of CJD (Hofman and Wientjens 1995). The attraction of an ecological study is that it is quick to do since it usually relies on data that is already available. However, there are problems as well. An ecological study cannot link exposure with disease in individuals. If Hofman and Wientjens had found that the incidence of CJD was higher in countries with greater exposure to BSE, they would still not have been able to demonstrate that the cases of CJD were actually in people who had eaten or been exposed in some way to infected cattle. Furthermore, there are always alternative explanations for observed correlations, since an ecological study cannot control for potential confounders. A confounder is a factor that is associated both with the exposure, and to the disease in question. For example, if CJD and BSE were both caused by a single environmental factor, one would expect there to be a correlation between exposure to BSE and incidence of CJD, but this would be because of confounding by the environmental factor rather than because BSE caused CJD.

In a *cross-sectional study*, exposure and disease status are measured at the same time in individuals in a defined population. With a rare disease like CJD, such an approach is impractical. Furthermore, since exposure and disease status is assessed at the same point in time, it may not be possible to distinguish the temporal relationship between them. Does eating beef cause CJD, or do people with CJD develop a craving for meat?

Each of the approaches described above can really provide no more than circumstantial evidence for a link between an exposure and a disease. More robust methods are required to provide better evidence. The strongest epidemiological research design is *the randomized controlled trial* (see Chapter 4), but it is rarely possible for such a method to be used in this context. In practice, the best epidemiological evidence that exposure to something causes a disease comes from case control and cohort studies.

Causality

So far in this chapter, epidemiological evidence has been considered in terms of association: for example, is smoking associated with lung cancer? What is much more useful to know is: does smoking *cause* lung cancer? Unfortunately, unlike laboratory science, definitive proof is not possible in epidemiology. Therefore, deciding about causation requires a judgement to be made about the circumstantial evidence that is available (Bradford-Hill 1965).

The first factor to consider is the *strength* of the association, which is indicated by the size of the relative risk. Thus, the strength of the association between smoking and lung cancer is very large (RR = 14.9), but the association between smoking and ischaemic heart disease is much weaker, though statistically significant (RR = 1.6) – see Table 3.2.

The second factor to consider is *consistency*. Have different types of study in different places and at different times shown the same association between exposure and the disease? For example, evidence that lying a baby prone is associated with sudden infant death syndrome comes from more than 10 case control studies between 1970 and 1992 in different countries and from a cohort study (Dwyer and Ponsonby 1992).

Third, it is important to ascertain the *temporal relationship* of the association. As Bradford-Hill put it: 'which is the cart and which is the horse?' (Bradford-Hill 1965). In some epidemiological investigations, such as ecological studies, cross-sectional surveys, and some case-control studies, it may not be possible to differentiate the one from the other.

Next, one needs to consider whether causation is *biologically plausible*. In other words, does it fit in with existing knowledge as to what is already known about the disease? For example, a case control study investigating leukaemia around the Sellafield nuclear plant found that there was an association between exposure of fathers to ionizing radiation before conception and leukaemia in their children (Gardner *et al.* 1990). While it is well recognized that radiation can lead to cancer, an effect on offspring requires some explanation. One explanation that Gardner *et al.* suggested was that radiation might have a direct effect on the sperm, to produce a mutation that would cause leukaemia in offspring. However, it has been questioned whether this is really plausible from basic biological and radiobiological principles (Notani 1990).

There is further evidence of a cause-effect relationship if a *dose-response relationship* can be demonstrated between the exposure and the disease. For example, in the British doctors study, the relative risk of lung cancer in current smokers compared to non-smokers rises depending upon how heavily they smoke (Doll *et al.* 1994). The relative risk of a light smoker (1–14 per day) is 7.5; the relative risk of a moderate smoker (15–24 per day) is 14.9; and the relative risk of a heavy smoker (more than 24 per day) is 25.4.

Next, evidence of *reversibility* should also be considered. If the risk factor is removed, does the frequency of the disease change? For example, in response to the epidemiological evidence suggesting a link between sudden infant death syndrome and prone sleeping position, in many countries there was a public campaign to educate mothers to lay their babies on their backs or sides. This was followed by dramatic reductions in the death rate from this syndrome, which could be attributed to changes in how babies were placed at night (Dwyer *et al.* 1995).

Conclusion

Observational studies have played, and continue to play, an important role in epidemiology and health services research. Their use in the evaluation of new drugs and therapies is overshadowed by the randomized trial (see Chapter 2) but they are indispensable tools in the ascertainment of risk factors in populations. Prospective cohort studies have advantages over the case control study, but they are time-consuming and often costly ventures. While case control studies are prone to bias they can, when carefully conducted, provide the first step to answering many important medical questions, and they can do so quickly and economically.

References

Barker, D.J.P., Gluckman, P.D., Godfrey, K.M., Harding, J.E., Owens, J.A. and Robinson, J.S. (1993) Foetal nutrition and cardiovascular disease in adult life, *Lancet*, 341: 938–41.

Barrett-Connor, E. and Bush, T.L. (1991) Estrogen and coronary heart disease in women, *Journal of the American Medical Association*, 265: 1861–7.

Bateman, D., Hilton, D., Love, S., Zeidler, M., Beck, J. and Collinge, J. (1995) Sporadic Creutzfeldt-Jakob disease in an 18-year-old in the UK, *Lancet*, 346: 1155–6.

Bennicke, K., Conrad, C., Sabroe, S. and Sorensen, H.T. (1995) Cigarette smoking and breast cancer, *British Medical Journal*, 310: 1431–3.

Blair, P.S., Fleming, P.J., Bensley, D., Smith, I., Bacon, C., Taylor, E., Berry, J., Golding, J., Tripp, J. and the Confidential Enquiry into Stillbirths and Deaths Regional Coordinators (1996). Smoking and the sudden infant death syndrome: results from 1993–5, case-control study for confidential inquiry into still births and deaths in infancy, *British Medical Journal*, 313: 195–8.

Bradford-Hill, A. (1965) The environment and disease: association or causation? *Journal of the Royal Society of Medicine*, 58: 295–300.

Britton, T.C., Al-Sarraj, S., Shaw, C., Campbell, T. and Collinge, J. (1995) Sporadic Creutzfeldt-Jakob disease in a 16-year-old in the UK, *Lancet*, 346: 1155.

Christensen, K., Vaupel, J.W., Holm, N.V. and Yashin, A.I. (1995) Mortality among twins after age 6: fetal origins hypothesis versus twin method, *British Medical Journal*, 310: 432–5.

Collaborative Group on Hormonal Factors in Breast Cancer (1996) Breast cancer and hormonal contraceptives: collaborative reanalysis of individual data on 53,297 women with breast cancer and 100, 329 women without breast cancer from 54 epidemiological studies, *Lancet*, 347: 1713–27.

Dillner, L. (1996) BSE linked to new variant of CJD in humans, *British Medical Journal*, 312: 795.

Doll, R. and Hill, A.B. (1954) The mortality of doctors in relation to their smoking habits – a preliminary report, *British Medical Journal*, i: 1451–5.

Doll, R., Peto, R., Wheatley, K., Gray, R. and Sutherland, I. (1994) Mortality in relation to smoking: 40 years' observations on male British doctors, *British Medical Journal*, 309: 901–11.

Dwyer, T. and Ponsonby, A.-L. (1992) Sudden infant death syndrome: insights from epidemiological research, *Journal of Epidemiology and Community Health*, 46: 98–102.

Dwyer, T., Ponsonby, A-L., Blizzard, L., Newman, N.M. and Cochrane, J.A. (1995) The contribution of changes in the prevalence of prone sleeping position to the decline in sudden infant death syndrome in Tasmania, *Journal of the American Medical Association*, 273: 783–9.

Fall, C.H.D., Osmonde, C., Barker, D.J.P., *et al.* (1995) Fetal and infant growth and cardiovascular risk factors in women, *British Medical Journal*, 310: 428–32.

Fleming, P.J., Blair, P.S., Bacon, C., *et al.* (1996) Environment of infants during sleep and risk of the sudden infant death syndrome: results of 1993–95 case control study for confidential inquiry into stillbirths and deaths in infancy, *British Medical Journal*, 313: 191–5.

Fraser, P., Carpenter, L., Maconochie, N., Higgins, C., Booth, M. and Beral, V. (1993) Cancer mortality and morbidity in employees of the United Kingdom Atomic Energy Authority, 1946–86, *British Journal of Cancer*, 67: 615–24.

Gardner, M.J., Snee, M.P., Hall, A.J., Powell, C.A., Downes, S. and Terrell, J.D. (1990) Results of case-control study of leukaemia and lymphoma among young people near Sellafield nuclear plant in West Cumbria, *British Medical Journal*, 300: 423–9.

Hemminki, E. (1996) Oral contraceptives and breast cancer, *British Medical Journal*, 313: 63–4.

Hofman, A. and Wientjens, D. (1995) Epidemiological evidence concerning a possible causal link, *British Medical Journal*, 311: 1418–19.

Hutton, J.L., Cooke, T. and Pharoah, P.O.D. (1994) Life expectancy in children with cerebral palsy, *British Medical Journal*, 309: 431–5.

Louik, C., Mitchell, A.A., Werler, M.M., et al. (1987) Maternal exposure to spermicides in relation to certain birth defects, *New England Journal of Medicine*, 317: 474–8.

Mant, J.W.F. and Vessey, M.P. (1995) Trends in mortality from primary liver cancer in England and Wales 1975–92: influence of oral contraceptives, *British Journal of Cancer*, 72: 800–3.

Matthews, K.A., Kuller, L.H., Wing, R.R., Meilahn, E.N. and Plantinga, P. (1996) Prior to use of estrogen replacement therapy, are users healthier than non-users? *American Journal of Epidemiology*, 143: 971–8.

Morabia, A., Bernstein, M., Heritier, S. and Khatchatrian, N. (1996) Relation of breast cancer with passive and active exposure to tobacco smoke, *American Journal of Epidemiology*, 143: 918–28.

Notani, N.K. (1990) Leukaemia and lymphoma among young people near Sellafield, *British Medical Journal*, 300: 877–8.

Phillips, A.N., Sabin, C.A., Elford, J., Bofill, M., Janossy, G. and Lee, C.A. (1994) Use of CD4 lymphocyte count to predict long term survival free of AIDS after HIV infection, *British Medical Journal*, 309: 309–13.

Swan, S.H., Shaw, G.M. and Schulman, J. (1992) Reporting and selection bias in case control studies of congenital malformations, *Epidemiology*, 3: 356–63.

Trichopoulos, D. and Katsouyanni, K. (1989) Oral contraceptives, tobacco smoking and breast cancer risk, *Lancet*, II: 158.

UK National Case-Control Study Group (1989) Oral contraceptive use and breast cancer risk in young women, *Lancet*, I: 973–82.

Vessey, M.P., McPherson, K. and Johnson, B. (1977) Mortality among women participating in the Oxford/Family Planning Association Contraceptive Study, *Lancet*, II: 731–3.

Vessey, M.P., Villard-Mackintosh, L., McPherson, K. and Yeates, D. (1989) Mortality among oral contraceptive users: 20-year follow up of women in a cohort study, *British Medical Journal*, 299: 1487–91.

Will, R.G., Ironside, J.W., Zeidler, M., et al. (1996) A new variation of Creutzfeldt-Jakob disease in the UK, *Lancet*, 347: 921–25.

4

Social surveys

Richard Layte and Crispin Jenkinson

Introduction

Social surveys are a method of social research in which investigators attempt
to gain a representative sample of a given population, or indeed may sample
the entire population, and gain data from self-report. A survey is an investigation in which information is systematically collected, but in which the
experimental method is not used (Abramson 1990). Such a definition, however, tends to refer to a wide number of research methods other than just
social surveys such as 'cohort studies' and 'case-control studies'. All of
these methods might usefully be grouped under the heading 'observational'
studies, as opposed to 'experimental studies' such as the randomized controlled trial (see Chapter 2). More narrowly, the term 'social survey' might
be taken to imply surveys of the population, or sub-groups of the population (e.g. people with a particular disease; ethnic minorities; people living
in a certain area, etc.), undertaken to gain information on, for example,
specific aspects of health, household management, education, employment,
etc. It is in this latter sense that 'social survey' is used in this chapter, while
a specific chapter in this book deals with cohort and case-control studies
(see Chapter 3). Data from social surveys tends to be collected in a standardized form that can be coded and analysed statistically. Such data may
be gained for the purposes of description and the generation and testing
of hypotheses. Consequently, social surveys can be descriptive, or analytic
in that they attempt to find the relationship between variables. However,
while analytic surveys may attempt to determine the association of variables, or may, in longitudinal designs, attempt to determine the effect of
a certain event, individuals are not randomly assigned to groups and consequently the study is observational rather than truly experimental. Some

1 Select a topic of study (e.g. health and lifestyles)
2 Undertake a review of the literature
3 Develop a set of issues to be addressed by the study.
4 Identify the population to be surveyed.
5 Carry out preparatory investigations (e.g. preliminary interviews with specialists in the area).
6 Draft a questionnaire, or select appropriate existing questionnaires.
7 Conduct a pilot study.
8 Finalize the questionnaire.
9 Select a sample of the population (if the study will not include the whole of a given population).
10 If appropriate, train interviewers to administer the instrument.
11 Collect data
12 Analyse data and write reports, etc.

Figure 4.1   The stages of conducting a survey (adapted from McNeill 1990)

established texts in the field assume that analytic surveys are experimental by nature (see, for example, Oppenheim 1966, 1992) but given there is no assignment of cases to groups this is unlikely to ever be the case. In this chapter the principles of survey research will be outlined, and the limitations and complexities of this apparently straightforward technique discussed. The basic steps in the planning and undertaking of a social survey are documented in Figure 4.1.

Planning a survey

Carrying out a survey can seem a relatively straightforward undertaking, requiring good organizational skills and some common sense. However, while it is probably fair to assume that most people could, given the appropriate level of funding, send out any number of questionnaires, the development of a properly conducted survey requires more than simply an ability to seal envelopes, or ask people questions! Appropriate questions have to be developed and piloted, or standardized questionnaires chosen; sampling techniques need to be considered in order to gain as representative a sample as possible and the issue of the mode of administration and its possible effect need to be carefully considered.

Sampling

Random sampling

Sampling is an important aspect of successful survey research. If the sample is not representative of the population from which it is drawn then the results gained from it cannot be generalized to the population level. One of the most famous studies of social mobility in England, undertaken by David Glass in the 1940s (Glass and Hall 1954), has been criticized for the very reason that the population characteristics did not seem to be reflected in the sample characteristics (Payne *et al.* 1977): the data indicated a reduction in the number of people entering white collar occupations, and consequently implied a contraction in these occupations, at a time when this section of the labour market had grown considerably. When one is trying to make claims about a population therefore, the importance of sampling cannot be underestimated. The most commonly adopted method of sampling is known as 'probability sampling' in which each person in the population has a known probability of being selected. Random sampling is the most familiar form of probability sampling, and is a technique whereby each sampling unit (e.g. an individual person) will have the same probability of being selected. When used without qualification random sampling is often referred to as 'simple random sampling'. Random sampling requires the following process: first, a sampling frame must be selected. This is usually a list containing all the people from which the sample is to be selected. Such a list may be all those people registered to vote in a given area or all those people registered with general practitioners in a given area. For example, in the Oxford Healthy Lifestyles Survey all patients on local Family Health Service Authorities (which at that time were the organizations that kept computerized lists of people registered with GPs) were used as the sampling frame (Wright *et al.* 1992). However, despite the fact one would hope that everyone in the country was accurately entered on electoral registers and general practice lists, the names that appear on a list rarely reflect the population perfectly accurately. They are often out of date, containing names of people who have moved out of the area or who have died. Furthermore, others will have moved into the area but not yet registered themselves on the electoral register or with doctors, and still others will not appear on such lists because they are homeless, never visit a doctor, have not replied to communications about their name and address, and so on. Ideally, some check should be done on the data in the sampling frame to determine that it is at least representative of the population it is meant to reflect. Thus, for example, one could run analyses to ensure that the social class distribution of the area was broadly comparable with data from the national census. If the two disagree substantially one may have considerable concern for the accuracy of the sampling frame. After the sampling frame has been selected, then the sample size should be determined. This is not an easy task, especially in those instances where power calculations (which indicate the ability of a study to determine relationships between variables being measured) cannot be made as there are no prior hypotheses about, for example, possible differences between certain groups of the population on a given variable or variables (see below). Pragmatically, most social survey research projects try to ascertain the largest sample that can be gained with the resources available. Once the sample size has been determined subjects are selected at random, usually from tables of random numbers, or using computer programs that generate random numbers.

Another form of probability sampling is 'systematic sampling'. Once the first case has been randomly selected the choice of all others is predetermined. A systematic sample is one gained by taking every 'nth' subject in a list containing the population to be sampled. Consequently, not all members of the population have the same chance of being selected for inclusion in the sample. Once the sample size as a percentage of the population, or 'sampling fraction', has been decided the random selection of the starting point determines the whole sample. Systematic sampling is likely to produce a more even spread of the sample over the population than does simple random sampling. This can lead to greater precision than does simple random sampling in those instances where the sample is ordered in some systematic way (e.g. by age). One particular problem of this sampling method concerns instances where the sampling interval coincides with some periodic interval in the list, but such periodicals are rare and generally easy to detect (Moser and Kalton 1972).

In instances where simple random or systematic sampling would create a sample too geographically spread then a method known as cluster sampling can be adopted. Cluster sampling is a method for gaining a sample from a population in two stages. This method takes advantage of the fact that most populations are structured in some way. For example, all people registered to vote constitute the national electorate. If this group is to act as the primary sampling frame it is possible to select a random group of local constituencies. Random sampling is used to select out groups to be included at the second stage and, technically, all subjects included in the selected samples are then surveyed. The advantage of this method is that it produces, as the name suggests, 'clusters' of respondents, thereby reducing interviewing and travelling costs. Simple random sampling of the national electorate would produce a list with potential respondents spread throughout the country, whereas cluster sampling will lead to clusters of places where respondents will be located. Cluster sampling is effectively a special case of 'multi-stage' sampling in which successive samples are taken. Thus, the national electorate may constitute the sampling frame, from which a random selection of local constituencies are selected, from which a random selection of local wards are drawn and, potentially, from which a random selection of respondents are chosen. Both cluster and multi-stage sampling increase the chance of sampling error with each stage in the process. Sampling error refers to inaccuracies in inferences about a population that have been derived from a sample survey. Thus, if a multi-stage sample selects more constituencies in the North of England than the South then the results are likely to reflect the views of people in the North rather than the South. The chance of such sampling error occurring increases substantially when samples are small. Multi-stage sampling was used in the national UK Health and Lifestyle Survey conducted by Blaxter and her colleagues (Blaxter 1990). In that study a three-stage sampling procedure was employed starting with a sampling frame based on electoral registers. To ensure that the resulting sample was not unrepresentative Blaxter compared the sociodemographic characteristics of the sample (of 9003 people) with data from the 1981 Census of England, Wales and Scotland. Broadly speaking she found the sample reflected the characteristics of the sample, although there was a shortfall in younger respondents and the elderly as well as a slight over-representation of women. However, on the basis of employment status, marital status, household composition and social class the survey seemed to mirror well the UK population.

It is possible that where a researcher wishes to compare sub-groups of the population, one or other of the groups is under-represented. To avoid this problem researchers can select samples of equal size within each of the groups. For example, one may wish to compare the attitudes to treatment of male and female heart attack survivors. However, a random sample would produce more men than women, given that heart attack is more common in males. Consequently, one may decide not to sample from the group as a whole, but to select random samples of equal size from the two sub-groups.

Non-random sampling

Ideally, to be able to extrapolate findings of surveys data should be collected from a randomly selected, representative sample. However, this can be very difficult to achieve in practice. Consequently, researchers sometimes adopt designs which simply include all the people in a given place at a given time (this is called 'opportunistic' sampling, though it should, perhaps more accurately be called 'haphazard'), or adopt a method called 'snowball sampling'. The latter technique, although unlikely to result in a truly representative sample, is useful in topics on surveys where the issue under discussion is either relatively rare or is a sensitive issue. Snowball sampling refers to getting an initial sample from either advertisements or via acquaintances and then requesting this sample to ask people known to them to join in the survey. An example of the use of such a method is Fitzpatrick et al.'s (1990) study on the behaviour of homosexual men. Many of the first participants were recruited by advertisements placed in clubs and bars. These initial respondents were then asked to ask friends and associates to come forward and take part in the study (Dawson et al. 1991; Fitzpatrick et al. 1990; Boulton et al. 1992).

Sample size

The sample size of a social survey is very important. 'Samples which are too small can prove nothing; samples which are too large can prove anything' (Sackett 1979). A small sample is likely to be unrepresentative of the population under investigation; furthermore true differences between any sub-groups of the sample are unlikely to reach statistical significance even if the sample is representative. On the other hand, while larger samples are more likely to be representative statistical tests on sub-groups are often likely to be statistically significant, yet not necessarily very meaningful. This latter consideration is particularly important in medical and health research given that it is possible to find differences between groups that are statistically significant but clinically or subjectively meaningless. For example, subjectively assessed health status between social classes I and II has been documented using established health assessment questionnaires (Jenkinson *et al.* 1993a, 1993b, 1996). The differences between the two groups may be statistically significant but there is very little evidence that they indicate any meaningful difference. A hypothetical example may be useful here. Imagine a survey of height in which it was found that one group of people were taller than another, and the difference statistically significant. However, everyone in one group was taller by a millimetre than everyone in the other group. Consequently, the difference is statistically significant (i.e. not a product of chance) but it is very unlikely this would have any real meaning to those in either group: the chances are they would never notice the difference in their daily lives.

One of the recurrent questions posed in survey research is how many subjects should be included in the sample. It is not an easy question to answer. In, for example, clinical trials and case-control studies principles exist for the calculation of sample size. In randomized controlled trials a researcher may know the typical outcome for people who are not treated and will make assumptions concerning the treatment effect. Thus, for example, in the MRC vitamin trial the researchers had beliefs about the efficacy of vitamin supplements on the effect of neural tube defects (MRC Vitamin Study Research Group 1991). They were thus able to hypothesize a difference between those receiving such a treatment and those not and calculate a sample size on the basis of such assumptions. However, very often survey research is descriptive in nature and the purpose of surveys is often not to test hypotheses, but to provide a description of a particular population.

In instances where a rough estimate can be made of the proportion in a population with some particular attribute the following formula can be used to estimate the sample size:

$$n = \pi(1 - \pi)/[\text{S.E. (p)}]^2 \qquad\qquad (\text{Equation 1})$$

where n = the sample size

π = proportion in the population with a particular attribute, and
S.E. (p) = the smallest *preferred* standard error

However, this calculation can lead to massive sample sizes, so the finite population correction (which corrects for the size of the population from which the sample will be drawn) can be applied:

$$n' = n/[1 + (n/N)]$$ (Equation 2)

where n is the solution of equation 1 (above), and
    N is the population size.

Of course simple equations such as those documented above are of little use when the purpose of a survey is to find the prevalence of some phenomena, and where one has no prior notion of the prevalence beforehand. Consequently, the tendency is for researchers to gain as large a sample size as possible given the constraints of time and resources at their disposal. While this can usually give reasonable assurance that the survey should be representative this is not something one can take for granted. A famous example of a large sample size producing a meaningless result was the 1936 Literary Digest survey of 10 million people which incorrectly forecast the outcome of the US Presidential election! In part this was due to the sampling frame, which was drawn from telephone directories, thereby excluding certain sections of the (voting) population, and non-response (only 20 per cent of mail ballots were returned). Consequently, the sampling frame may be unrepresentative as may be the respondents. One method of determining whether a sample is representative is to compare its composition with that of some known aspect of the characteristics of the target population. Thus, for example, in the Oxford Health and Lifestyles Survey (Wright *et al.* 1992) certain demographic aspects of the target population were compared with census data for that region. Thus the social class characteristics of the area were compared with that gained from the survey and were found to be similar. This would give one some confidence that the sample was representative.

Questions, answers and mode of administration

Questions and answers

The design of questionnaires may not seem, to most people, to be an undertaking requiring training, and considerable time and resources. A modicum of common sense, a word processor and some paper would seem to be all that is required. However, most people are also familiar with questionnaires that they have found boring, confusing and, sometimes, downright incomprehensible! Perhaps, similar to the case of common sense, everyone believes that they are better equipped to design questionnaires than anyone else. Fortunately, there are principles laid down for the design and validation of questionnaires which can provide some form of quality assurance.

The requirements of questions included in surveys has been documented by Stone (1993), who claims that they should be appropriate, intelligible, unambiguous, unbiased, 'omnicompetent' (by which he seems to mean that response categories should cover all possible responses to the question), piloted and ethical. Such requirements seem little more than common sense, but other techniques which can assess whether a questionnaire is valid (i.e. produces results which reflect the phenomena they purport to be measuring) and reliable (i.e. produces the same results in the same situations at different times). The issues of reliability and validity are dealt with in Chapter 5 which discusses these requirements in relation to measures designed to assess health status and quality of life; however, the issues apply to questionnaires in general.

Mode of administration

The basic instrument for the collection of survey data is the questionnaire. This can be administered either face to face, or over the phone, or can be sent in the post. Not only do these different methods of administration differ in the percentage of people who will agree to take part in the study but evidence suggests that they also differ in the responses given by people to questions. Face-to-face interviewing is often the preferred method of administration, but while it is often associated with higher numbers of people agreeing to take part in the study (de Vaus 1991), it is both costly and brings with it a number of complications. Certainly there is a considerable body of evidence that the characteristics of the interviewer as well as their expectations can have a substantial effect upon responses (Groves 1989).

Non-response

One of the major problems of social surveys, especially when conducted via the post, is non-response. The problem is not, in general, that non-response provides a lower sample size but rather that the sample gained may not be representative of the population from which it was drawn, or, put another way, non-respondents may differ from the respondents in some important and/or systematic fashion. Certainly, it has been consistently found that those with higher levels of education and in higher social classes are more likely to respond. Researchers undertaking a survey, especially when sent by post, should attempt to ensure as a high a response rate as possible. There are three areas over which researchers have limited control when undertaking a survey: the population, the topic and the sponsorship of the survey. However aspects of survey design are amenable to change and methods exist to increase participation in mail surveys. These are well documented in the literature, and will not be re-rehearsed in any depth here.

Suffice to say, response envelopes, covering letters informing people of the purpose of the survey and possible inducements are all methods for increasing response. These issues are covered in greater depth in most social survey texts, such as the now classic texts by Cartwright (1983) and Moser and Kalton (1972).

Missing data

Related to the problem of non-response is missing data, i.e. data missing from questionnaires that have been returned. Pilot studies should be undertaken to determine if certain questions have higher levels of non-response than others, and if so attempts should be made to make changes. However, it is inevitable that respondents will not complete every question, especially in postal surveys. For the most part there is precious little that can be done about missing-data although some methods have been recommended for imputing such missing information. For example, some established questionnaires, such as the SF-36, which is designed to measure self-reported functioning and well-being over eight areas of health status, have recommended algorithms for substituting data that has been omitted by respondents (Ware *et al.* 1993). However, the use of data substitution algorithms is not highly recommended: it is researchers trying to guess what respondents would have answered to questions, which somehow seems to do away with asking the questions in the first place! Nevertheless, practical considerations sometimes make this a necessity (see below).

Conducting a social survey: an example

As the previous sections of this chapter have shown, the primary aim when conducting a social survey is to collect a representative sample of responses from any given population. However, there is always a tension between this aim and the practicality of carrying it out. For example, although probability sampling theory dictates that sampling units should be randomly distributed across the area within which the population is located, this demand is, in reality impractical since interviewers would spend inordinate amounts of time travelling between interviews. This section will describe at length one example of how practical feasibility was combined with methodological rigour in the planning and execution of an ongoing, nationally representative social survey – the British Household Panel Study (from here on referred to as the BHPS), and how this survey may serve so as to illuminate the complex relationship between health and employment status.

The BHPS is being carried out by the Economic and Social Research Council Centre on Micro-Social Change at the University of Essex and seeks to further our understanding of social and economic change at the individual and household level in Britain. The survey is longitudinal in design, that is, it is designed to be carried out every year until at least 1999. It is also a 'panel survey' as it will return to the same individuals every year. This design will allow researchers to follow individuals and households over time and thus 'identify, model and forecast changes, their causes and consequences in relation to a range of socio-economic variables' (Taylor *et al.* 1996). Since social surveys are not experimental, it is often very difficult to separate the causal relationship between variables which are sampled at the same time (in a so-called 'cross-sectional' survey). With a longitudinal panel survey on the other hand, researchers will be able to test for relationships between variables while controlling for the affects of others. One example is the relationship between unemployment and health (Whelan 1994). It has been repeatedly observed that the unemployed have a lower health status than the employed, but it has always been impossible to prove that the ill-health followed the unemployment and not the other way around. The BHPS contains a battery of questions which deal with physical and emotional health and a full and detailed account of each individual's work life since leaving school.

The BHPS is a valuable source of data, but more important in the context of this chapter is the complexity of the data sought (i.e. nationally representative individual and household interviews over an extended period) and the practical methodology that was employed to make the survey a reality. As in the earlier part of this chapter, we will divide the analysis of the methodology of the BHPS into sections dealing with sample selection, sample size and the problems of missing and reweighting the data.

Sample selection

Since the BHPS was intended to survey a representative sample of individuals and households in Great Britain, a sampling methodology had to be employed which would balance the need for the final sample to be representative of the entire British sample of households while not being prohibitively expensive to the Economic and Social Research Council. Luckily, the research team could draw upon the experience and lessons learnt in carrying out past government social surveys of households such as the General Household Survey (GHS). In practice, the sample design of the BHPS was very close to that employed in the GHS – a two-stage clustered probability design with systematic sampling – and used the same sampling frame. Let's examine each of the elements in that description and relate them to the sections outlined earlier.

Successful sample selection can only be made from a sampling frame (i.e. a list of the population to be surveyed) which includes all of the population. If categories of persons, households or areas are missing, no amount of statistical wizardry can make the results representative. The BHPS team used the small users Postcode Address File (PAF) for Great Britain south of the Caledonian Canal (excluding Northern Ireland). This frame is accepted as the best for sampling households since it is almost completely inclusive in its coverage of addresses, and it is regularly updated (Wilson and Elliot 1987; Butcher 1988).

With the appropriate sample frame, the next stage is to construct a sampling procedure that ensures that the final units of analysis will be representative of the population along the dimensions of interest to the researcher or researchers. In the case of the BHPS, there were to be a number of uses to which the survey was to be put and thus a large number of dimensions along which sampling could be carried out. However, since most researchers using the survey would be interested in the relationship between socio-economic and demographic variables, it makes sense that the sample should be representative of the British population in terms of its socio-demographic structure. In reality, it would be hoped that certain socio-demographic characteristics (such as age) would be randomly distributed and thus would not pose too many problems in terms of sample selection. These characteristics are all at the individual or household level, but to make a random sample selection of households at this point could lead to a very widespread distribution of interviewees (i.e. the sample would not be 'clustered' into specific geographical locations). Therefore, the sample selection was split into two stages: the first based upon a stratified primary sampling unit (PSU) of 250 postcode sectors systematically selected, and the second upon a systematic selection of delivery points or addresses within these sectors.

In the first stage, 250 postcode sectors were selected (with an average of 2500 delivery points each) by stratifying the population of delivery points into an ordered list by region and three socio-demographic variables and then systematically sampling the required number. Thus, all PSUs were ordered into 18 national regions (after making sure that each PSU contained at least 500 households, and if not grouped with other smaller PSUs) within which PSUs were then stratified into a rank order according to the proportion of heads of households in professional or managerial positions. Each stratified region was then split into 'major strata', or smaller units, the number of which depended upon the size of the region. Each major strata was then ranked once again, this time by the proportion of the population of pensionable age, and then split into 'minor strata' that were re-ranked either by the proportion of the population employed in agriculture (if rural) or the proportion of the population under pensionable age and living in single person households (if urban). This rather complicated stratification procedure ensured that when the systematic selection process was initiated, the outcome would not be skewed by periodic effects in the list (remember that systematic sampling chooses a starting integer and then chooses every nth subject depending on this starting value).

The second stage of the sampling procedure was to select households from each of the 250 PSUs selected in the first stage. Since each PSU was a specific geographical area, the final selection of households would be clustered, thus making the process of getting to interviews easier for the research team. Inside each PSU, selection of households could now be easily accomplished by using a systematic sampling procedure similar to that employed in the first stage. However, to ensure that the final list of households to be included was of the highest quality, selection was left as late as possible so that the most recent list of addresses could be used. The late stage of the address selection meant that some of the PSUs had increased or decreased in size since the initial ranking procedures had been carried out and this needed to be taken into account when setting the final number of households to be selected from each PSU.

Another sample problem arose at the point at which the interviewer appeared at the front door of the house: each address could have multiple households in residence. To take account of this, each interviewer was instructed to sample up to three of the households within the address and take details of the unsampled households so that weights could be applied to the data later (see last section). This procedure does, however, assume that the interviewer can discern individual households. In practice they employed the standard definition of a household used by the Office of National Statistics (which was created in 1996 by the amalgamation of the Central Statistical Office and the Office of Population Surveys and Censuses): 'One person living alone or a group of people who either share living accommodation or share one meal a day and who have the address as their only main residence.'

Since the BHPS is a longitudinal survey, rules needed to be constructed as to how new individuals would enter the survey at subsequent waves so as to preserve the representativeness of the survey. The sample for wave two consisted of all eligible adults in all households where at least one interview was obtained at wave one, regardless of whether that individual had been interviewed in the first wave. This meant that people who were not interviewed in a household at wave one could now be included in wave two or subsequent waves. Households who refused to take part in the survey at wave one were also approached again in an effort to recruit them into the sample. Individuals would also be recruited into the survey if an original sample member moved in with them (as a household), or they moved in with an original sample member.

Sample size

The sample for the BHPS was intended to be nationally representative, but the exact way in which this would translate into a set number of respondents would depend on the proportion of the British population with a specific attribute. The BHPS is a general social survey, thus there is no specific criterion upon which this equation could be built. As such, the decision was made to sample the maximum number of households possible, given the funding available, which turned out to be around 5000.

Weighting and missing data

Even the most rigorous and careful social surveyor can still find that households or individuals carefully selected and tentatively approached can refuse to take part in the survey. Such 'non-response' could lead to systematic inaccuracies in the survey sample and thus to the survey as a whole being unrepresentative. However, if the characteristics of the individuals or households which do not respond are known, it is possible to construct 'weights' for the sample which can be applied during the analysis of the data to correct for any bias introduced by non-response. In the BHPS, weights were constructed to deal with non-response at both the household and individual level.

A 'weight' is a value attached to a sample unit (i.e. a variable with a specific value in a data set of 'cases' made up of variables') which can be used (usually by a statistical program on a computer) to increase or decrease the numbers of cases with different characteristics, depending on the non-response characteristics of the survey. Thus, weights are applied to responding households in order to compensate for non-responding households. If weights are not applied to a sample, the assumption is automatically being made that means, proportions and relationships between variables in the responding households are identical to those in the non-responding households. The value of the weight is dictated by the known or assumed characteristics of the non-responding units, therefore in the case of the BHPS, non-responding households were put into two classes: one where the type of dwelling was known and one where it was unknown. If the type was unknown, a weighting class, or value was calculated using the socioeconomic group stratifier used at the first stage of the sample selection (the proportion of heads of households in professional or managerial positions). Within each class, the responding households were then weighted by a factor that made the total number of households for a given class equal to the total number of responding and non-responding households in that class. If the type of dwelling was known, the weighting classes were subdivided once again according to the type of accommodation (i.e. detached, semi-detached, etc.).

Although there may be data for households, some individuals within the household may not be available or may refuse to take part. As at the household level, this non-response may mean that the individuals actually sampled are not an accurate sample of the population of individuals as a whole. Accurate weights can be constructed if the characteristics of the non-responding individuals are known. This would usually not be possible, but the BHPS implemented an 'interview by proxy' methodology which asked other members of the household to answer simple questions about the socio-economic and demographic status of the non-responding person. Using this data and other data about the household, a statistical model was constructed which estimated the probability of a person giving a full interview, a proxy interview or no interview. The estimates from this model were then used to weight the known individuals in the survey.

Since the BHPS is a panel survey, i.e. it returns to the same sample of people every year, weights also had to be constructed for each subsequent wave of the survey. In essence, these weights are identical to those applied to wave one. However, more complex weights had to be devised which could be used in the analysis of information from multiple waves. These 'longitudinal weights' had to take account of the different sampling characteristics of each new wave since households or individuals from one wave may not necessarily appear in a later wave (refusal and moving away are the main reasons for loss, but as in any population some respondents will die or be admitted to institutions and thus not be re-sampled). In the same way, the weights also had to take account of new additions to the sample such as new entrants to a household. The longitudinal respondent weight selects out cases who gave a full interview at all waves in the current file (the weight has thus to be recalculated at each new wave) and these cases are re-weighted to take account of previous wave respondents lost at the current wave.

The weights to be attached to respondents to the current wave are calculated in a two step procedure. First, all respondents whose current status was known (even if they had died or were now outside of the remit of the sample) were weighted to take account of those whose status was now unknown because they could not be traced. Second, all respondents giving a full interview were weighted to take account of those who refused, gave a proxy interview or were otherwise unable to respond. Weighting was calculated using a set of computer algorithms which analysed the household and available variables associated with none response.

Data imputation

An earlier section of this chapter discussed the problem of missing data and the measures that can be taken to minimize it at the pilot stage of the survey. It is a sad fact of social survey research that whatever measures are undertaken, respondents will still miss items within the survey that may be crucial to the analysis at hand. This problem is especially significant when using statistical modelling since missing data on one variable in the analysis may mean that a case is removed from the whole analysis. Imputation is a method of dealing with this problem which although not totally satisfactory, may still be better than simply deleting cases from the analysis. This latter approach makes the strong assumption that responding cases are an accurate sample of the population and are randomly distributed. It is easy to think of variables such as income where this assumption would lead to systematic bias.

Imputation techniques use different models with defined assumptions to gain a best estimate of the data which is missing. In the BHPS, imputation was used to obtain important income variables. Two main imputation techniques were used in the BHPS: 'hot-deck' imputation and regression imputation.

Hot-deck imputation is very similar to the process used to calculate weights using weighting classes. As when weighting, the sample is divided into categories which are predictive of the variable that is missing for some cases. Missing data is then replaced using the value of the cases without missing data in the same class. This method was used extensively in the BHPS to replace categorical money variables such as the band within which a personal income fell.

In regression imputation an ordinary least squares regression model (OLS) is constructed containing both missing and non-missing cases which seeks to predict a variable of interest (i.e. one with missing values) using other variables. When the model with the highest explained variance is reached (highest R^2) for both valid and missing cases, a 'fitted value' or estimate is taken from the model of the true value of the variable for each missing case. Since OLS regression models deal with 'continuous quantities', they are ideal for estimating and imputing financial data such as income.

Since the best estimate of the value of a variable for a case in one wave is probably the value of the variable in another wave, cross-wave information was used to augment the imputation procedures just outlined. It must be remembered, however, that imputation is simply a technique for minimizing response bias and not a way of improving accuracy by increasing the available sample size.

Conclusions

The BHPS provides an interesting practical example of the social survey techniques outlined in this chapter. Its need to be nationally representative means that it employed a two stage sampling procedure taking cases from a national sampling frame. However, practical considerations meant that the final sample was collected from a number of 'clusters' around Britain where interviewers would find it easier to access respondents without travelling long distances between interviews. Unfortunately, the best laid plans do not always work perfectly, thus we have seen how remedial measures such as weighting and imputation were used to make the sample as representative as possible.

This chapter has highlighted the potential pitfalls and complexities of what is perhaps the most apparently straightforward form of social research.

Given that so many claims in the medical literature and elsewhere are based upon results from social surveys it is essential that anyone reading such reports view them with caution and determine the methods of sampling, weighting, etc. used. For those planning a social survey the potential complexities and pitfalls should not be underestimated.

References

Abramson, J.H. (1990) *Survey Methods in Community Medicine.* Edinburgh: Churchill Livingstone.

Blaxter, M. (1990) *Health and Lifestyles.* London: Routledge.

Butcher, R. (1988) The use of the post-code address file as a sampling frame, *The Statistician*, 37: 15–24.

Boulton, M., Hart, G. and Fitzpatrick, R. (1992) The sexual behaviour of bisexual men in relation to HIV transmission, *HIV Care*, 4: 165–75.

Cartwright, A. (1983) *Health Surveys in Practice and in Potential.* London: Kings Fund.

de Vaus, D.A. (1991) *Surveys in Social Research* (3rd edn). London: UCL Press.

Dawson, J., Fitzpatrick, R., McLean, J., Hart, G. and Boulton, M. (1991) The HIV test and sexual behaviour in a sample of homosexually active men, *Social Science and Medicine*, 32: 683–8.

Fitzpatrick, R., McLean, J., Dawson, J., Boulton, M. and Hart, G. (1990) Factors influencing condom use in a sample of homosexually active men, *Genitourinary Medicine*, 66: 346–50.

Glass, D. and Hall, J.R. (1954) Social mobility in Britain: a study of intergenerational changes in status, in D. Glass and J.R. Hall (eds) *Social Mobility in Britain.* London: Routledge and Kegan Paul.

Groves, R.M. (1989) Actors and questions in telephone and personal interview surveys, in E. Singer and S. Presser (eds) *Survey Research Methods: A Reader.* Chicago: University of Chicago Press.

Jenkinson, C., Coulter, A. and Wright, L. (1993a) Short Form 36 (SF36) health survey questionnaire. Normative data for adults of working age, *British Medical Journal*, 306: 1437–40.

Jenkinson, C., Wright, L. and Coulter, A. (1993b) *Quality of Life Measurement in Health Care.* Oxford: Health Services Research Unit, University of Oxford.

Jenkinson, C., Layte, R., Wright, L. and Coulter, A. (1996) *The UK SF-36: An Analysis and Interpretation Manual.* Oxford: Health Services Research Unit, University of Oxford.

McNeill, P. (1990) *Research Methods.* London: Routledge.

Moser, C.A. and Kalton, G. (1972) *Survey Methods in Social Investigation.* London: Heinemann Educational.

MRC Vitamin Study Research Group (1991) Prevention of neural tube defects: results from the MRC Vitamin Study, *Lancet*, 338: 132–7.

Oppenheim, B. (1966) *Questionnaire Design and Attitude Measurement.* New York: Basic Books.

Oppenheim, B. (1992) *Questionnaire Design, Interviewing and Attitude Measurement.* London: Pinter.

Payne, G., Ford, G. and Robertson, C. (1977) A reappraisal of social mobility in Britain, *Sociology*, 11: 289–310.

Sackett, D. (1979) Bias in analytic research, *Journal of Chronic Diseases*, 32: 51–63.

Stone, D.H. (1993) Design a questionnaire, *British Medical Journal*, 307: 1264–6.

Ware, J.E., Snow, K.K., Kosinski, M. and Gandek, B. (1993) *The SF36 Health Survey Manual and Interpretation Guide*. Boston, Mass.: The Health Institute, New England Medical Center.

Whelan, C.T. (1994) Social Class, Unemployment and Psychological Distress, *European Sociological Review*, 10, 1: 49–61.

Wilson, P.R. and Elliot, D.J. (1987) An evaluation of the post-code address file as a sampling frame and its uses with the OPCS, *Journal of the Royal Statistical Society (a)*, 150(3): 230–40.

Wright, L., Harwood, D. and Coulter, A. (1992) *Health and Lifestyles in the Oxford Region*. Oxford: Health Services Research Unit.

5

Patient assessed outcomes: measuring health status and quality of life

Crispin Jenkinson and Hannah McGee

Introduction

'Doctors use a variety of technologies – thermometers, blood tests, X-rays, magnetic imaging machines, endoscopes – to determine what ails you. But to find out how you feel, about all they can do is ask' (Winslow 1992). This assertion appeared in the *Wall Street Journal* and might at first glance seem unremarkable, if not even trivial, but the article went on to document the fact that in recent years attempts have been made to *systematically* collect data on subjective well-being from patients. This chapter will begin by introducing this topic, and outlining the uses information gained directly from patients may have. It will then document the desired measurement properties of instruments and potential limitations in this area of research.

The purpose of medical care

The primary aim of medical care is to improve or maintain the overall functional capacity and general health of patients. Medical care has historically concentrated on the diagnosis and treatment of physiological and anatomical conditions (Wasson *et al.* 1992). For the most part this approach has tended to overlook global functioning, well being, and quality of life. Traditionally, evaluation of medical treatment has relied upon measures of morbidity and mortality, while medical practitioners have based judgements for intervention on traditional clinical, radiological and laboratory measures (Albrecht 1994). This is anomalous given that clinically assessed outcomes of treatment do not always reflect those of patients (Blazer and

Houpt 1979; Jenkinson 1994a). However, over the past few decades there has been a gradual shift away from this approach, and increasingly there is incorporation of patient based data into the evaluation of care (Geigle and Jones 1990; Jenkinson 1995).

The recognition of the patient's point of view as central to the monitoring and evaluation of medical care has brought with it numerous approaches to the measurement of subjective well being. The purpose of such evaluation is to provide more accurate assessments of individuals' or populations' health and the benefits and harms that may result from medical care (Fitzpatrick *et al.* 1992a). The ideal outcome of treatment is a return to the normal or usual quality of life for a given age and medical condition (Ware 1993; Silver 1990). To evaluate the outcome of treatments subjective health measures can be utilized. However, there are a wide variety of applications of health status measures, and the requirements of measures differ across these applications. Before considering the nature of subjective health measures it is worth considering the variety of applications in which data gained directly and systematically from the patients perspective could be of value.

Applications of health status measures

Subjective accounts of functioning and well-being can be used in a variety of ways in the evaluation of health and medical care. Health status measures have been advocated as appropriate tools for the screening of patients needing particular care or attention (Fitzpatrick 1994). For example, health status measures were more accurate than traditional measures of health state in predicting long-term morbidity and mortality in rheumatoid arthritis (Leigh and Fries 1991). However, the data made available from such questionnaires should never be the sole grounds on which treatment decisions should be based. It has been suggested that before standardized health measures are routinely incorporated into clinical practice for individual patient assessment, and the evaluation of treatment options, then score confidence intervals must be fully documented (McHorney *et al.* 1994). The less reliable an instrument (i.e. the greater the level of measurement error) the wider the confidence intervals around any individual score. For example, the short form 36 health survey questionnaire (SF-36), which has been the subject of considerable validation (Brazier *et al.* 1992; Jenkinson *et al.* 1993; Jenkinson *et al.* 1996a; Ware and Sherbourne 1992; Ware *et al.* 1993) has been found to manifest wide confidence intervals. Wide confidence intervals call into question the validity of using brief multi-item scales for individual patient assessment. However, it has been suggested that on an individual basis health status data can act as an adjunct to the standard clinical interview, and may be useful for informing medical practitioners of the well-being of individual patients in their care.

This was one of the possible applications suggested by the designers of the Nottingham Health Profile (NHP) (Hunt *et al.* 1986), although no studies have documented its use in this manner. However, the Dartmouth COOP charts were designed with this purpose in mind (Nelson *et al.* 1990; Nelson *et al.* 1996; Wasson *et al.* 1992). Studies suggest that both patients and clinicians believe the use of the charts has led to improved interaction, and better treatment (Kraus 1991).

At the level of group analysis perhaps the most obvious use for standardized health measurement profiles is as outcome measures in randomized controlled trials. While the use of such measures in randomized control trials has been relatively limited their use in this arena of outcomes research is growing (Spilker 1996). One potential problem with the use of such measures in trials relates to the difficulties in determining meaningful differences on health assessment measures. This problem has probably been one reason for the relatively slow uptake of subjective health outcomes as primary end point measures in clinical trials and the relative paucity of trials including such measures has in turn been suggested as one reason why many clinicians have been unwilling to utilize such measures in clinical practice (Bergner *et al.* 1992). In many instances clinical trials that have claimed to utilize quality of life instruments have done so with measures that are often limited in the range of dimensions covered, and have not been psychometrically validated (Aaronson 1989). For results to be meaningful in such studies it is imperative that psychometrically validated measures covering appropriate domains must be used. Such measures now exist and are increasingly being utilized in audit, and routine evaluation of health care (Wasson *et al.* 1992). Routine systems to collect outcomes have been successfully demonstrated in England (Bardsley and Coles 1992) and America (Lansky *et al.* 1992). Such systems have proved acceptable to clinicians, although widespread utilization of 'outcomes management' systems has been slow to get off the ground. In part this is due to a lack of an agreement on what standardized measures should be used, and concern as to what, if any, effect such measurement will have upon clinical practice (Wasson *et al.* 1992).

Perhaps the most emotive use for health status measures is in the arena of cost containment and prioritization. When utilized in cost utility studies measures are required from which a single figure can be derived, which can then be used to rank order treatments, or indeed patients. The most famous attempt that has as yet been made to derive a set of priorities on the basis of a cost benefit analysis was the Oregon experiment (Oregon Health Services Commission 1991). It utilized the quality of well-being scale (Kaplan *et al.* 1987) and produced results that were so counter-intuitive that informal procedures were used to reorder the resulting list. The value of utility measures in prioritization is discussed more fully in this book in the chapter by Katherine Watson (Chapter 8).

Health status measures also permit the monitoring of populations health, or sub-samples within the population (Ware 1992). Furthermore, comparisons of the health status of different countries can also be undertaken (Orley and Kuyken 1994). Thus, there is currently interest in developing measures that can be used across cultures. This is the thrust of the work being undertaken by, for example, the WHOQOL Group (Szabo 1996) and the IQOLA Group (Aaronson et al. 1992). The development of such instruments is not without its difficulties. It is certainly not enough to simply translate an instrument from one language to another. Careful checks are required to ensure that the meaning of questions remains the same. This can mean that it is actually necessary to ask somewhat different questions in different cultures to ensure that the same underlying concept is being tapped (Bullinger et al. 1995). Even more problematic is the possibility that issues of importance in one culture in relation to health are unimportant elsewhere (Hunt 1995). However, if these problems can be overcome the potential exists of not only comparing the quality of life of different countries, which seems an undertaking of limited value, but also undertaking large multi-centre cross-cultural trials that incorporate self-perceived health as a major outcome measure.

In the evaluation of medical care health assessment questionnaires can be used for a variety of purposes. It is important to realize, however, that different types of evaluation require different methods of assessment. A questionnaire such as the Sickness Impact Profile (SIP), of which the Anglicized version is the Functional Limitations Profile (FLP) (Bergner et al. 1981; Patrick and Peach 1989), contains 136 questions and is thus not appropriate for routine monitoring, or as an adjunct to the clinical interview, as it is simply too long and takes too much time for patients to complete and score. Similarly, cost benefit analyses require single index figures to be gained from health assessment questionnaires, and the use of multi-dimension questionnaires such as the SF-36 cannot be used for this purpose, although work is underway to attempt to gain a single index utility based figure from the profile of scores this measure produces (Brazier et al. 1994). When considering undertaking some form of evaluation of the quality of life of patients careful and informed choice of instruments is essential.

Requirements of measures

It would be naive to assume that designing a health assessment measure, or indeed any, questionnaire is an easy task (Oppenheim 1992). A number of issues must be considered when designing a questionnaire. Instruments must be reliable, valid and sensitive to change.

Reliability

Questionnaires must be reliable over time. Thus, they should produce the same, or very similar results, on two or more administrations to the same respondents, provided, of course, there is good reason to believe that the health status of the patients has not changed. The difficulty with such a method of validating a questionnaire is that it is often uncertain as to whether results that may indicate a questionnaire is unreliable are in fact no more than a product of real change in health status. Due to the potential difficulties in gaining an accurate picture of reliability in this way, many researchers adopt the Cronbach's alpha statistic (Cronbach 1951), to determine internal reliability. Internal reliability refers to the extent to which items on a scale are tapping a single underlying construct, and therefore there is a high level of inter-item correlation. Assuming that such high levels of inter-item correlation are not a product of chance, it is commonplace to assume that a high alpha statistic indicates the questionnaire is tapping an underlying construct and hence is reliable. There is, however, disagreement as to whether such a method can be viewed as appropriate for assuming a questionnaire is reliable over time (Ruta *et al.* 1993; Sheldon 1993).

Validity

Essentially there are four aspects to validity. Face validity, content validity, criterion validity and construct validity.

Face validity

Face validity refers to whether items on a questionnaire superficially appear to make sense, and can be easily understood. This may seem a simple enough test for a questionnaire to pass, but there are ambiguities on some of the most respected and well utilized measures. For example, the FLP requests respondents to complete the questionnaire with reference to today. They are thus asked to affirm or disaffirm items on the basis of how they are feeling today. The basis of this judgement should, further, be related to their health. Let us take the example outlined in the FLP itself. It concerns the ability to drive. The statement given is 'I am not driving my car'. Thus, if a respondent cannot drive a car today, and this is due to a health complaint then they should affirm the question 'I am not driving my car'. If they are not driving because they never learnt to do so, then they must answer this question in the negative. Thus, respondents are asked to make two judgements for each response. It could be argued that in such a long questionnaire (136 items) respondents may well forget or ignore the initial rubric. However, even if this were not the case, some questions do not make any sense on the basis of the rubric; for example, the item 'I have attempted suicide'. Respondents must tick 'Yes' or 'No' to this item. Further, they must not tick 'Yes' if they have attempted suicide today, but did so because their spouse has been killed in a car accident (this is, after all, not a problem with *their* health). Maybe it would be legitimate to tick 'Yes' if the respondent reasoned that their mental health had been adversely affected by a relative's death, and they had attempted it today (just before filling in the questionnaire, in fact). There are more of these confused requests on the FLP. For example, respondents are clearly told to answer questions on the basis of today, and to only affirm questions which reflect some problem caused by health. This seems a tall order for some of the items, for example the item 'I sleep or doze most of the time, day and night' sounds very much like a question relating to a broader time period than just the activities engaged in today. Questions such as these must make researchers sit back and take stock of how such questions are interpreted (or reinterpreted) by respondents if results from such instruments are to be of any meaningful use whatsoever. Further some items on the FLP can be influenced by place of administration. It has been suggested that individuals are more likely to affirm certain statements when in hospital than elsewhere. For example, items such as 'I stay in bed most of the day' are more likely to be affirmed in hospital than, for example, at home, though the need to stay in hospital may be induced by hospital requirements rather than by state of health per se (Jenkinson *et al.* 1993b; Ziebland *et al.* 1992). The FLP is certainly not the only questionnaire at which such criticisms can be aimed. The SF-36, which has gained increasingly in popularity and use, contains this item: The rubric reads: 'During the past 4 weeks, have you had any of the following problems with your work or other regular activities as a result of any emotional difficulties (such as feeling depressed and anxious)?'

There are a number of items, of which one of them is: 'Didn't do work or other activities as carefully as usual (answer Yes or No).'

Thus, respondents are informed in the rubric that the following items are a list of problems. The item would make perfect sense if it was phrased as 'I worked less carefully than usual'. However, in its present form it is difficult to know whether a 'Yes' or 'No' affirms the item's content. A respondent could tick 'Yes' assuming that this affirms the item's content. Alternatively, to tick 'No' in order to affirm the item would be grammatically more appropriate (and a double negative).

Content validity
Content validity refers to choice of, and relative importance given to, items on a questionnaire. In a matter as fundamental as the selection of items a number of approaches are available to the potential designer. Broadly speaking, items can be developed by the researcher, or from studies of lay or patient populations, or any combination of these.

Both the NHP and SIP were developed on the basis of surveys of health perceptions of non-medically trained populations, with items weighted by a psychometric scaling technique. Hunt *et al.*, the designers of the NHP, claimed that the scoring and weighting for seriousness of items on many health assessment questionnaires often reflect the values of the physician and not those of the lay person. As such they claimed that items tapping *subjective* health status should be generated from studies of lay people (Hunt *et al.* 1986).

The NHP is a short, easily administered questionnaire designed to over-come the potential criticism of many pre-existing instruments that both the domains and the questions contained in them are more a reflection of the assessments of clinicians and academic researchers than of lay people. To overcome this problem, Hunt and her colleagues undertook a great deal of research upon lay people in order to ascertain what they believed to be the most salient dimensions of health that could be affected by illness. Six distinct dimensions emerged: pain, social isolation, energy, sleep disturb-ance, mobility, and emotional reactions. Lay people were then asked to generate items that could be incorporated into these dimensions. Large numbers of statements were gained. A small number were then selected and weighted for inclusion in the questionnaire. To undertake this process, Hunt *et al.* utilized a method similar to that which had been used by Bergner and her colleagues in the development of the SIP (Bergner *et al.* 1976, 1981).

There are 38 questions on the first section of the NHP (designed to assess subjective health state), and each item on the questionnaire carries a specific weight, ascribed to it by the developers, by an attitude scaling technique developed by Thurstone early this century (Thurstone 1928). Respondents can affirm all or none, or indeed any number, of the state-ments, as the developers claim they all tap an underlying attribute on any given dimension. It has been suggested that it is misleading to use a scaling technique such as Thurstone's method to attempt to scale statements that are, or could be viewed as, factual (Edwards 1957). The NHP contains factual statements, or ones that certainly could be viewed in this light (e.g. 'I'm unable to walk at all'). It is because of this that the NHP contains illogical groups of (factual) statements. It is possible, for example, to gain higher scores (indicating worse health) for less severe symptoms on the mobility dimension of the NHP. Some of the statements contained in the mobility section of the NHP logically preclude subjects responding to other items. For example, an affirmation of the statement 'I'm unable to walk at all' (with a weight value of 21.30) technically precludes positive responses to some other aspects of mobility. For example, if a respondent affirms the statement that they are unable to walk, they should not, logically, be able to affirm the statements 'I can only walk about indoors' (weight 11.54), and 'I have trouble getting up and down stairs and steps' (weight 10.79), which make a total score of 22.33. Thus the score of a respondent with walking difficulties may exceed that of someone who is unable to walk at all. Such an outcome can make the results gained from a questionnaire such as the NHP difficult to interpret (Jenkinson 1991; Jenkinson 1994b).

Criterion validity

Criterion validity refers to the ability of an instrument to correspond with other measures. While subjective health assessment questionnaires are constructed with the intention of measuring subjective perceptions a large number of items for such questionnaires have been designed by clinicians and researchers themselves. There exists the potential criticism, therefore, that such questionnaires may reflect more the interests of clinical judgement than those of patients themselves. For example, the Stanford Arthritis Center Health Assessment Questionnaire (Fries et al. 1980, 1982) and the Arthritis Impact Measurement Scales (Meenan et al. 1980) were developed in this way. To then attempt to provide information on the validity of the questionnaire by using existing clinical measures is to fall into the trap twice. Thus a clinician who designs a questionnaire and validates its scoring properties on the basis of existing medical and clinical measures could stand accused of not paying sufficient attention to the very phenomena they wish to measure, namely *subjective* (non-clinical) assessment. For example, in developing the AIMS, Meenan et al. (1982) argue that

> the most commonly used measures, such as joint count and ESR, address disease activity only. The ARA Functional Classification, and Katz's Activities of Daily Living Scale, focus on functional abilities. These approaches fall far short of conceptualising or measuring health in the WHO sense of a physical, psychological and social state. Despite their long-standing use and widespread acceptance, disease activity and functional measures of outcome also have significant shortcomings as measurement tools. They have been accepted and disseminated primarily because they appear to be objective, and very little work has been done on documenting their measurement properties. The work which has been done, in fact, suggests that they are far from perfect.
> (Meenan 1982: 785)

Thus, here Meenan seems to be claiming that existing measurement tools for rheumatoid arthritis are far from perfect. This prompts him and his colleagues to develop a more refined questionnaire that will cover areas currently not tapped by existing medical assessments. He then uses clinical data to support the construct validity of the new instrument

> In the discriminant analysis, the clinical and health status measures were very similar in their ability to discriminate among the groups and between the treatment and no treatment. This provides further

evidence that the health status measures performed as well as standard measures in this trial.

(Meenan *et al.* 1984: 1351)

In this example we see that, on the one hand, measures such as clinical assessments are viewed as inaccurate and warranting further investigation, while on the other, these measures can be used to bolster the case for the measurement properties of the AIMS. In the absence of a gold standard such practice has become commonplace. However, when items have been selected by clinicians rather than from surveys of lay people or patient groups, such results provide only limited support for the construct validity of the instrument. Put another way, the fact that the items of the questionnaire were chosen by Meenan and his colleagues (the dexterity and pain items were developed by Meenan, and other items were adapted from Katz's Index of Independence of Activities of Daily Living (Katz *et al.* 1963, 1970; Katz and Akpom 1976) the RAND instruments developed by Ware and his colleagues (Ware *et al.* 1980) and the Index of Well Being (Kaplan *et al.* 1976)) and can be found to associate with existing clinical variables is perhaps to suggest that this instrument taps the dimensions of interest to clinicians. Indeed, an updated AIMS questionnaire, the AIMS2, contains somewhat different items on the basis that not all appropriate dimensions of interest to patients were covered (Meenan *et al.* 1992). This would provide some support for the claim that questionnaires should be developed, at least in part, on surveys of lay people or appropriate patient groups. Certainly, this principle has been used in the development of other generic (Hunt *et al.* 1986) as well as disease-specific measures (for example, Guyatt *et al.* 1987a; Peto *et al.* 1995).

Construct validity

Construct validity refers to the ability of an instrument to confirm expected hypotheses. Thus one would expect those who are ill, who are in lower social classes, and/or who make more frequent visits to their GP to gain scores indicating worse health than those who are well, in higher social classes and rarely visit their GP. Preliminary validation of questionnaires involves ensuring questionnaires can discriminate between such groups (Hunt *et al.* 1985, 1986; Brazier *et al.* 1992; Jenkinson 1993a, 1996a; Ware *et al.* 1993).

Sensitivity to change

Sensitivity to change or 'responsiveness' is an important requirement of health status measures when utilized to evaluate the impact of medical interventions (Guyatt *et al.* 1987b). In general, most attention in the development of health status questionnaires has been aimed at examination of the reliability and construct validity of measures (Fitzpatrick *et al.* 1993).

However, recent work suggests that different measures can provide different pictures of change (Fitzpatrick *et al.* 1992b). This is largely due to item content, which in part reflects the way in which items were selected (e.g. from patient interviews, or physician judgements) and the primary purpose of the instrument (e.g. the NHP was designed primarily as a population survey tool, while many disease specific measures are designed with outcome evaluation of treatment as their primary objective). Measures can reflect different conceptualizations of illness, health and disability (Ziebland *et al.* 1993). Many instruments often contain similarly labelled dimensions; these are not necessarily tapping the same aspects of the attribute. Thus, for example, the social dimension on the Arthritis Impact Measurement Scales asks respondents about social interactions over a longer time span than the FLP. The FLP is therefore more sensitive to recent small changes in social interactions than the Arthritis Impact Measurement Scales.

Overview of measures

Broadly speaking, there have emerged two general approaches to the measurement of health status. The first is an attempt to develop instruments that provide a single global score of well-being. These are designed in such a way as to permit all items on a questionnaire to be summed into a single health index. The other method is the development of questionnaires designed to measure a number of dimensions of health status.

Single index measures of health status

Single index measures of health status are designed to provide a single scale of health states. Perhaps the most famous example of such a measure is that described by Rosser (1988). This measure, designed initially to place in perspective the magnitude of change achieved in clinical trials, consists of two dimensions, disability and distress, in the form of a matrix. There are eight levels of disability and four levels of distress. For each combination of distress and disability the Rosser Index provides a single figure. The figures in the matrix were developed by Rosser on the basis of a project where 70 subjects, including doctors, nurses, psychiatric patients and healthy volunteers were asked to rank illness states and estimate relative severity. While this scale gains a single index figure of health state, and, when used in routine clinical practice it takes only a few seconds for those familiar with its use to complete, it has to be borne in mind that the original weighting exercise, which produced the matrix, was undertaken on a very small sample. The valuations, therefore, are unlikely to reflect those of the population as a whole.

While the Rosser Index was essentially developed for completion by physicians and staff, and not patients, attempts have been made to develop self-completion single index measures. An attempt to gain a single index value of health state from the perspective of the patient is the Quality of Well Being Scale (QWB). The complex method of developing this question-naire has been described fully elsewhere (Kaplan and Anderson 1987). The intention of this index is to combine mortality, morbidity and the benefits and side effects of treatment into a single global score. Such a global score can permit for the comparison of health states and treatments. Its value in comparing disease states is, however, dependent on gaining reliable prognoses. Without this latter information it is not possible to calculate potential 'well years' accruing from treatments. Another limitation of this questionnaire is its length. It can take up to 15 minutes to complete, and the developers suggest it is administered by an interviewer, as the self-completion version resulted in unreliable data (Anderson *et al.* 1986). As such, the QWB does not lend itself to easy use in clinical settings, or for routine evaluation of care.

Attempts have been made to gain a questionnaire that is both short, easy to complete and a reliable indicator of health state. This has been a ven-ture that has had few successes, though the Health Measurement Question-naire (HMQ), which was derived from the Rosser Index, and the EuroQol have both had their advocates. The HMQ is a relatively brief, easy to complete questionnaire that elicits information on dimensions of mobility, capacity for self-care, constraints on usual activities, social relationships and perceived stress. A single index figure is derived from responses to these domains. More information on this questionnaire is provided in Kind and Gudex (1991). A more widely used measure is the EuroQol EQ-5D (EuroQol Group 1990; Rosser and Sintonen 1993; Kind 1996). The EuroQol EQ-5D was developed by a multidisciplinary group of researchers from five European countries (EuroQol Group, 1990). There are five questions cover-ing the areas of mobility, self-care, usual activity, pain/discomfort and anxiety/depression. Each question has three response categories; level 1 – 'no problems', level 2 – 'some problems' and level 3 – 'inability or extreme problems'. Overall health state can ostensibly be calculated from responses to these items. For example, the response set '11111' indicates no problems with any of the five areas, and subsequently perfect overall health. There are in total 243 possible health states (i.e. 3^5), and weighted values have been assigned to each of these on the basis of national and international surveys (van Agt *et al.* 1994). A single overall score can also be gained from the EuroQol thermometer, on which respondents mark their overall perceived health from 'Worst imaginable health state' to 'Best imaginable health state'. The development of the EuroQol is covered in detail in this text by Katherine Watson in Chapter 8.

All of the above single index measures are based upon questionnaires which include fixed format items. However, a number of researchers have begun to analyse the possibility of asking patients to individually nominate areas of their life which have been adversely affected by health state, and to then assess the extent of this impact. The results from each of the items selected is then aggregated to form a single index figure. A variety of methodologies to this approach exist, but in essence they all permit each individual to select and weight their own chosen areas (McGee *et al.* 1991; Ruta *et al.* 1994). Such a procedure has the advantage of not imposing pre-existing definitions of health state upon respondents (Ruta and Garratt 1994; Ruta *et al.* 1994). Research in this area has been undertaken in a number of groups including patients undergoing orthopaedic surgery, HIV positive patients, arthritis patients and patients reporting low back pain (Tugwell *et al.* 1990; McGee *et al.* 1991; O'Boyle *et al.* 1992; Ruta and Garratt 1994; Ruta *et al.* 1994; Hickey *et al.* 1996). Such methods are, like many research projects attempting to gain single index figures of health state, still in their infancy and hence not widely applied. A number of issues need to be addressed, such as whether respondents should select new dimensions each time they complete the questionnaire in longitudinal studies, whether aggregating potentially unrelated dimensions is an appropriate methodology and whether patients should select dimensions from a list (which perhaps does away with the whole philosophy of this approach) or simply select from any areas they think important. Such issues are at present receiving attention from a number of researchers, and while the generalized applicability of this new technique seems a long way off, it is an interesting and potentially worthwhile new approach to the whole field of subjective health measurement.

Health status profiles

Health status profiles are measures that tap a number of dimensions of functioning and well-being. Many instruments that have been developed are illness specific or are aimed at tapping a specific aspect of ill-health (such as pain or depression). However, the search for short comprehensive health status measures, which are able to detect differences between illness groups, and which are sensitive to changes over time, has produced remarkably few regularly utilized, and psychometrically validated, instruments. For example, the McMaster Health Index Questionnaire (Chambers 1988, 1993) has been used infrequently, evidence for the psychometric reliability and validity of the Functional Status Questionnaire (Jette *et al.* 1986) is very limited, the Duke-17 (Parkerson *et al.* 1991) has been rarely used and the Duke UNC Profile (Parkerson *et al.* 1981) has been criticized on psychometric grounds (Wilkin *et al.* 1992, 1993). The most frequently reported generic health measures have been the Sickness Impact Profile (Bergner *et al.* 1976, 1981) the Functional Limitations Profile (Patrick and Peach 1989), the Nottingham Health Profile (Hunt *et al.* 1985, 1986), and, more recently, the COOP Charts (Wasson *et al.* 1992; Nelson *et al.* 1996),

Functional limitations profile (FLP)/sickness impact profile (SIP)	Nottingham health profile (NHP)	Short form 36 (SF-36) health survey	Short form 12 (SF-12) health survey	Coop charts
No of items: 136	No of items: 38	No of items: 36	No of items: 12	No of items: 9
No of dimensions: 12	No of dimensions: 6	No of dimensions: 8	No of dimensions: recommended for the derivation of the two summary scores although the original eight tapped in the SF-36 can be obtained (this is not recommended)	No of dimensions: 9
Dimensions: Ambulation Body care and movement Mobility Household management Recreation and pastimes Social interaction Emotion Alertness Sleep and rest Eating Communication Work	Dimensions: Energy Pain Emotional reactions Sleep Social isolation Physical mobility	Dimensions: Physical functioning Role limitations due to physical problems Role limitations due to emotional problems Social functioning Mental health Energy Pain Health perception	Dimensions: Designed to provide the PCS and MCS (see SF-36 column), but can provide eight dimensions of SF-36	Dimensions: Physical fitness Feelings Daily activities Social activities Change in health Overall health Social support Quality of life Pain
Other: • The FLP is the anglicized version of the SIP. • An overall single index score can be derived from the FLP/SIP, as can a psycho-social dimension score and a physical dimension score. • Note scoring rules differ slightly for the FLP and SIP.	Other: • The original NHP contained a second section but the developers no longer recommend its use (Hunt and McKenna 1991) • A single index (the NHP distress index) can be created from a sub-set of the items (see McKenna et al. 1993).	Other: • Two summary scores can be derived from the SF-36: the physical component summary (PCS) and mental component summary (MCS). For further information see Ware et al. 1994; Jenkinson et al. 1996a.	Other: • The developers do not recommend the SF-12 for use where the eight dimensions are required, but in instances when only the PCS and MCS scores are required (see SF-36 column). The SF-12 was designed to provide these scores yet in a shorter form instrument.	Other: • There is only one item per dimension. • The charts were intended for use in the clinical interview. • A version for children has been developed (see Nelson et al. 1996).

Figure 5.1 Properties of some commonly used generic health status measures

and the Short-Form 36 (SF-36) (Brazier *et al.* 1992; Ware and Sherbourne 1992; Ware *et al.* 1993, 1994; Jenkinson 1996a, 1996b) and Short-Form 12 (Ware *et al.* 1995a; Ware *et al.* 1995b; Ware *et al.* 1996). These measures cover a wide variety of dimensions of health status and are not primarily designed to give a single index of health status but to provide a profile of scores. However, for all these measures methods of data reduction have been suggested (see Figure 5.1 for attributes of these questionnaires).

Discussion

Single index figures of health status appeal to those who wish to compare different treatments and interventions. However, while such single index figures give the impression of comparability between illness states and treatments they may do so unfairly. For example, the EuroQol (EuroQol Group 1990; Kind 1996) questionnaire does not contain a dimension evaluating sleep disturbance, and a treatment aimed primarily at improving this dimension of health may not appear to have been efficacious if assessed by this measure.

Single index figures gained from patient generated measures, such as those of Ruta and Garratt (1994) and O'Boyle *et al.* (1992), may overcome the above criticism. Essentially, the dimensions chosen by patients are seen as paramount; so if a patient is primarily concerned about the impact of illness on their sleep patterns, this will be incorporated in the measure. However, difficulties arise here. At initial interview a patient may claim their quality of life in five areas is affected. At follow up, these areas may have improved, so if the patient completes the questionnaire using the same dimensions chosen at time one an improvement in health status will be apparent. However, side-effects of drug treatment may have influenced other aspects of the respondent's life, and the patient's overall quality of life may not have improved at all. When using such a measure it is therefore appropriate to also include a generic instrument so as to ensure as wide as possible coverage of health related dimensions.

Generic measures, such as the FLP/SIP, the SF-36 Health Survey Questionnaire and the NHP, indicate clearly which dimensions of health status are being measured, but the dimensions included may not be appropriate in the assessment of every intervention. For example, the FLP, despite having 12 dimensions, lacks a specific category measuring pain. Results from generic measures can, of course, be compared with data from other populations and illness groups. For example, normative data can be used to compare the health status of a particular patient group with that of the general population (Ware 1993). However, it is still important that disease specific measures are used alongside such generic measures, as disease specific measures are, by their very nature, likely to tap particular aspects of ill health that are unique to particular illnesses.

Ceiling and floor effects must be considered. The NHP has been criticized because it detects only the severe end of ill health, and thus most respondents score zero on many, if not all, of the six dimensions of the questionnaire (Kind and Carr-Hill 1987). The items on the questionnaire were chosen to represent severe health states, and so individuals who have mild to moderate illness may not be detected with this instrument. In a study of change over time, respondents with minor ailments may improve, but if their initial score on dimensions of the NHP was zero, such improvement may not be detected (floor effect). Similarly, respondents may score as maximally ill on a health measurement questionnaire. However, the extent of their illness state may still not be fully reflected in the questionnaire. Such severely ill respondents would fall beyond the measurement range. Thus, while these patients may improve over time, it is still possible they may continue to score as maximally ill on the questionnaire (ceiling effect). Such floor and ceiling effects are more likely to be found on instruments with small numbers of items (Bindman *et al.* 1990).

Related to floor and ceiling effects is another important aspect of health status measures: sensitivity to change or 'responsiveness'. For health status measures to be useful in evaluating the impact of medical interventions they must be 'sensitive'. It is thus imperative, when selecting a measure, to determine the exact nature of the questions asked and the time scales utilised. For example, a questionnaire such as the NHP, designed to tap the extreme end of ill health, is unlikely to be sensitive to small changes in health status among patients with minor illnesses.

Furthermore, in longitudinal studies it is important that the mode of administration of questionnaires is kept consistent. For example, due to the nature of some of the items in the FLP, respondents may gain higher scores in hospital than as out-patients or when at home, and such scores may not actually reflect health state. Items such as 'I stay in bed more' are more likely to be affirmed in hospital, and may not accurately reflect the impact of the illness per se on a person's life (Jenkinson *et al.* 1993b).

Conclusion

It is important to note that subjective health measurement questionnaires are not designed to be used as substitutes for traditional measures of clinical endpoints. On the contrary, they are intended to complement existing measures and to provide a fuller picture of health state than can be gained by medical measures alone. However, to be useful such measures must be carefully chosen. Health status measures can provide a useful adjunct to the data traditionally obtained from mortality and morbidity statistics, or from traditional clinical and laboratory assessments, but careful consideration must be given to the choice of measures. At present it seems reasonable to assume that health status measures may permit scientific questions to be answered fully in the context of clinical trials, and, in time, they may find their way into routine use. However, the results obtained from such measures must be made intuitive and meaningful to clinicians, as well as to researchers, and adequate care must be taken to ensure appropriate measures tapping relevant domains are being utilized. Subjective health status measurement could provide much needed data on the impact of clinical interventions on the day to day lives of patients; done without due care of the pitfalls, however, such data could be irrelevant, or misleading.

References

Aaronson N. (1989) Quality of life assessment in clinical trials: methodologic issues, *Controlled Clinical Trials*, 10: 195–208S.

Aaronson, N.K., Acquadro, C., Alonso, J., Apolone, G., Bucquet, D., Bullinger, M., Bungay, K., Fukuhara, S., Gandek, B., Keller, S., Razavi, D., Sanson-Fisher, R., Sullivan, M., Wood-Dauphinee, S., Wagner, A. and Ware, J.E. (1992) International Quality of Life Assessment (IQOLA) Project, *Quality of Life Research*, 1: 349–51.

Albrecht, G. (1994) Subjective health assessment, in C. Jenkinson (ed.) *Measuring Health and Medical Outcomes*. London: UCL Press.

Anderson J.P., Bush J.W. and Berry C.C. (1986) Classifying function for health outcome and quality of life evaluation, *Medical Care*, 24: 54–69.

Bardsley, M. and Coles, J. (1992) Practical experiences in auditing patient outcomes, *Quality in Health Care*, 1: 124–30.

Bergner, M., Bobbitt, R.A., Kressel, S., Pollard, W.E., Gilson, B.S. and Morris J.R. (1976) The Sickness Impact Profile: conceptual formulation and methodological development of a health status measure, *International Journal of Health Services*, 6: 393–415.

Bergner, M., Bobbitt, R.A., Carter, W.B. and Gilson B.S. (1981) The Sickness Impact Profile: development and final revision of a health status measure, *Medical Care*, 18, 787–805.

Bergner, M., Barry, M.J., Bowman, M.A., Doyle, A., Guess, H.A. and Nutting, P.A. (1992) Where do we go from here? Opportunities for applying health status assessment measures in clinical settings, *Medical Care*, 30 (Supplement): MS219–MS230.

Bindman, A.B., Keane, D. and Lurie N. (1990) Measuring health changes among severely ill patients: the floor phenomenon, *Medical Care*, 28: 1142–52.

Blazer, D. and Houpt, J. (1979) Perception of poor health in the healthy older adult, *Journal of the American Geriatrics Society*, 27: 330–4.

Brazier, J.E., Harper R., Jones, N.M.B., O'Cathain, A., Thomas, K.J., Usherwood, T. and Westlake, L. (1992) Validating the SF-36 health survey questionnaire: new outcome measure for primary care, *British Medical Journal*, 305: 160–4.

Brazier, J.E., Usherwood, T., Harper, R. and Jones, N. (1994) Deriving a single index measure for health from the short-form 36 (SF36) health survey. Paper presented at the Society for Social Medicine Conference, September 1994, University of Leeds.

Bullinger, M. (1995) in I. Guggenmoos-Holzmann, K. Bloomfield, H. Brenner and U. Flick (eds) *Quality of Life and Health: Concepts, Methods and Applications*. Berlin: Blackwell-Wissenschafts.

Chambers, L. (1988) The McMaster Health Index Questionnaire – an update, in S.R. Walker and R.M. Rosser (eds) *Quality of Life: Assessment and Application*. Lancaster: MTP.

Chambers, L. (1993) The McMaster Health Index Questionnaire – an update, in S.R. Walker and R.M. Rosser (eds) *Quality of Life Assessment: Key Issues in the 1990s*. London: Kluwer.

Cronbach, L.J. (1951) Coefficient alpha and the internal structure of tests, *Psychometrica*, 16: 297–334.

Edwards, A. (1957) *Techniques of Attitude Scale Construction*. Englewood Cliffs, NJ: Prentice-Hall.

EuroQol Group (1990) EuroQol – A new facility for the measurement of health related quality of life, *Health Policy*, 16: 199–208.

Fitzpatrick, R. (1994) Applications of health status measures, in C. Jenkinson (ed.) *Measuring Health and Medical Outcomes*. London: UCL Press.

Fitzpatrick, R., Fletcher, A., Gore, S., Jones, D., Spiegelhalter, D. and Cox, D. (1992a) Quality of life measures in health care. I: applications and issues in assessment, *British Medical Journal*, 305: 1074–7.

Fitzpatrick, R., Ziebland, S., Jenkinson, C., Mowat, A. and Mowat, A. (1992b) The importance of sensitivity to change as a criterion for selection of health status measures, *Quality in Health Care*, 1: 89–93.

Fitzpatrick, R., Ziebland, S., Jenkinson, C., Mowat, A. and Mowat, A. (1993) A comparison of the sensitivity to change of several health status measures in rheumatoid arthritis, *Journal of Rheumatology*, 20: 429–36.

Fries, J.F., Spitz, P.W., Kraines, R.G. and Holman, H.R. (1980) Measurement of patient outcome in arthritis, *Arthritis and Rheumatism*, 23: 137–45.

Fries, J.F., Spitz, P.W. and Young, D.Y. (1982) The dimensions of health outcomes: the health assessment questionnaire, disability and pain scales, *Journal of Rheumatology*, 9: 789–93.

Geigle, R. and Jones, S.B. (1990) Outcomes measurement: a report from the front, *Inquiry*, 27: 7–13.

Guyatt, G.H., Berman, L.B., Townsend, M., Pugsley, S.O. and Chambers, L. (1987a) A measure of quality of life for clinical trials in chronic lung disease, *Thorax*, 42: 773–8.

Guyatt, G., Walter, S. and Norman, G. (1987b) Measuring change over time: assessing the usefulness of evaluative instruments, *Journal of Chronic Diseases*, 40: 171–8.

Hickey, A.M., Bury, G., O'Boyle, C., Bradley, F., O'Kelly, D. and Shannon, W. (1996) A new short form quality of life measure (SEIQoL-DW): application in a cohort of individuals with HIV/AIDS, *British Medical Journal*, 313: 29–33.

Hunt, S. (1995) Cross-cultural comparability of quality of life measures, in I. Guggenmoos-Holzmann, K. Bloomfield, H. Brenner and U. Flick (eds) *Quality of Life and Health: Concepts, Methods and Applications*. Berlin: Blackwell-Wissenschafts.

Hunt, S., McEwen, J. and McKenna, S. (1985) Measuring health status: a new tool for clinicians and epidemiologists, *Journal of the Royal College of General Practitioners*, 35: 185–88.

Hunt, S., McEwan, P. and McKenna, S. (1986) *Measuring Health Status*. London: Croom Helm.

Hunt, S. and McKenna, S. (1991) *The Nottingham Health Profile User's Manual*. Manchester: Galen Research and Consultancy.

Jenkinson, C. (1991) Why are we weighting? A critical analysis of the use of item weights in a health status measure, *Social Science and Medicine*, 32: 1413–16.

Jenkinson, C. (1994a) Measuring health and medical outcomes: an overview, in C. Jenkinson (ed.) *Measuring Health and Medical Outcomes*. London: UCL Press.

Jenkinson, C. (1994b) Weighting for ill health: the Nottingham health profile, in C. Jenkinson (ed.) *Measuring Health and Medical Outcomes*. London: UCL Press.

Jenkinson, C. (1995) Evaluating the efficacy of medical treatment: possibilities and limitations, *Social Science and Medicine*, 41: 1395–403.

Jenkinson, C., Coulter, A. and Wright, L. (1993a) Short Form 36 (SF36) health survey questionnaire. Normative data for adults of working age, *British Medical Journal*, 306: 1437–40.

Jenkinson, C., Layte, R., Wright, L. and Coulter, A. (1996a) *The UK SF-36: An Analysis and Interpretation Manual*. Oxford: Health Services Research Unit, University of Oxford.

Jenkinson, C., Layte, R., Wright, L. and Coulter, A. (1996b) Evidence for the sensitivity of the SF-36 health status measure to inequalities in health, *Journal of Epidemiology and Community Health*, 50: 377–80.

Jenkinson, C., Ziebland, S., Fitzpatrick, R., Mowat, A. and Mowat, A. (1993b) Hospitalisation and its influence upon results from health status questionnaires, *International Journal of Health Sciences*, 4: 13–18.

Jette, A.M., Davies, A.R., Cleary, P.D., Calteins, D.R., Rubenstein, L.V., Fink, A., Kosekoff, J., Young, R.T., Brook, R.H. and Delbonco, T.L. (1986) The Functional Status Questionnaire: reliability and validity when used in primary care, *Journal of General and Internal Medicine*, 1: 143–9.

Kaplan, R.M., Bush, J.W. and Berry, C.C. (1976) Health status: types of validity and the Index of Well-Being, *Health Services Research*, 11: 478–507.

Kaplan, R.M. and Anderson, J.P. (1987) The quality of well-being scale: Rationale for a single quality of life index, in S.R. Walker and R. Rosser (eds) *Quality of Life: Assessment and Application*. Lancaster: MTP/Kluwer.

Katz, S. and Akpom, C.A. (1976) Index of ADL, *Medical Care*, 14: 116–18.

Katz, S., Ford, A.B., Moskowitz, R.W., Thompson, H.M. and Svec, K.H. (1963) Studies of illness in the aged. The Index of ADL: a standardised measure of biological and psychosocial function, *Journal of the American Medical Association*, 185: 914–19.

Katz, S., Downs, T.D., Cash, H.R. and Grotz, R.C. (1970) Progress in development of the Index of ADL, *Gerontologist*, 10: 20–30.

Kind, P. (1996) The EuroQol Instrument: an index of health related quality of life, in Spilker, B. (ed.) *Quality of Life and Pharmacoeconomics in Clinical Trials* (2nd edn). Philadelphia: Lippincott-Raven.

Kind, P. and Carr-Hill, R. (1987) The Nottingham Health Profile: a useful tool for epidemiologists? *Social Science and Medicine*, 25: 905–10.

Kind, P. and Gudex, C. (1991) *The HMQ: Measuring Health Status in the Community. Centre for Health Economics Discussion Paper, Number 93*. York: University of York, Centre for Health Economics.

Kraus, N. (1991) *The InterStudy Quality Edge*, Vol. 1, No. 1. Excelsior, Minneapolis: InterStudy.

Lansky, D., Butler, J.B.V. and Frederick, W.T. (1992) Using health status measures in the hospital setting: from acute care to 'outcomes management', *Medical Care*, 30 (Supplement): MS57–MS73.

Leigh, P. and Fries, J. (1991) Mortality predictors among 263 patients with rheumatoid arthritis, *Journal of Rheumatology*, 18: 1298–306.

McGee, H.M., O'Boyle, C.A., Hickey, A., O'Malley K. and Joyce, C.R.B. (1991) Assessing the quality of life of the individual: the SEIQoL with a healthy and gastroenterology unit population, *Psychological Medicine*, 21: 749–59.

McKenna, S., Hunt, S. and Tennant, A. (1993) The development of a patient-completed index of distress from the Nottingham health profile: a new measure for use in cost-utility studies, *British Journal of Medical Economics*, 6: 13–24.

McHorney, C.A., Ware, J.E. and Lu, J.F. The MOS 36-Item short-form health survey (SF-36): III. (1994) Tests of data quality, scaling assumptions, and reliability across diverse patient groups, *Medical Care*, 32: 40–66.

Meenan, R.F., Gertman, P.M. and Mason, J.H. (1980) Measuring health status in arthritis: the Arthritis Impact Measurement Scales, *Arthritis and Rheumatism*, 23: 146–52.

Meenan, R.F., Gertman, P.M., Mason, J.H. and Dunaif, R. (1982) The Arthritis Impact Measurement Scales: further investigations of a health status measure, *Arthritis and Rheumatism*, 25: 1048–53.

Meenan, R.F., Anderson, J.J., Kazis, L.E., Egger, M.J., Altz-Smith, M., Samuelson, C.O., Willkens, R.F., Solsky, M.A., Hayes, S.P., Blocka, K.L., Weinstein, A., Guttadauria, M., Kaplan, S.B. and Klippel, J. (1984) Outcome assessment in clinical trials: evidence for the sensitivity of a health status measure, *Arthritis and Rheumatism*, 27: 1344–52.

Meenan, R.F., Mason, J.H., Anderson, J.J., Guccione, A.A. and Kazis, L.E. (1992) AIMS2: the content and properties of a revised and expanded Arthritis Impact Measurement Scales health status questionnaire, *Arthritis and Rheumatism*, 35: 1–10.

Nelson, E.C., Landgraf, J.M., Hays, R.D., Wasson, J.H. and Kirk, J.W. (1990) The functional status of patients: how can it be measured in physicians' offices? *Medical Care*, 28: 1111–26.

Nelson, E.C., Wasson, J.H., Johnson, D.J. and Hays, R.D. (1996) Dartmouth COOP functional assessment charts: brief measures for clinical practice, in B. Spilker (ed.) *Quality of Life and Pharmacoeconomics in Clinical Trials* (2nd edn). Philadelphia: Lippincott-Raven.

O'Boyle, C., McGee, H., Hickey, A., O'Malley, K. and Joyce, C.R.B. (1992) Individual quality of life in patients undergoing hip replacement, *Lancet*, 339: 1088–91.

Oppenheim, A.N. (1992) *Questionnaire Design, Interviewing and Attitude Measurement.* London: Pinter.

Oregon Health Services Commission (1991) *Prioritization of Health Services.* Salem: Oregon Health Commission.

Orley, J. and Kuyken, W. (eds) (1994) *Quality of Life Assessment: International Perspectives.* Berlin: Springer-Verlag.

Parkerson, G.R., Broadhead, W.E. and Chiu-Kit, J. (1991) The Duke Health Profile: a 17-item measure of health and dysfunction, *Medical Care,* 28: 1056–69.

Parkerson, G.R., Gehlbach, S.H., Wagner, E.H., James, S.A. and Clapp, N.E. (1981) The Duke-UNC Health Profile: an adult health status instrument for primary care, *Medical Care,* 19: 806–28.

Patrick, D. and Peach, H. (1989) *Disablement in the Community.* Oxford: Oxford University Press.

Peto, V., Jenkinson, C., Fitzpatrick, R. and Greenhall, R. (1995) The development of a short measure of functioning and well-being for patients with Parkinson's disease, *Quality of Life Research,* 4: 241–8.

Rosser, R.M. (1988) A health index and output measure, in S.R. Stewart and R.M. Rosser (eds) *Quality of Life: Assessment and Application.* Lancaster: MTP.

Rosser, R.M. and Sintonen, H. (1993) The EuroQol quality of life project, in S.R. Stewart and R.M. Rosser (eds) *Quality of Life Assessment: Key Issues in the 1990s.* London: Kluwer.

Ruta, D. and Garratt, A. (1994) Health status to quality of life measurement in C. Jenkinson (ed.) *Measuring Health and Medical Outcomes.* London: UCL Press.

Ruta, D., Garratt, A., Abdalla, M., Buckingham, K. and Russell, I. (1993) The SF-36 health survey questionnaire: a valid measure of health status, *British Medical Journal,* 307: 448–9.

Ruta, D., Garratt, A., Leng, M., Russell, I. and Macdonald, L. (1994) A new approach to the measurement of quality of life: the Patient Generated Index (PGI), *Medical Care,* 32: 1109–23.

Spilker B. (ed.) (1996) *Quality of Life and Pharmacoeconomics in Clinical Trials.* New York: Lippincott-Raven.

Szabo, S., on behalf of the World Health Organization Quality of Life (WHOQOL) Group (1996) The World Health Organization Quality of Life (WHOQOL) assessment instrument in B. Spilker (ed.) *Quality of Life and Pharmacoeconomics in Clinical Trials* (2nd edn). Philadelphia: Lippincott-Raven.

Thurstone, L. (1928) Attitudes can be measured, *American Journal of Sociology,* 33: 529–54.

Tugwell, C., Bombardier, C., Buchanan, W., Goldsmith, C., Grace, E., Bennett, K., Williams, J., Egger, M., Alarcon, G.S., Guttadauria, M., Yarboro, C., Polisson, R.P., Szydlo, L., Luggen, M.E., Billingsley, L.M., Ward, J.R. and Marks, C. (1990) Methotrexate in rheumatoid arthritis: impact on quality of life assessed by traditional standard item and individualized patient preference health status questionnaires, *Archives of Internal Medicine,* 150: 59–62.

van Agt, H.M.E., Essink-Bot, M., Krabbe, P.F.M. and Bonsel, G.J. (1994) Test-retest reliability of health state valuations collected using the EuroQol questionnaire, *Social Science and Medicine,* 39: 1537–44.

Wasson, J., Keller, A., Rubenstein, L., Hays, R., Nelson, E., Johnson, D. and the Dartmouth Primary Care COOP Project (1992) Benefits and Obstacles of

Health Status Assessment in Ambulatory Settings: the Clinician's Point of View, *Medical Care*, 30 (Supplement): MS42–MS49.

Ware, J.E. (1992) Measures for a new era of health assessment, in A.L. Stewart and J.E. Ware (eds) *Measuring Functioning and Well-Being*. London: Duke University Press.

Ware J. (1993) Measuring patients' views: the optimum outcome measure. SF36: a valid, reliable assessment of health from the patient's point of view, *British Medical Journal*, 306: 1429–30.

Ware, J.E., Brook, R.H., Stewart, A.L. and Davies-Avery, A. (1980) *Conceptualisation and Measurement of Health for Adults in the Health Insurance Study: Vol. I, Model of Health and Methodology*. Santa Monica, California: RAND Corporation.

Ware, J.E., Kosinski, M. and Keller, S.D. (1994) *SF-36 Physical and Mental Health Summary Scales: A User's Manual*. Boston, Massachusetts: The Health Institute, New England Medical Center.

Ware, J.E., Kosinski, M. and Keller, S.D. (1995a) *SF-12: How to Score the SF-12 Physical and Mental Health Summary Scales* (2nd edn). Boston, Massachusetts: The Health Institute, New England Medical Center.

Ware, J.E., Kosinski, M. and Keller, S.D. (1995b) A 12-item short-form health survey. Construction of scales and preliminary tests of reliability and validity, *Medical Care*, 34: 220–33.

Ware, J.E., Kosinski, M. and Keller, S.D. (1996) SF-12: an even shorter health survey, *Medical Outcomes Trust Bulletin*, 4: 2.

Ware, J.E. and Sherbourne, C.D. (1992) The MOS 36-Item Short-Form Health Survey 1: conceptual framework and item selection, *Medical Care*, 30: 473–83.

Ware, J.E., Snow, K.K., Kosinski, M. and Gandek, B. (1993) *The SF36 Health Survey Manual and Interpretation Guide*. Boston, Mass.: The Health Institute, New England Medical Center.

Wasson, J., Keller, A., Rubenstein, L., Hays, R., Nelson, E., Johnson, D. and the Dartmouth Primary Care COOP Project (1992) Benefits and obstacles of health status assessment in ambulatory settings: the clinician's point of view. *Medical Care*, 30: (Supplement): MS42–MS49.

Wilkin, D., Hallam, L. and Doggett, M. (1992) *Measures of Need and Outcome for Primary Health Care*. Oxford: Oxford University Press.

Wilkin, D., Hallam, L. and Doggett, M. (1993) *Measures of Need and Outcome for Primary Health Care* (rev'd edn). Oxford: Oxford University Press.

Sheldon, T. (1993) Reliability of the SF-36 remains uncertain, *British Medical Journal*, 307: 125–6.

Silver, G.A. (1990) Paul Anthony Lembcke, MD, MPH: A pioneer in medical care evaluation, *American Journal of Psychiatry*, 80: 342–8.

Winslow, R. (1992) Questionnaire probes patients' quality of life, *The Wall Street Journal*, July 7, B1 and B4.

Ziebland, S., Fitzpatrick, R. and Jenkinson C. (1992) Assessing short term outcome, *Quality in Health Care*, 1: 141–2.

Ziebland, S., Fitzpatrick, R. and Jenkinson, C. (1993) Tacit models of disability in health assessment questionnaires, *Social Science and Medicine*, 37: 69–75.

6

The assessment of patient satisfaction

Ray Fitzpatrick

Introduction

In the most obvious sense, when any care is provided by a health professional to a patient, it is important to take account of how that care is viewed and valued by the patient. If a historical view is taken of the development of health care, it becomes clear that there have been periods where consideration of the patient's wishes has been so paramount that it actually inhibited the development of scientific medicine (Jewson 1974). However, many would argue that, in the first half of the twentieth century, medicine became so concerned by biomedical and technological aspects of disease that the opposite extreme was reached, of frequent neglect of patients' wishes and preferences. Most recently, health care systems have sought to achieve a balance in services that are on the one hand effective and scientific evidence-based and on the other hand sensitive to patients. Maxwell (1984) identified six dimensions in terms of which we judge the quality of a modern health service: access, relevance to need, effectiveness, equity, efficiency and social acceptability. The last dimension encompasses patient satisfaction. It is becoming clearer that these are desirable properties that often have to be traded-off against each other. For example, the drive for efficiency in the complex modern hospital seeking to provide cost-effective services to large numbers of patients may jeopardize satisfaction at the level of the individual patient. For this reason we have to assess the impact of services in terms of patient satisfaction as well as health outcomes. This chapter reviews the evidence that the processes of care can influence patient satisfaction. It is then explained how the concept of patient satisfaction has been defined and measured. Methodological considerations are reviewed which influence the accuracy with which patients' views are assessed.

Reasons for assessing patient satisfaction

Patient satisfaction has become the subject of investigation in the health care systems of Europe and North America for a variety of reasons. In the first place, it is seen as an important indicator of the quality of health care. For this reason purchasers, providers and planners of health services seek to obtain evidence of patients' views of the quality of care received that may be used in the continuous process of monitoring and improving care. In the United Kingdom this approach received momentum from the Griffiths report on NHS management which criticized the NHS for failing to obtain and act upon systematic feedback from its customers (DHSS 1983). Although it was acknowledged that there are specific difficulties in treating patients with health problems as if they were consumers of a product, the report nevertheless argued strongly for the greater use of surveys of patients' opinions. Added impetus to this emphasis was given by the White Paper of the Secretary of State, *Working for Patients* (Secretary of State for Health 1989), and by documents of the NHS Management Executive such as *Local Voices* (NHSE ME 1992), both of which made assessment of patients' views a priority. In the USA such applications have been more extensively developed, so that consumer reports are now published ranking health care plans according to their patients' views (Rubin *et al.* 1996). There has therefore been a strong climate of opinion to involve patients in assessing the quality of care. The greatest concern in this context is to obtain measures that are feasible and can be used on a regular basis to monitor the quality of services.

A second and related reason has been the growth of health service research. This application differs from the first in that patient satisfaction measures were needed in a research context to provide valid and generalizable results from health service research studies. Robust measures of patient satisfaction have been needed that could be used to examine alternative forms of providing health care in randomized or observational trials. Particularly in North America, patients' views came to be used as measures of outcome in trials of alternative methods of funding health care (Murray 1986), and of alternative treatments (Deyo *et al.* 1986).

The third and ultimately the most important reason for measuring patient satisfaction is that there is increasing evidence of its contribution to other outcomes that are of great importance to purchasers and providers of health care. A variety of studies have found that patients who are dissatisfied are more likely not to reattend for further care (Weiss and Senf 1990; Orton *et al.* 1991). Dissatisfied patients are also less likely to comply with treatment regimes (Korsch *et al.* 1968; Fitzpatrick and Hopkins 1981). There is also a range of evidence that links lower levels of patient dissatisfaction with poorer health outcomes, although, as is discussed below, there are difficulties in identifying the causal direction of such evidence (Deyo and Diehl 1986; Hall *et al.* 1990).

Table 6.1   Dimensions of patient satisfaction

• Humaneness	• Cost
• Informativeness	• Facilities
• Overall quality	• Outcome
• Competence	• Continuity
• Bureaucracy	• Attention to psychosocial problems
• Access	

What is patient satisfaction?

A variety of models have been proposed to understand and explain patient satisfaction. Included in such approaches are the work of Linder-Pelz (1982) who used a psychological approach of value-expectancy theory and Fox and Storms (1981) who used discrepancy theory. However, none of these attempts formally to produce a theoretical basis for patient satisfaction have been convincing and it is not surprising that clear and explicit definitions are also therefore lacking (Williams 1994). However it is clear that most approaches view patients' experiences as including *cognitive evaluations* together with *emotional reactions* to their care (Fitzpatrick 1993). Patients at a cognitive level appraise the value of treatment received, while arriving at some positive neutral or negative response.

Although at the level of measurement, there are arguments for the use of global or single item measures that summarize patients' overall level of satisfaction, detailed research has shown that patients are capable of making quite complex and differentiated judgements of the quality of their care so that the construct is most usefully considered as multi-dimensional (Table 6.1). Thus patients may hold distinct and independent views on the one hand as to whether the health professionals from whom they have received care are humane and have good interpersonal skills, and on the other hand regarding the costs or accessibility of services. The multi-dimensional nature of patients' views is found from those studies that use factor-analytic methods to explore underlying dimensions of lists of questions about patients' views. Ware and Snyder (1975) asked a sample of respondents from Illinois households to respond to 80 questionnaire items about their health care. Factor analysis revealed four distinct dimensions of views in the sample: doctor's conduct, availability of care, continuity and convenience and financial accessibility.

Hall and Dornan (1988a) in their systematic review of patient satisfaction studies, found that some dimensions were far more likely to be studied than others. For example, patients' views about the humaneness of health professionals were investigated in 65 per cent of studies and informativeness in 50 per cent of studies, whereas patients' views about outcomes were only studied in 6 per cent of studies and views about attention received for psychosocial problems in only 3 per cent of studies. How investigators define patient satisfaction and which aspects they choose to investigate can therefore have a substantial influence on levels of satisfaction observed. Hall and Dornan (1988b) found that average levels of patient satisfaction across studies were much higher where measures focused upon health professionals' humaneness compared to other dimensions such as costs, bureaucracy and attention to psychosocial problems.

Relationships with processes of care

One important test of the validity and, ultimately, the value of measures of patient satisfaction is consideration of the range of aspects of health care that have been shown to influence patients' views. It is important to look for evidence where aspects of health care have been measured independently of patients' views to obtain the most robust evidence. This is to place particular emphasis upon those studies where one is not solely reliant on patients' own judgements of what has influenced their views; researchers have independently assessed processes of care. The following are areas where such robust studies have shown aspects of care to influence patient satisfaction.

Interpersonal skills

How skilled health professionals are in interacting with their patients can substantially influence patient satisfaction. DiMatteo and colleagues (1980) studied 71 doctors working in a New York community hospital. They were asked to perform two experimental tasks. First, they had to judge the emotions portrayed by actors in a film specifically made for the study. Second, they were asked to demonstrate a range of emotions that were then rated by other study participants. Subsequently, patients actually attending the clinics of study doctors were asked to assess independently their doctor's interpersonal skills and technical competence. Doctors' scores for interpreting emotions from, for example non-verbal cues were found to be significantly related to patients' satisfaction with interpersonal skills but not with technical competence.

Other studies have tried to specify more directly what the interpersonal skills are that are most appreciated by patients. Stiles and colleagues (1979) tape-recorded the consultations of 19 doctors providing general medical care in an American hospital and then subsequently asked their patients to complete a questionnaire about satisfaction with care. Rating scales were used to judge the dialogue between patients and doctors. Patient satisfaction with doctors' interpersonal skills were highest when the form of dialogue in consultations was independently assessed from tape-recordings to facilitate the patient in talking about their health problems in their own terms rather than following a rigid closed-ended sequence of medical questions. This approach to consultations is often referred to as a patient-centred style of communication in which questions are asked by the doctor using open-ended questions and the doctor facilitates the expression of patients' concerns and feelings about their presenting problem. A study in which independent ratings were made of Canadian primary care physicians' patient centredness from tape-recordings of their consultations found that the more patient centred they were, the greater were patients' levels of satisfaction (Henblest and Stewart 1990). Not all evidence points in this direction. A London based study with a similar design to the Canadian study found that, when patients were randomized either to receive a conventional style of consultation or to receive one in which the GP was more patient centred, conventional care produced higher levels of satisfaction (Savage and Armstrong 1990). It may be that such sudden shifts of behaviour by their GP surprised patients. For current purposes it is of less importance what constitutes 'patient centred care'. It is more essential to appreciate a substantial body of evidence linking behaviour of the health professional independently measured with subsequent views expressed by the patient.

Information giving

The ability on the part of health professionals to communicate relevant amounts and quality of information to the patient has received particular attention. A meta-analysis of a series of studies in which consultations were independently assessed and patients' views separately elicited after the consultation found that overall information giving had the biggest single effect of all health professional behaviours in influencing patient satisfaction (Roter 1989). This evidence from observational studies is supported from experimental evidence. Ley and Spelman (1967) report a study in which junior doctors in both medical and surgical firms were randomly assigned to communicate with inpatients in one of three ways. In the experimental arm, they were to make a particular effort to elicit patients' concerns. In an attention placebo arm, they were to spend more time communicating with patients but with no particular focus. The control arm involved routine care. In the medical but not the surgical patients, higher satisfaction was reported by patients receiving experimental compared with other forms of communication.

Technical competence

It is often argued from survey evidence that patients may be able competently to judge the interpersonal skills of health professionals but not aspects of technical competence (Sira 1980). To some extent this must be the case since many very technical procedures are performed by health professionals that few experts are sufficiently knowledgeable to evaluate. Nevertheless, there is evidence that patients' views, as expressed in well-designed surveys may correspond with what health professionals consider appropriate care. Baker (1993) asked 100 patients in each of eight surgeries to complete a satisfaction questionnaire. Their views about the quality and professional standards of the practices were significantly associated with the judgements made by an external professional assessor.

The organization of health care

Patients' views have been shown to correlate with a number of organizational features of their health care. Thus in the Medical Outcomes study, the views of over 17,000 patients were elicited in simple satisfaction questionnaires (Rubin *et al.* 1996). Patients attending more traditional solo-practitioners rated all aspects of the quality of their care higher than patients attending health maintenance organizations (HMOs). These differences remained after adjustment for patients' demographic and health status characteristics. One immediate consequence of these reactions noted by the investigators was the significantly greater readiness of dissatisfied patients to change their source of health care. Although a number of other studies have suggested that patients are less satisfied in the United States with the newer and somewhat more bureaucratic forms of health care such as HMOs compared to traditional practices, there is also interesting evidence that the longer they stay with new services such as HMOs the more likely it is that levels of satisfaction reach those achieved in more traditional settings (Ross *et al.* 1981).

Over 7000 patients attending the practices of 126 different GPs were asked to complete a patient satisfaction questionnaire (Baker 1996). The larger the list size, the absence of a personal list system (in which patients register with a named GP) and its being a training practice were all characteristics that decreased patients' expressed satisfaction independently of patients' own characteristics.

Time

It might reasonably be argued that a common denominator of many of the aspects of care that have been shown to have an independent effect on patient satisfaction is the simple parameter of time. It is not surprising that several studies have assessed the effect of this variable. Two studies of British primary care adopted the same basic research design of non-systematic allocation of patients to appointments of varying lengths and used the same patient satisfaction questionnaire as outcome measure (Morrell *et al.* 1986; Ridsdale *et al.* 1989). There was a trend in the direction of longer consultations producing higher levels of patient satisfaction but differences by appointment length were not great and few differences in dimensions of satisfaction were significant. However, in a third study (Howie *et al.* 1991), GPs had some flexibility as to whether patients received a longer consultation compared to the earlier studies in which time was rigidly maintained. In this study, length of consultation was significantly correlated with patient satisfaction, suggesting that when appropriate longer consultations are appreciated.

In this section it has not been the intention to identify the determinants of patient satisfaction, since in almost every field reviewed evidence is still incomplete. Rather it has been shown how wide ranging is the evidence of factors that have been shown by independent measurement to influence patient satisfaction. From this evidence it is clear that accurate assessment of views is essential better to identify aspects of health care appreciated by patients.

Questionnaire items versus scales

Three quite distinct approaches exist to assess patients' views of health care. Two of these approaches are based on fixed choice questionnaires. A third approach uses in-depth interviews to generate either qualitative or quantitative data. The role of in-depth interviews is considered in a later section. Here we consider two ways in which fixed choice questionnaires can be used. In one approach, questionnaire items may be said to stand alone and the focus of the survey is upon specific answers to specific questions. In a second approach questionnaire items are scored and summed into scales and the focus of attention is upon analysis of scale scores.

Focus upon specific questions

There is a very substantial tradition of survey research associated in particular with Ann Cartwright in the UK, in which carefully sampled nationally representative respondents report their views and experiences of primary care and hospital services (Cartwright 1964, 1967; Cartwright and Anderson 1981). In this tradition of survey research attention is given to obtaining accurate estimates of views by obtaining representative samples with high response rates. In addition, questionnaires are carefully piloted to eliminate ambiguous or difficult questions. As Cartwright (1983) has argued, much of the emphasis in such surveys is upon asking patients in as precise and comprehensible way as possible about whether they have had particular experiences in the course of their care. To take a specific example, Cartwright (1964), in order to find out about the communication of information in hospitals, included in the questionnaire to a national sample of respondents who had been inpatients the following: 'In general did you ask about things or did people tell you of their own accord?' In the survey, 45 per cent said they mainly asked, 40 per cent said they were told, 7 per cent said they neither asked or were told and 8 per cent did not give an answer. The item addresses the issue of how readily hospital staff volunteer information to patients. Other questions in the survey asked respondents about which, if any, staff gave them information, how early they were woken up in the mornings and whether they found the time too early.

Such surveys have influential effects on health policy. They provide representative responses reporting how commonly specific problems or experiences occur in hospitals or general practice. This tradition has been continued in work such as is reported by Bruster and colleagues (1994) who surveyed over 5000 patients from 36 randomly sampled NHS hospitals. They argue that asking patients to judge their satisfaction with services produces positively skewed data which gives a misleadingly optimistic picture of patients' experiences. Instead, they argue, patients should be asked questions focusing on the specific experiences and problems, regardless of subjective response. Thus, they found that 11 per cent of patients had operations cancelled, 34 per cent were not informed of the results of tests and 44 per cent had no discussion with their doctor about discharge. Furthermore, the rate of such problems varied significantly from one geographical area of England to another. The same survey questionnaire has also been used in the United States and Canada so that international comparisons can be made of the quality of hospital care in different systems (Cleary et al. 1991; Charles et al. 1994).

The wording of such questionnaire items is crucial since what is asked shapes how respondents interpret the question and give their answers. An illustration of this problem is provided by a series of surveys of randomly selected respondents who had received hospital care in Scotland (Cohen et al. 1996). The investigators found that slight differences in the wording of questions between surveys changed the apparent levels of reported problems. For example, while 5.6 per cent of respondents agreed with the statement 'I was not encouraged to ask questions', 23.9 per cent in another survey disagreed with the statement 'You were encouraged to ask questions about your treatment'. The investigators rule out the possibility that differences might be due to patient characteristics or response rate and conclude that respondents found it more difficult to agree with a negative statement about their care than to disagree with a positive statement. As will be argued later, normative value inhibiting criticism of health professionals are very strong.

The emphasis of this first approach is upon questionnaire items that particularly focus upon specific experiences and are less concerned with the respondent's subjective response to the experience. If patients report that they are regularly woken at 5.00 a.m. in hospital or never informed about test results, these are seen as undesirable experiences in common sense terms and it is unnecessary to elicit views such as satisfaction. However, it is possible to use individual questionnaire items with evaluative components effectively. Rubin and colleagues (1996) asked over 17,000 respondents to rate on a simple five-point scale ('excellent' to 'poor') the overall quality of their last visit to the doctor. This single item produced significant differences in the evaluations by patients of solo practices compared with doctors working in multi-specialty or health maintenance organizations. The single evaluative item was also significantly associated with likelihood of patients subsequently changing their health care provider.

Focus upon scale scores

A second and quite different tradition derives from psychometric approaches to the measurement of human subjective states. In essence this approach holds that no single item is likely accurately to assess an individual's view or attitude towards a phenomenon. Instead a number of deliberately chosen items together will provide a better approximation to underlying views.

An excellent example to illustrate what is involved in the development of such scales is provided by Richard Baker's work (1990; 1993) in developing two questionnaires for use in primary care: a Consultation Satisfaction Questionnaire (CSQ) to assess patients' views of their consultations with the GP and a Surgery Satisfaction Questionnaire (SSQ) assessing broader aspects of the practice as a whole. From the available literature he developed a list of 126 questionnaire items on the consultation, that might contribute to the CSQ. Items were eliminated in an iterative series of exercises on the basis of poor response from patients, highly skewed response and in later stages principal components analysis of patterns of answers to versions of the questionnaire from samples of patients. This form of statistical analysis is intended to group together items measuring a single or similar underlying construct and separate out items measuring different constructs. As a result he obtained a questionnaire with 16 items that contributed to one of four scales: general satisfaction, professional care, depth of relationship and perceived length of consultation. Thus the scores of three items were summed to produce the overall scale score for 'perceived length of the consultation'. This version of the questionnaire and its scale scores were then subjected to further analyses along principles outlined below to establish reliability and validity. The questionnaire has subsequently shown differences in satisfaction scores of patients in practices with larger list sizes and no personal list system (Baker 1996).

The principle advantages of the psychometric approach are twofold: (i) that greater attention can be given to estimating reliably the 'true' underlying views of patients and (ii) that finer gradations of score can be achieved when multiple items are summed to assess a construct, thus increasing possible sensitivity to differences of experience. The principle disadvantages are (i) that it is a time-consuming approach beyond the resources of many users of surveys and (ii) that scale scores provide a less intuitive result for audiences of surveys than distributions of answers to single direct questions.

Reliability and validity

Reliability

Most evidence has been presented for patient satisfaction questionnaires developed from within the psychometric tradition. This is to be lamented since the value of simple and direct questions in the first tradition identified above would be even further enhanced if more evidence were available on reliability and validity. With regard to reliability far more attention has been given to the internal reliability of scales than to whether they are reproducible (as examined by test-retest). The Consultation Satisfaction Questionnaire described above had very satisfactory levels of both internal and test-retest reliability. The complexities of examining this dimension are illustrated by Savage and Armstrong (1990) who found that patients' satisfaction with a GP consultation was significantly lower when reassessed after one week. In such situations it is very difficult to distinguish between measurement error in the questionnaire and real shifts in patients' views as they reflect further on a health care experience. As Stimson and Webb (1975) showed with qualitative evidence from in-depth interviews with respondents at several points after a general practice consultation, patients continue to evaluate and re-evaluate consultations particularly as they appraise benefits to health and obtain interpretations from their family and other sources of advice.

Validity

The validity of patient satisfaction questionnaires is not easy to establish. Content validity is best established by drawing up questionnaire items on the basis of exploratory interviewing to establish how patients in a particular group view the services they receive. Patients should also be involved in commenting on drafts of questionnaires in terms of omissions and other problems. Construct validity is a more formal way of examining an instrument, that is examining whether it has expected relationships with other variables considered theoretically related. Ware and Hays (1988) examined the construct validity of alternative forms of a patient satisfaction questionnaire by whether they were associated with compliance with medical regimen and with whether respondents would recommend the service to friends. Evidence that instruments predict changing health service provider

Table 6.2   Advantages of self-completed versus interview based
questionnaires

• Sensitivity to patients' concerns	• More scope to follow-up
• Flexibility in covering topics	non-response
• Rapport	• Standardization of task
• Clarification of ambiguities of items	• No 'interviewer bias'
or of reasons for views	• Anonymity
• Respondent adherence to task	• Low cost of data gathering
	• Less need for trained staff

may also be considered evidence of validity (Rubin *et al.* 1996). More
demanding still is to examine convergent and discriminant validity. Fitzpatrick and colleagues (1987) examined the validity of a patient satisfaction questionnaire for use in a back pain clinic. The instrument contained
three scales assessing the humaneness and art of care, the technical quality of care and an efficacy scale (to assess satisfaction with outcomes of
care). It was postulated that changes in patient symptoms of back pain
over time should correlate most with the efficacy scale and least with the
art and humaneness scale, since changes in symptoms would be an element
in judgements about the efficacy of the clinic but not in judging personal
skills of the doctor. These predictions were confirmed.

Methods of data gathering

Most patient satisfaction questionnaires with fixed choice format can be
completed by respondents without the involvement of an interviewer so
that they are feasible to send by post. However, there are a number of
reasons why it may be advantageous to collect such data by means of an
interviewer. The advantages and disadvantages of collecting structured data
by interviewer or self-completion are summarized in Table 6.2. On balance there would seem to be few circumstances where a well developed
and piloted questionnaire should not produce accurate results and a good
response rate if postally administered.

The stronger case for using interviews in the context of patient satisfaction
research is made for the use of in-depth interviews gathering qualitative
data (the third approach identified above). Some indeed argue that structured patient satisfaction questionnaires have produced a quite distorted
impression of how patients view their health care and that only more in-
depth interviews uncover dissatisfaction and the grounds for such negative
responses (Stimson and Webb 1975; Williams 1994). Two forms of in-depth
interview to assess patient satisfaction have proved particularly useful: the
non-schedule standardized interview and critical incident technique.

Non-schedule standardized interviews

This form of interview allows the interviewer to collect data in an informal and unstructured way that maximizes expression of personal concerns by the respondent. However, data are collected with a clear agenda of issues that the investigator needs to cover. Tape-recorded interviews are analysed and coded according to scales to assess subjects of concern. This approach was used to examine patients' experiences of neurological care for chronic headache (Fitzpatrick and Hopkins 1983; 1993). Patients were reluctant to criticize neurologists in the terms usually used in patient satisfaction questionnaires. Nevertheless, it was possible to make simple ratings of interviews that clearly distinguished a range of responses to clinic attendance from viewing it as successful through to severe disappointment. From other data collected, it was possible to explain disappointed reactions as arising from failures of neurologists to reassure or, in other cases inappropriate referrals of patients hoping to prevent their headaches by lifestyle advice from neurologists with no expertise in this area. These simple ratings of success and disappointment were also significant predictors of symptomatic improvement when patients were reassessed one year later (Fitzpatrick and Hopkins 1983).

Critical incident technique

Critical incident technique has been extensively applied to assess patients' views of health services. Like other in-depth interviews, it requires trained interviewers to talk respondents through the sequence of experiences that are involved in a hospital stay or visit to general practice in ways that encourage expression of positive and negative aspects of such experiences (Flanagan 1954). The most important aspect of this technique is identifying aspects of respondents' stories that produce the most negative (or positive) responses. For example, from a sample of respondents who had attended an outpatient clinic, it was possible to reconstruct that the experience of getting to and from the outpatient clinic produced more negative incidents in patients' accounts than did their narratives of the consultation and medical treatment received (Pryce-Jones 1993).

Methodological problems

There are a number of methodological problems that seem to reoccur commonly and that need to be taken account of when designing studies that include patient satisfaction as a primary concern. They do not necessarily jeopardize the investigation of patient satisfaction but may, if ignored, lead to misleading results.

Positive skew

Hall and Dornan's systematic review (1988b) of studies shows that if scores are standardized to 0–100 range, the mean level of satisfaction score across studies is 0.76. Analysed in a slightly different way the mean proportion of positively satisfied patients was found to be 81 per cent. A second meta-analysis, of studies of patient satisfaction and primary care, has also found very positively skewed data (Wensing et al. 1994). The vast majority of patients select positive responses in such surveys. It is difficult to determine whether this is due to high quality care per se or to the normative values that clearly surround discussion of doctors, nurses and medicine and which patients recognize as inhibiting more critical comments (Fitzpatrick and Hopkins 1983). The most obvious implication of this is that quantitative analysis of such data needs to be approached with caution. Also quite small numbers of dissatisfied patients will be found if studies recruit small samples. This may be important if it is intended, for example, to find a difference in levels of satisfaction between different forms of providing care.

Effects of health status and psychological well-being

A number of studies have an association between poorer health status and dissatisfaction with health care (Fitzpatrick 1993). It is impossible in most of the evidence to disentangle different possible explanations for this association. At one extreme, patients with poorer health outcomes may attribute this to the quality of their care, even when such attributions are unwarranted. At the other extreme, there may be real differences in the quality of care that lead to both dissatisfaction and poorer health status. Sensky and Catalan (1992) draw together evidence for what may be a third and most plausible form of explanation for the association, namely that patients with poor psychological mood (either primary or as a consequence of ill-health) may have cognitive biases that lead to particularly negative judgements of the value of their health care.

Influence of demographic variables

To some extent responses to patient satisfaction questionnaires may reflect not the quality of actual experiences of treatment but more generalized attitudes and orientations to health. In other words, variations in satisfaction levels may reflect patients' characteristics rather than the service being evaluated. Hall and Dornan (1990) show that across studies, age is by the most consistent variable to have this effect; older patients usually express more positive satisfaction. Baker (1996) suggests more complex interactions of age with other characteristics in influencing satisfaction levels. Again it is difficult to interpret this consistent finding of age and positive satisfaction, although it is more likely to be due to a cognitive perceptual effect rather than to the possibility that older individuals receive higher quality care. In any case, demographic variables need to be controlled for when interpreting possible relationships of satisfaction to types of care or treatments.

Conclusion

Although the patient's distinctive viewpoint is now widely recognized to be a vital element in the evaluation of health services, there is still no consensus about optimal ways of capturing this perspective. Rather as in the field of health status measurement, there needs to be far more research on the relative merits of shorter and simpler instruments that, while losing some content validity, may still be advantageous in terms of response rates, study feasibility and overall generalizability. Such practical approaches need to be explored in the context of large trials and health service evaluations, but there is still an important role for the exploratory in-depth method that informs us of how patients experience health care. Both approaches are needed to ensure that patients' views are appropriately assessed in the evaluation of health care.

References

Baker, R. (1990) Development of a questionnaire to assess patients' satisfaction with consultations in general practice, British Journal of General Practice, 40: 487–90.

Baker, R. (1993) Use of psychometrics to develop a measure of patient satisfaction for general practice, in R. Fitzpatrick and A. Hopkins (eds) Measurement of Patients' Satisfaction with their Care. Royal College of Physicians of London, 57–76.

Baker, R. (1996) Characteristics of practices, general practitioners and patients related to levels of patients' satisfaction with consultations, British Journal of General Practice, 46: 601–5.

Bruster, S., Jarman, B., Bosanquet, N., Weston, D., Erens, R. and Delbanco, T. (1994) National survey of hospital patients, British Medical Journal, 309: 1542–9.

Cartwright, A. (1964) Human Relations and Hospital Care. London: Routledge & Kegan Paul.

Cartwright, A. (1967) Patients and their Doctors. London: Routledge & Kegan Paul.

Cartwright, A. (1983) Health Surveys in Practice and in Potential. London: King Edward's Hospital Fund for London.

Cartwright, A. and Anderson, R. (1981) General Practice Revisited. London: Routledge & Kegan Paul.

Cleary, P., Edgman-Levitan, S., Roberts, M., Moloney, T., McMullen, W. and Walker, J. (1991) Patients evaluate their hospital care: a national survey, Health Affairs, 10: 254–67.

Charles, C., Gauld, M., Chambers, L., O'Brien, B., Haynes, R. and Labelle, R. (1994) How was your hospital stay? Patients report about their care in Canadian hospitals, *Canadian Medical Association Journal*, 150: 1813–22.

Cohen, G., Forbes, J. and Garraway, M. (1996) Can different patient satisfaction survey methods yield consistent results? Comparison of three surveys, *British Medical Journal*, 313: 841–4.

Deyo, R. and Diehl, A. (1986) Patient satisfaction with medical care for low back pain, *Spine*, 11: 28–30.

Deyo, R., Diehl, A. and Rosenthal, M. (1986) How many days of bed rest for acute back pain? A randomised clinical trial, *New England Journal of Medicine*, 315: 1064–70.

DiMatteo, M., Taranta, A., Friedman, H. and Prince, L. (1980) Predicting patient satisfaction from physicians' non-verbal communication skills, *Medical Care*, 18: 376–87.

Fitzpatrick, R. (1993) Scope and measurement of patient satisfaction, in R. Fitzpatrick and A. Hopkins (eds) *Measurement of Patients' Satisfaction with their Care*. London: Royal College of Physicians of London, 1–18.

Fitzpatrick, R., Bury, M., Frank, A. and Donnelly, T. (1987) Problems in the assessment of outcome in a back pain clinic, *International Disability Studies*, 9: 161–5.

Fitzpatrick, R. and Hopkins, A. (1981) Patients' satisfaction with communication in neurological outpatient clinics, *Journal of Psychosomatic Research*, 25: 329–34.

Fitzpatrick, R. and Hopkins, A. (1983) Problems in the conceptual framework of patient satisfaction research: an empirical exploration, *Sociology of Health and Illness*, 5: 297–311.

Fitzpatrick, R., Hopkins, A. and Harvard-Watts, O. (1983) Social dimensions of healing, *Social Science and Medicine*, 17: 501–10.

Fitzpatrick, R. and Hopkins, A. (eds) (1993) *Measurement of Patients' Satisfaction with their Treatment*. London: Royal College of Physicians of London.

Flanagan, J. (1954) The critical incident technique, *Psychological Bulletin*, 5: 327–58.

Fox, J. and Storms, D. (1981) A different approach to socio-demographic predictors of satisfaction with health care, *Social Science and Medicine*, 15A: 557–63.

Hall, J. and Dornan, M. (1988a) What patients like about their medical care and how often they are asked: a meta-analysis of the satisfaction literature, *Social Science and Medicine*, 27: 935–9.

Hall, J. and Dornan, M. (1988b) Meta-analysis of satisfaction with medical care: description of research domain and analysis of overall satisfaction levels, *Social Science and Medicine*, 27: 637–44.

Hall, J. and Dornan, M. (1990) Patient sociodemographic characteristics as predictors of satisfaction with medical care: a meta-analysis, *Social Science and Medicine*, 30: 811–18.

Hall, J., Feldstein, M. and Fretwell, M. (1990) Older patients' health status and satisfaction with medical care in an HMO population, *Medical Care*, 28: 261–70.

Henblest, R. and Stewart, M. (1990) Patient-centredness in the consultation. 2: Does it really make a difference?, *Family Practice*, 7: 28–33.

Howie, J., Porter, M., Heaney, D. and Hopton, J. (1991) Long to short consultation ratio: a proxy measure of quality of care for general practice, *British
Journal of General Practice*, 41: 48–54.

Jewson, N. (1974) Medical knowledge and the patronage system in eighteenth
century England, *Sociology*, 8: 369–85.

Korsch, B., Gozzi, E. and Francis, V. (1968) Gaps in doctor–patient communications: 1. Doctor–patient interaction and patient satisfaction, *Paediatrics*, 42:
955–71.

Ley, P. and Spelman, M. (1967) *Communicating with the Patient*. London, Staples
Press.

Linder-Pelz, S. (1982) Toward a theory of patient satisfaction, *Social Science and
Medicine*, 16: 577–82.

Maxwell, R. (1984) Quality assessment in health, *British Medical Journal*, 288:
1470–2.

Morrell, D., Evans, M., Morris, R. and Roland, M. (1986) The 'five minute'
consultation: effect of time constraint on clinical content and patient satisfaction, *British Medical Journal*, 292: 870–2.

Murray, J. (1986) A follow-up comparison of patient satisfaction among
pre-paid and fee-for-service patients, *Journal of Family Practice*, 26: 576–
81.

NHS Management Executive (1992) *Local Voices*. London: London Department of
Health.

Orton, M., Fitzpatrick, R., Fuller, A., Mant, D., Mlynek, C. and Thorogood,
M. (1991) Factors affecting women's response to an invitation to attend for
a second breast cancer screening examination, *British Journal of General
Practice*, 41: 320–3.

Pryce-Jones, M. (1993) Critical incident technique as a method of assessing patient
satisfaction, in R. Fitzpatrick and A. Hopkins (eds) *Measurement of Patients'
Satisfaction with their Care*. London: Royal College of Physicians of London, 87–98.

Ridsdale, L., Carruthers, L., Morris, R. and Ridsdale, R. (1989) Study of the effect
of time availability on the consultation, *Journal of the Royal College of
General Practitioners*, 39: 488–91.

Ross, C., Wheaton, B. and Duff, R. (1981) Client satisfaction and the organization
of medical practice: why time counts, *Journal of Health and Social Behavior*,
22: 243–55.

Roter, D. (1989) Which facets of communication have strong effects on outcome:
a meta-analysis, in M. Stewart and D. Roter (eds) *Communicating with
Medical Patients*. London: Sage, 183–96.

Rubin, H., Gandek, B., Rogers, W., Kosinski, M., McHorney, C. and Ware, J.
(1996) Patients' ratings of outpatient visits in different practice settings,
Journal of the American Medical Association, 270: 835–40.

Savage, R. and Armstrong, D. (1990) Effect of a general practitioner's consulting
style on patients' satisfaction: a controlled study, *British Medical Journal*,
301: 968–70.

Security of State for Health (1989) *Working for Patients*. London: HMSO.

Sensky, T. and Catalan, J. (1992) Asking patients about their treatment, *British
Medical Journal*, 305: 1109–10.

Sheldon, T. (1993) Measuring patients' views of their health. Reliability of the SF36 remains uncertain, *British Medical Journal*, 307: 125–6.

Sira, Z.B. (1980) Affective and instrumental components in the physician–patient relationship: an additional component of interaction theory, *Journal of Health and Social Behaviour*, 21: 170–80.

Stiles, W., Putnam, S., Wolf, M. and James, S. (1979) Interaction exchange structure and patient satisfaction with medical interviews, *Medical Care*, 17: 667–79.

Stimson, G. and Webb, B. (1975) *Going to See the Doctor: The Consultation Process in General Practice*. London: Routledge & Kegan Paul.

Ware, J. and Snyder, M. (1975) Dimensions of patient attitudes regarding doctors and medical care services, *Medical Care*, 13: 669–79.

Ware, J. and Hays, R. (1988) Methods for measuring patient satisfaction with specific medical encounters, *Medical Care*, 26: 393–402.

Weiss, B. and Senf, J. (1990) Patient satisfaction survey instrument for use in health maintenance organisations, *Medical Care*, 28: 434–45.

Wensing, M., Grol, R. and Smits, A. (1994) Quality judgements by patients on general practice care: a literature review, *Social Science and Medicine*, 38: 45–53.

Williams, B. (1994) Patient satisfaction: a valid concept? *Social Science and Medicine*, 38: 509–16.

7

Qualitative research methods

Sue Ziebland and Lucie Wright

Introduction

This chapter is concerned with two qualitative methods which are relatively widely used in health and health services research: observation and in-depth interviewing. The first two sections describe, separately, the unique features of these methods and how they have been used in research in a health setting. The final section details aspects of analysis and issues of validity and reliability which are shared by the two approaches.

Qualitative research in the medical literature

The range of methods which are described generically as qualitative research (including in-depth interviewing, ethnography and observation) share a perspective which complements and contrasts with the focus of quantitative methods (such as surveys, trials and experiments). Qualitative methods are used when there is a need to understand the meaning and interpretation of aspects of society, drawing on the experiences and expressions of those who are being studied. Qualitative methods are particularly useful for developing an understanding of how people behave and how social systems operate in a natural context. This is achieved through a combination of observation, exploration of the ways in which people interpret their experiences and reflection on the impact of the research process. The methods are often used to explore the range of views and behaviour prior to designing research methods for surveys based on representative population samples, but they may also be usefully employed to help interpret the results of quantitative studies. Applications of qualitative research methods are certainly not confined to circumstances where they can be combined with quantitative methods. As will be demonstrated in this chapter, they are also invaluable in their own right. In health and health services research this could include the management of health care; patients' and carers' experience of health and illness; features of the clinical consultation; and the culture, development and training of health workers.

In recent years some qualitative researchers have made considerable efforts to explain the value of the methods to a wide audience in health and health services research (Murphy and Mattson 1992; Britten and Fisher 1993; Pope and Mays 1995). While there is growing evidence of enthusiasm for research methods which are not based on the positivist model (from which quantitative scientific research is derived) there remain considerable misunderstandings about what counts as qualitative research. This confusion is apparent in any search of the published literature or conference abstracts where a remarkable array of papers describe their methods as 'qualitative'. The statement 'This qualitative study . . .' precedes reports of studies which share no discernible features of qualitative design. The focus of the qualitative research question and the methods which are employed are quite distinct from survey and trial methods. An open question on a self-completion questionnaire, a personal interview with a structured interview schedule or a study based on subjective matters does not make a qualitative study. A survey cannot be reclassified as a qualitative study in a last ditch attempt to salvage some publishable results. As Fitzpatrick and Boulton point out, 'research based on a small number of respondents should not be considered qualitative just because the sample size is too small to assess statistical significance. This is more likely to prove to be an inadequate quantitative study' (Fitzpatrick and Boulton 1994).

Qualitative methods have been used in medical sociology and in social and educational research for decades and there is increasing evidence that the medical and epidemiological mainstream is at least willing to inspect the field. Examples from the last few years attest this disposition: in 1992 at the Society for Social Medicine conference Catherine Pope and Nick Mays enacted an entertaining dialogue representing the mutual incomprehension inherent in the quantitative/qualitative polarities. This was subsequently published as a paper in the British Medical Journal (Pope and Mays 1993). A 1992 paper in *Family Practice* (Murphy and Mattson 1992) and an editorial in the *British Journal of General Practice* (Britten and Fisher 1993) both highlighted the value of qualitative research in primary care. The following year medical sociologists Ray Fitzpatrick and Mary Boulton drew attention to the 'exciting range of qualitative methods capable of providing basic understanding of the processes and outcomes of health care' in a review of qualitative methods in Quality in Health Care (Fitzpatrick and Boulton 1994) and an editorial in the *Journal of Epidemiology and Community Health* considered 'Why we need qualitative research' (Black

1994). In 1995, the *British Medical Journal* published a series, edited by Pope and Mays, which described a range of qualitative research methods. These included interviewing (Britten 1995), observation, (Mays and Pope 1995) case studies (Keen and Packwood 1995) focus groups (Kitzinger 1995) and consensus methods (Jones and Hunter 1995) and two introductory chapters by the series editors, one of which specifically addressed the difficulties which medical researchers might have in assessing rigour in qualitative research (Mays and Pope 1995).

In 1995 Mildred Blaxter began a process to produce a set of criteria for evaluating qualitative research, in recognition of the difficulty which some editors of medical and epidemiological journals may have in deciding which qualitative papers should be sent for peer review. There is not universal agreement that producing such checklists will be helpful to qualitative research, but the process has opened discussion about issues of reliability and validity in research and, hopefully, provides reassuring evidence that there are consensual standards. This may be particularly important when the methods are unfamiliar and regarded with suspicion by those who have been trained in another research tradition.

The next two sections of this chapter describe the approaches of qualitative observation and in-depth interviewing.

Qualitative observation

This section is concerned with the combination of methods which are used in ethnographic research. Qualitative observation studies involve collecting detailed information about behaviour in a natural, rather than experimental, setting. While some counting of occurrences may be appropriate to the research design, the research aim is exploratory and will therefore be primarily in the form of unstructured field notes, memos and transcripts of speech, for which numerical analysis is rarely applicable.

The methods have been widely used in medical sociology and health services research, yet the objectives, style and reporting of qualitative observation may seem alien to those who are more familiar with trials or survey research or the similarly named 'observation studies' of medical research. In this section we intend to describe salient features of design and analysis which will assist in planning and reading ethnographic studies.

Ethnographic methods are often used either to study groups that are perceived as unusual, alien or deviant, or to provide a new way of looking at phenomena which are taken for granted or routine. However, the ethnographer's perspective need not be limited to these extremes. For example, Strong and Robinson (1990) were neither working with the commonplace nor the exotic when they conducted their case study of organizational changes in the NHS, which they described as a 'policy ethnography'.

The researchers did not adopt the naive stance of the outsider: they were well informed, familiar with the culture and the in-depth interviews in this study often resembled discussions between experts.

While there are questionnaire designs and interviewing techniques which may help to minimize the disparity between what people do and what they say they do, a description of occurrences in a natural setting tells a more convincing story than is possible when relying on questionnaire responses alone. This advantage of observational research methods is all the more applicable if the researcher is conducting their research *in cognito*, as a covert participant observer. If the subjects are aware that they are being observed they may alter their behaviour, perhaps from increased self-consciousness, or to present themselves in a favourable light; or to adhere to official rules of comportment. Some classic research in health settings has been conducted by 'under cover' researchers who gained access by working as staff, e.g. Goffman's (1961) study which was undertaken while he was working in a mental hospital (as an assistant to the athletic director). Having an additional role to perform, especially if the researcher is 'under-cover' will inevitably sometimes interfere with the process of data collection, but may be the only way to achieve naturalistic observations in the setting of interest. A more recent example is a study of condom use in motels in Nicaragua (Gorter 1993). The study included a comparison of the effectiveness of different ways of distributing condoms to sex workers and their clients. Researchers working as cleaners or receptionists searched the waste-bins in the bedrooms for used condoms after each couple had departed. Given that there was no other obvious way of disposing of used condoms in the rooms, absence of a condom was taken as evidence of non-use.

Posing as a patient in a mental hospital may be an even more extreme covert role than taking a job of work to gain access to a research environment. A controversial use of the pseudo patient in a research study is Rosenhan's work 'On being sane in insane places' (1973), which described the diagnostic and subsequent experiences of eight 'sane' people who gained secret admission to psychiatric hospitals. All presented with the same symptoms, the complaint that they were hearing voices. None was recognized as an impostor and, despite behaving in a 'normal' and cooperative manner and not complaining of symptoms again after admittance, the average length of time to discharge was 19 days, with a range from seven to 52 days. Unsurprisingly, the covert nature of Rosenhan's work did nothing to endear him (or the wider research community) to the profession of psychiatry. Covert participant observation has rather fallen from favour because of the difficult ethical issues involved. There are often ethical problems if researchers pose as health care workers or patients. There may be additional concerns about the misuse of resources if the deception continues long-term.

The other end of the observation spectrum is overt and non-participant observation, where the role of the researcher is acknowledged and the aim is to impact as little as possible on the setting. When observations are conducted in an overt and non-participant manner, it may be argued that the longer the observer is present in the setting (or the less informed are the subjects about the true purpose of the research) the more naturalistic will be the observations. Strong, as a non-participant observer, by conducting 'fly on the wall' research on hundreds of paediatric consultations in Britain and the United States was able to detail the complex rules which make up the institutionalized roles of patients and doctors (Strong 1979). Prior to Pope's work on the management of waiting lists it was assumed that waiting lists functioned as more or less orderly queues. This assumption proved to be misplaced and her research showed how an outside observer using qualitative observation techniques is able to reflect on organizational details which may escape those who are closely involved (Pope 1991).

Lofland observes that many ethnographies have arisen from the researcher's personal biography (Lofland and Lofland 1984). Observations may be overt or covert, participant or non-participant. Some aspects of the research role will be eased through familiarity with the setting, although the dangers of 'going native' may be all the more acute. Barrie Thorne was an antiwar activist when the field work for 'Protest and the problem of credibility' was conducted and Julius Roth was a patient in a tuberculosis hospital when he did the fieldwork for his study 'Timetables: structuring the passage of time in hospital treatment and other careers' (Roth 1963). While the qualitative researcher may see the research possibilities of an extended illness episode, such opportunities are unlikely to be actively sought.

Gaining access

Negotiating access to the naturalistic research setting is a vital part of ethnographic observation. Settings which are likely to be of interest to the health researcher are rarely characterized by entirely open access. A waiting room in an out-patients' department or GPs surgery is certainly an environment with less restricted access arrangements than an operating theatre, but observations which are curtailed on the public side of the clinician's door will have a limited scope. Failed research is rarely reported and many ethnographic research projects may have ground to a halt or veered off on a 'path of least resistance' (Lee 1993) as a result of difficulties which occur when trying to gain access. Dowell comments that it is an area of social dynamics which is worthy of research in itself (Dowell et al. 1996). Access will need to be negotiated at the appropriate levels within the hierarchy and at each gatekeeping encounter it may be necessary to accept the imposition of conditions on the research. These may involve methodological restrictions; the negotiation of a reciprocal arrangement where access is allowed on the condition that the gatekeeper's research agenda is (also) addressed; and an agreement that the gatekeeper has the final say in any resultant publications (Lee 1993). It should be noted that while gatekeepers in relatively powerful positions are able to impose restrictions in an overt manner, those at other levels in the hierarchy may be even more effective in scuppering the process if they have not been appropriately consulted or if the researcher antagonizes staff whose cooperation is essential.

The precise context of the access is given due importance in reporting qualitative research. The following extract from Paul Atkinson's *Medical Talk and Medical Work* demonstrates how, even to those with international reputations, enthusiastic local sponsors and sabbatical leave as visiting scholars with honorary hospital appointments, this stage is of primary importance in shaping the study.

I arranged to pass through the university city in which the teaching hospital is located . . . and was thus able to negotiate my access there before I embarked on my precious fieldwork. In the interim I had also begun to negotiate access with equivalent medical services in a British teaching hospital. Having had the possibilities of work in both Haematology and Pathology services opened up in the US, I approached the equivalent departments in a British setting. My experiences with both specialities, in Britain and the USA, were similar and determined the precise outcome of the research. The pathologists I approached were, at best, lukewarm and at worst chose not to respond to any overtures I made. Even the senior pathologist in the American hospital – who had apparently agreed to my research in general terms – proved unwilling or unable to go as far as to set up any practical access to his colleagues. The reception offered by the haematologists, on the other hand, was entirely accommodating. Not only were the respective Chiefs of Service sympathetic to my proposed research, but they were able to indicate just how I could establish a practical presence with some of their colleagues, and to observe their everyday work.

(Atkinson 1995: 3)

Once access has been achieved, the importance of establishing (and deserving) the trust of participants in the research setting cannot be over-emphasized. If rich data is to be gained it is important that investigators act in a manner which will maximize the information which is made available to them. Lofland discusses ways in which the problems of 'getting along' may be minimized with regard to stance and style. The stance which most fieldworkers take is, they suggest, 'trust combined with a healthy dose of scepticism'. In many situations the researcher's style will be successful if it combines a non-threatening demeanour with what the authors describe as a display of 'socially acceptable incompetence' (Lofland and Lofland 1984).

Logging data

Field notes and interview transcripts are likely to make up the bulk of the data in an ethnographic study, but researchers will also use photographs, maps, sound recordings and document collection. Ethnographic observation relies heavily on the skills of the researcher in immersing themselves in the field and describing their material. Field notes should be as rich a source as possible and depend on the observational abilities of the researcher, the accuracy of their notes, the frequency and comprehensiveness of writing up and their attention to detail.

Lofland stresses the importance of thoroughness in data logging:

the task of naturalistic researchers is not so much to 'procure' data for recording as it is to register the social events unfolding or the words being spoken before them. The researcher does not only (or mainly) wait for 'significant' (sociologically or otherwise) events to occur or words to be said and then write them down. An enormous amount of information about the settings under observation or the interview in progress may be apprehended in apparently trivial happenings or utterances and these can be indispensable grist for the logging mill. Understandably then, the complaint of the novice investigator (or the boast of the professional) that he or she 'didn't make any notes because nothing important happened' is viewed in this tradition as either naive or arrogant, or both.

(Lofland and Lofland 1984: 46)

Wherever it is possible audio (or video) tape recording has the potential to provide the richest source of data, although in some circumstances there will be justifiable concerns about the impact of the technology on the behaviour being observed. Consent should always be obtained and in an interview will rarely be refused if confidentiality is assured and the tape recorder is presented as an aid which 'just means that I don't have to write everything down'. The impact of recording equipment on the dynamics of the setting must be carefully considered and the need for detail must be balanced against preservation of the naturalistic setting. Atkinson was given permission by the participants to use a small recorder to capture the detail of medical talk during ward rounds. The precision which was neces- sitated by his study simply could not have been achieved with field notes, no matter how swiftly written. However, it is very difficult to produce high quality transcriptions of talk in such settings, characterized as they are by 'high levels of interruption and overlapping talk . . . normally consisting of two or three participants . . . marked by quite high levels of simultaneous talk, mutual interruption and other perturbations' (Atkinson 1995: 11).

In those circumstances where respondents do prefer to speak off the record and unrecorded, detailed notes should be written up as soon as possible after each interview or set of observations. However the data is collected, protection of confidentiality must be carefully considered. Code names or numbers should always be used with the data and any reference to real identity kept as a hard copy in a locked cabinet.

Counting

Whether or not it is deemed appropriate to count instances as part of a qualitative study must depend on the focus of the study. Silverman has illustrated how counting the number of questions asked in a consultation by parents whose children were about to undergo surgery added to his understanding of the clinic. Parents reported in interviews that they did not feel able to ask questions when there were many staff present, but counting revealed that they actually asked more questions when the consultant had colleagues or students present than when alone. It was suggested that when the consultant broke off their interaction with the parents to address their colleagues it gave time for the parents to think of questions. The dissatisfaction which was evident from the interviews combined with the parents' need to reflect before phrasing questions, led to a change in the organization and timing of the clinics. The success of these changes was demonstrated in an evaluation (Silverman 1993).

While counting or timing some events may be an important addition to some studies, it has been suggested that it is probably unwise to try and include the collection of masses of quantitative data while making naturalistic observations. An approach which relies on quantifying occurrences or phenomena requires a rather different frame of mind from that needed to identify its major qualitative features – attempting the two pursuits simultaneously could be counterproductive. Erving Goffman refers to this concern when describing his fieldwork in a mental hospital:

> Desiring to obtain ethnographic detail regarding selected aspects of patient social life I did not employ usual kinds of measurements and controls. I assumed that the role and time required to gather statistical evidence for a few statements would preclude my gathering data on the tissue and fabric of patient life.
>
> (Goffman 1961: xi)

Methods of analysing data from qualitative observation and issues of reliability and validity share much in common with data from interviews. These will therefore be discussed together in the final section of the chapter.

Interviewing

In general usage the term 'interview' can be defined as a conversation or questioning of a person. This dictionary definition reflects, for research, the diversity of the interview technique – ranging from a 'guided conversation' (Lofland and Lofland 1984) to a structured questioning of the interviewee. This diversity is largely determined by the degree of structure imposed within the interview. That is, the extent to which the wording of questions posed are established and consistent and the extent to which they are asked in the same order. Conventionally, interviewing is typically characterized as ranging in structure from depth interviewing (which is relatively unstructured) through semi-structured interviewing, to structured or standardized interviewing.

The diversity of interviewing, however, is determined not only by the degree of structure. In addition, approaches to interviewing vary in terms of the number of people being interviewed at a time. The most common interview conducted within research is the one-to-one interviewer and interviewee format. However, group interviewing, common within market research, is being utilized increasingly in health related research. Also interviews may be conducted face-to-face with the interviewee or by telephone. They may be brief one-off events or lengthy and conducted on several occasions with each respondent or group (Fontana and Frey 1994).

In other words, there is a diversity of approaches to research interviewing. In qualitative studies the methods will be used to generate narrative, as opposed to numerical data. In this section, qualitative interviewing – semi- and unstructured – conducted individually and within groups will be discussed in the context of health and health services research.

Individual interviews

As mentioned the qualitative interviewer may take a semi- or unstructured approach to addressing the research question. Using a semi-structured approach a set of pre-determined questions are asked. However, the order of questions may be varied between respondents and answers are probed by the interviewer where necessary. In this way the researcher can adapt the research to the respondent's level of comprehension and articulacy (Fielding 1992). Using a semi-structured approach to interviewing requires prior knowledge and understanding of the research topic in order to know the pertinent questions to cover.

Such a priori knowledge is not a prerequisite of unstructured interviewing. The aim of in-depth interviewing is to elicit the interviewee's perspective, rather than that imposed by the researcher. According to Marshall and Rossman, the fundamental assumption underlying this approach is that: 'the participant's perspective on the phenomenon of interest should unfold as the participant views it, not as the researcher views it' (Marshall and Rossman 1995: 80). This does not imply that the interview is a free for all with each interviewee talking on anything and everything. Rather the interview takes the form of a 'guided conversation' where the interviewer has a list or 'interview guide' (Fielding 1992) comprising topics to cover.

Group interviews

As with individual one-to-one interviews, the format of group interviews can vary in their degree of structure depending on the research topic and the purpose of the study. Fontana and Frey describe group interviewing as 'essentially a qualitative data gathering technique that finds the interviewer/ moderator directing the interaction and inquiry in a very structured or very unstructured manner, depending on the interview's purpose' (Fontana and Frey 1994). It allows for a different perspective on the research topic than that yielded by one-to-one interviewing because it explicitly draws on the interaction between participants (Kitzinger 1994) and on interpretations of events that reflect group input (Frey and Fontana 1993).

Two forms of qualitative group interviewing will be outlined – focus groups and nominal group techniques. Jones and Hunter have recently distinguished between these two methods as follows: 'the nominal group technique focuses on a single goal . . . and is less concerned with eliciting a range of ideas or the qualitative analysis of the group process per se than is the case in focus groups' (Jones and Hunter 1995).

Focus groups

'A focus group is a carefully planned discussion designed to obtain perceptions on a defined area of interest in a permissive, non-threatening environment' (Krueger 1994: 6). Typically, this involves six to 12 participants in each group in at least three groups the members of which come together in a 'focused' discussion of the topic.

Although focus groups originated in social science (Merton and Kendall 1946) until recently their use has been largely limited to market research (Morgan 1988; Fontana and Frey 1994). More recently still, focus groups have found favour among health and health services researchers to examine people's experiences of disease and of health services and to explore attitudes and needs of staff (Kitzinger 1995). One example, where extensive use of focus groups has been made, is a study conducted by Kitzinger and colleagues to explore how media messages are processed by audiences and how understandings of AIDS are constructed (Kitzinger 1994, 1990). Here 52 groups were conducted with 351 participants (Kitzinger 1994).

Nominal groups

Nominal Group Technique (NGT) is a method for structuring small group meetings that allows individual judgements about a topic or issue to be pooled effectively and used in situations in which uncertainty or disagreement exists about the nature of a problem and possible solutions.

(Moore 1994: 10)

The technique is useful in identifying problems, exploring solutions and establishing priorities (Moore 1994). In health related research it has been used as a way of dealing with conflicting scientific evidence – largely to examine the appropriateness of interventions, but also it has been used in education, in training and in the identification of measures for clinical trials (Jones and Hunter 1995). One example of its use in health related research was conducted by Carney and colleagues who employed NGT to identify problems faced by community nurses in meeting local people's need for care (Carney et al. 1996). Typically, the nominal group meeting is structured in seven stages. First, participants write down their views on the topic. Second, each then gives one of these views to the facilitator who records it on a flip chart. Third, the written suggestions are grouped where similar and discussed by the group. Next each member of the group ranks each idea. The rankings are then presented to the group, after which the overall ranking is discussed and reranked. Lastly, the final rankings are tabulated and fed back to the group (Jones and Hunter 1995). This voting procedure can give the impression that the final result indicates group consensus, but usually the main outcome is the generation of ideas (Moore 1994).

Interviewing in health research

As already mentioned in the introduction to this chapter, until recently health and health services research has relied primarily on quantitative research methods (Fitzpatrick and Boulton 1994; Rifkin 1995). However, examples of published research in medical, nursing and social science journals reveal the multiplicity of applications for qualitative interviewing within this field. The application of qualitative interviewing methods can be found within a variety of health-related contexts, for example in primary care, in secondary care, in management and in policy making and evaluation.

It has been argued that qualitative methods have particular relevance to general practice research because they share many of the commitments of family medicine (Murphy and Mattson 1992); for example, a focus on the individual rather than the disease, consideration of the patient in their social context of family and community and concern for the meaning of events or symptoms to those individuals who experience them. In addition, the central method of collecting information about the patient in general practice is the interview. As Brody points out, respect for the use of narrative as a mode of inquiry should be common to both primary care medicine and the social sciences (Brody 1991: 130).

Research interviewing skills and clinical history taking are not, however, identical and training is required to avoid producing poor research (Britten and Fisher 1993). Qualitative interviewing has been utilized in a secondary care context relating to in-patient, out-patient and accident and emergency care and services.

Strong and Robinson describe how qualitative data collection can also be understood to be part of the health service manager's everyday work:

He or she walks the patch, chats with other staff, goes to meetings, scrutinises documents, watches how others behave, swap notes with friends and other observers; in short, uses qualitative methods to get to all those many parts that numbers cannot always reach – the feel of personalities, relationships, emotions, language, politics, customs, the comedy and the pathos, the mundane and the exotic, the real and the formal structures, the actual and the claimed behaviour, the whole and not just the part.

(Strong and Robinson 1990: 7)

In relation to policy making and evaluation, qualitative interviewing techniques can be utilized to elicit the views and opinions of the general public, service users and providers, and those in the policy making and implementation process. Recently, there have been attempts to involve members of the public in policy decision making regarding priority setting. One example, using both qualitative and quantitative data, was recently published in the British Medical Journal by Lenaghan and colleagues who conducted a pilot study into citizens' juries as a way of setting health service priorities (Lenaghan *et al.* 1996).

Qualitative interviewing can be conducted, then, in a variety of health related contexts. In the remainder of this section on interviewing, examples will be provided of the appropriate application of qualitative interviewing within a range of contexts.

Exploratory studies

First, qualitative interviewing can be used as a method of exploring a research area. This may be where there is a lack of existing research or may be where the aim is to develop further understanding of a topic. A good example of this latter application of qualitative interviewing is provided by Williams and Calnan (1994). They conducted 40 face-to-face in-depth interviews with general practitioners (GPs) to explore their views, attitudes and opinions towards coronary heart disease (CHD) prevention. Although CHD prevention in general practice is not a new research topic by any means, what the authors of this study were able to explore was the divergence between the official rhetoric from government and professional organizations regarding prevention and rank and file GPs' ideas, feelings and behaviour towards prevention. Their concern, therefore, was not to quantify levels and determinants of GP involvement but to describe and explore GPs' perspectives on prevention. Tape recorded, transcribed and thematically analysed face-to-face interviews enabled the researchers to achieve these aims.

As an exploratory stage, interviews may be used also to develop ideas and possibly research hypotheses rather than to gather facts and statistics (Oppenheim 1992: 67). They may be used to identify key variables to be operationalized quantitatively (Patton 1987: 37) and thus may be used as a preliminary stage in a quantitative study. One example of using qualitative interviewing as a preliminary stage to a quantitative survey is provided by O'Brien's 'Portland Men's Study', a psychosocial study of gay and bisexual men at risk for HIV (O'Brien 1993). In this study a series of focus groups were conducted, this qualitative stage contributed to the development of the subsequent quantitative study in a number of ways. First, it enabled the researchers to learn the language the men used to discuss their private emotional and sexual experiences. Second, they were able to collect information about experiences which illustrated the concepts under study. Third, focus group members could be consulted about recruitment to the survey. Finally, this stage built support for the study among members of the local community.

Sensitive topics

A second broad area where qualitative interviewing is utilized is when the research is of a sensitive nature. Lee defines sensitive research topics as those which have the potential to pose a threat to those involved (Lee 1993: 4). In-depth interviewing can be used to minimize such potential threats, although as Lee points out there is no reason why in-depth interviewing will be any less uncomfortable for interviewer and respondent broaching sensitive topics than for survey researchers and respondents (Lee 1993: 102). However, there are many examples of where qualitative interviewing has been used for topics of a sensitive nature within health research.

Perhaps one obvious topic area, where the content is of a sensitive nature is research relating to sex and sexual behaviours. As well as this topic being of a very personal and private nature it can be sensitive because 'the presence of a researcher is sometimes feared because it produces a possibility that deviant activities will be revealed' (Lee 1993: 6). Kitzinger's work with focus groups has already been mentioned. However, it is worth stressing that she used this technique to conduct research on the potentially sensitive topic of how and why people's understandings of AIDS are constructed. Focus groups were carried out with a variety of populations, for example, with play group mothers, with prison officers, with retirement club members, and with lesbians (Kitzinger 1994). So, while it may be assumed that this method would be contraindicated in researching sensitive topics Kitzinger argues that 'group work can actively facilitate the discussion of taboo topics because the less inhibited members of the group break the ice for shyer participants' (Kitzinger 1995).

Research can be sensitive 'where members of some group to be studied are powerless or disadvantaged, they may fear exploitation or degradation, or be sceptical about research' (Lee 1993: 7) or where the subject matter relates to 'deeply personal experience' (Renzetti and Lee 1992). An example of the application of qualitative interviewing which is sensitive in both of these respects is provided by Bowes and Domokos (1996). They carried out in-depth interviews with Pakistani women in Glasgow about their experiences of maternity care. The researchers point out that while a number of quantitative surveys of women's views of maternity services have been conducted, a consistently low response rate is found among South Asian women, whereas work which has utilized qualitative approaches has been more successful. Bowes and Domokos employed in-depth interviews with very little direct questioning to create the potential for women to shape the interviews themselves giving them more control over and power within the interview. In addition, this method created the potential for women to talk in as much depth as they felt comfortable with about a topic which was difficult to talk about. The researchers report that 'in many ways, we were disappointed with the data' (p. 57) as women did not speak about the topic if they preferred not to, for example if a subject upset them. However, this study was an attempt to empower women within the research process itself, which is an ethical approach to a doubly sensitive area.

Understanding of experiences, meanings, behaviours, attitudes and views
Perhaps where qualitative interviewing is most extensively employed is to explore and understand in depth peoples' experiences, meanings, behaviours, attitudes and views. In relation to health research this approach has been used to examine experiences of illness and the meaning attached to that experience, particularly of chronic illness. It has been used to examine health behaviour, as well as to explore attitudes and views to aspects of health care including treatment, services and health policies.

Kelleher's study of people with diabetes used qualitative interviewing to examine the experience of a chronic illness (Kelleher 1988). Analysis of semi-structured interviews with 30 adult diabetics revealed three strategies which were adopted to cope with, or adapt to, living with diabetes. Kelleher concludes that it would be helpful to people with diabetes if health carers addressed the cognitive problem of what it means to an individual as well as the practical problems of managing diabetes.

Focusing on health behaviour, Britten's study of patients' ideas about medicines provides another example of how understanding of the patient's perspective has the potential for positive changes in health care (Britten

1994). She conducted semi-structured interviews with 30 general practice patients and revealed a number of reasons for non-adherence to prescribed medication. These reasons, she concludes, should be explored by GPs before writing a prescription to help them to assess the appropriateness of proposed treatment for the individual patient concerned.

Qualitative interviewing has been used extensively to consider attitudes and views about treatment and care. Good examples of this application can be found in the work of Pound and colleagues in their examination of stroke survivors' evaluations of their health care (Pound *et al.* 1995a), their views on their admission to hospital (Pound *et al.* 1995b) and their views on the benefits of physiotherapy (Pound *et al.* 1994). Forty in-depth interviews were conducted with men and women who previously had been admitted to hospital with stroke. Analysis revealed that patients used a combination of criteria to evaluate their care involving aspects of the process of care, such as the quality of interaction with health professionals, as well as the outcome of that care. The in-depth interviews were combined with a quantitative patient satisfaction survey. The survey was able to provide evidence of people's dissatisfaction with services, while the qualitative work was able to suggest some answers to *why* people were dissatisfied (Pound *et al.* 1995a).

There are examples of studies of attitudes and views towards health policies which have utilized qualitative interviewing. Dicker and Armstrong's study of views of priority setting in health care, for example, used semi-structured interviews with 16 general practice patients to develop understanding of how the public approaches the problem of determining priorities (Dicker and Armstrong 1995). Ayres, on the other hand, used in-depth interviews with 18 GPs to elicit their views on rationing and priority setting (Ayres 1996).

Exploring in depth issues arising from quantitative work
Finally, qualitative interviewing may be appropriate to examine in depth issues or problems identified in quantitative work; Pound's study described above is one example. Another is the issue of women's smoking behaviour. Surveys have identified an upward trend in young women's smoking (e.g. Wright *et al.* 1992), a trend which Graham calls 'the feminization of adolescent smoking' (Graham 1989). Qualitative work has explored the context in which women smoke allowing for greater depth of understanding of the reasons why this pattern may be occurring (Graham 1987; Daykin 1993). Graham's research utilized a diary method, while Daykin's study employed in-depth interviews to consider the contexts in which 25 young women smoke. Such research enables those working in health promotion to go beyond the identification of young women's smoking as a problem identified by epidemiological and survey research and to take into account the psycho-social and economic circumstances in which young women smoke.

This section has identified and given examples of some of the diverse uses to which both individual and group qualitative interviewing can be applied within health and health services research. The final section of this chapter will discuss issues of validity and reliability pertinent to qualitative research using interviewing or observational methods.

Issues of validity and reliability in qualitative research

Recent efforts to improve the standard of survey and trial research have included the production of guidelines for the design, conduct and reporting of studies. Checklists may be useful to those who need to review funding applications, referee papers for publication or prepare their own research reports. In order to help and hearten those who are unfamiliar with the issues of validity and rigour in qualitative methods, attempts have been made to develop criteria for evaluating qualitative research.

Qualitative research does not rest on some of the absolutes of trial or survey design, which means that checklists should not be applied in a prescriptive manner. At the stage of writing a grant proposal, for example, it will not be known *precisely* how many in-depth interviews may be required to reach a saturation point in the data, while if a trial is being conducted a power calculation will provide a very exact figure about the numbers needed in the control and intervention groups to detect a statistically significant difference. There are a number of approaches to validating qualitative analysis, but since they do not have universal applicability, the important point is that validity is addressed and the approach is appropriate. For example, in some studies respondent validation will be expedient, while in others it would be unsuitable. We suggest that checklists are no substitute for experience of the particular research methods. This is equally true of checklists for quantitative studies where some items, e.g. 'have appropriate statistical tests been used?' may be unanswerable by the non-specialist reader. However, they may be very useful as *aides-mémoires*, focusing attention on each stage of the research process and on good practice in writing reports.

In this section we discuss some of the issues of validity and reliability in qualitative research. These are considered under the subheadings design, data collection, analysis and reporting.

Design

The methods which are used should be appropriate to the research question. Very broadly, if the question is of the 'how often' variety, a quantitative method will be needed, while 'why' and 'what' and 'how', exploring process and subjective meanings, is the main purpose of qualitative methods (Pope and Mays 1995). However, too blunt a distinction can be misleading since counting is sometimes an entirely appropriate feature of an ethnographic study and surveys can certainly be designed to address complex causal relationships.

Sampling

Sample selection is important in qualitative research, even though the object of the study is not to generate statistically significant findings. While it is not relevant to use power calculations to determine the size of the sample, there are requirements appropriate to the aims of the research. Sampling will sometimes be conducted to provide as broad a range as possible, according to the researchers' understanding of factors which might affect the observations or the perspective of individual or group interviewees. These may include the type of institution; whether a rural or urban location; the sex, age and ethnic group of respondents and so on.

Where interviews are conducted in a group, particular attention should be paid to the composition of the sample for each group interview. It is often recommended that each group ideally should be composed of individuals who are strangers to each other to avoid biases and to avoid the formation of sub-groups conducting conversations between themselves. However, as Morgan points out the rigid application of this 'rule' would make it very difficult to conduct focus groups in a number of situations (Morgan and Krueger 1993), for example within organizations such as general practices, or within small communities. The most important design strategy to address this issue is to rely on a trained moderator to meet the potential problems posed by groups of acquaintances rather than to avoid them altogether (Morgan and Krueger 1993).

Snowball sampling involves asking respondents to pass details of the research and contact numbers on to other individuals who may be willing to participate. This method of sampling is particularly relevant when the individuals being studied may be known to each other, but not accessible through any known sampling list. Examples may include gay men and illegal drug users and groups whose confidentiality would be compromised if they were sampled through their medical records, e.g. immunization 'refusers' or users of complementary therapies.

The term 'theoretical sampling' which is often referred to in qualitative research does not, as may be supposed, distinguish it from 'actual sampling'. It is an approach whereby the purpose of the research (such as developing a theory or explanation) guides the sampling and data collection procedure. An initial set of observations or interviews will be conducted and analysed to guide the next stage of the research, which may include modifications in approach or sampling, in response to initial findings and the development of the explanation. One of the ways in which observational methods and semi-structured interviewing differ from quantitative methods is that it is entirely acceptable (indeed, it is seen as a strength of the method) to make adjustments to the sampling procedure while the data is being collected. This is possible because field work and analysis take place concurrently and issues which arise from the analysis can be explored further and tested by, for example, recruiting more of a particular type of patient or observing specific clinics.

Data collection

A report of qualitative research should state how the interviewer or field worker presented themselves in the setting. In much health and health services research it is important that the researcher is known to be independent of the medical setting. This is particularly true if respondents are encouraged to speak openly about features of their health care. An assurance of confidentiality may be insufficient to avoid the problem since patients may be swayed by their interlocutor's (real or supposed) professional identity. If more than one interviewer or field worker was used, issues of comparability should be considered.

The importance of a well trained moderator in group interviewing has been stated already, but is worth emphasizing in the context of data collection. The transcription of group interview recordings is rendered virtually impossible if several people within the group talk simultaneously resulting in the loss of sections of data for analysis. A skilled facilitator should be able to minimize the occurrence of this as well as tactfully encouraging quiet members to contribute while restraining dominant ones (Krueger 1993).

Where recordings are made transcriptions can be made at several levels of detail. To transcribe the entire data set at a level suitable for conversational analysis (every utterance and pause precisely documented) will be inappropriately thorough for many research purposes. It may not be considered important to transcribe fully all of the interviewers statements, although her/his prompts and explanations will often be consequential in the analysis. The number of seconds taken up in a pause, or the length of a sigh or burst of laughter are all potentially important additions to the transcript and will often be considered necessary detail. As the analysis progresses it may be decided that certain sections of the interview do not need to be fully transcribed. Whenever feasible, all original recordings should be retained as unedited tapes, so that independent verification of the transcripts is possible.

Anonymized tape recordings and detailed fieldnotes may provide valuable material for subsequent analysis, perhaps in the light of new theoretical developments (Weaver 1994) or in combination with comparable data sets. There is considerable potential for secondary analysis of qualitative data, for which central archives are now available.

Analysis

Coding

Coding is an essential part of qualitative data analysis, but is quite a different procedure from the coding stage of survey research. In qualitative analysis the coding is concerned with the relationship between chunks of data and categories or emerging themes, whereas in survey research it will involve the substitution of numerical codes for responses (e.g. 1 for 'yes'; 2 for 'no'; 3 for 'don't know'). The object of coding textual data from interview transcripts or field notes is to ensure that all of the data which is relevant to each category can be identified and examined. Glaser and Strauss described the process in their classic *The Discovery of Grounded Theory* (1967): 'The analyst starts by coding each incident in his data into as many categories of analysis as possible, as categories emerge or as data emerge that fit in an existing category' (1967: 105).

Traditional methods of qualitative data analysis have relied heavily on coloured pens, card systems, filing cabinets and cutting and pasting. The methods are undoubtedly laborious, but certainly retain contact with the data in its raw state, which could be a spur to creativity. The availability of word-processing packages (especially in Windows) has offered considerable advantages to researchers using textual data. Coding and retrieval of text is simplified through word-processing 'search' techniques and a split screen facilitates gathering, copying and pasting chunks of text into different files.

Word processors can be enormously helpful in searching large amounts of text for specific terms. The frequency with which particular words or phrases appear in a piece of text is of interest in some areas of research; for example, analysis of political speeches and mass media research. Content analysis of this sort requires an unambiguous, pre-defined coding system and aims to produce counts which may be tabulated and analysed using standard statistical techniques. It is distinct from the techniques of qualitative analysis in which data is coded or indexed in order to ensure that nothing relevant is lost to subsequent examination, not to reduce it to frequencies or cells in a table. This difference in analytic approach results from the theory building focus of interpretative research for which predefined coding, counting and tests of statistical significance are simply not germane.

Computer-assisted analysis

The evolution of computer software for analysing qualitative data has been welcomed as an important development with the potential to improve the rigour of analysis (Kelle 1995). The current software offers functions which enable more complex organization and retrieval of data than that possible with word-processing software.

Recent packages which have been designed to assist in the analysis of unstructured textual data all have 'code and retrieval' functions and several other uses which will be recognizable to researchers. These include the ability to define variables which can be used for selective retrievals (e.g. to examine separately by gender or age group excerpts referring to a particular phenomenon); to use algorithms to identify co-occurring codes in a range of logically overlapping or nesting possibilities; to attach comments and theoretical notes to sections of the text as 'memos'; to add new codes if and when required and join together existing codes. Most of the packages also provide counts of code frequencies.

These functions are all concerned with organizing and accessing the data, which are only the initial stages in qualitative analysis. It has also been suggested that computer-assisted analysis can help the researcher to build theoretical links, search for exceptions and examine 'crucial cases' where counter-evidence might be anticipated. A systematic search for 'disconfirming evidence' can be assisted by using Boolean operators (such as OR, AND, NOT) to examine the data. An examination of the context of the fragments may be achieved either through considering which other codes are attached to the data or by displaying the immediate context of the extract by including the lines of text which surround it. This function should particularly appeal to researchers who are concerned about the decontextualization which can result from fragmenting the data into coded chunks. The Hypersoft package (Dey 1993) uses what the developer calls 'hyperlinks' to capture the conceptual links which are observed between sections of the data, and protect the narrative structure from fragmentation.

There are many potential benefits to using a software package to help with the more laborious side of textual analysis but, as ever, some caution is advisable. One of the criticisms which is levelled at qualitative researchers is that the samples are too small and unrepresentative: the prospect of computer-assisted analysis may persuade researchers (or their funders) that they can manage much larger amounts of data and increase the 'power' of their study. Qualitative studies, which are not designed to be representative in terms of statistical generalizability, may gain little from an expanded sample size except a more cumbersome data set. The nature and size of the sample should be directed by the research question and analytic requirements, not by the available software. In some circumstances, a single case study design may be the most successful way of generating theory. Lee and Fielding (1995) warn against the assumption that using a computer package will make analysis less time-consuming, although it is hoped that it may make the process more demonstrably systematic. The essential tasks of studying the text, recognizing and refining the concepts and coding the data are inescapably the work of the researcher. A computer package may be useful for gathering together chunks of data, establishing links between the fragments, organizing and reorganizing the display and helping to find exceptions, but no package is capable of perceiving a link or defining an appropriate structure for the analysis.

Testing the validity of the findings

In addition to the methods mentioned above (e.g. systematically searching for disconfirming evidence within the data) two other approaches are widely recommended to address the validity of the findings. These are 'triangulation' and 'respondent validation'. It is important to note that these will only be applicable in some circumstances. Silverman goes further and suggests these methods are 'usually inappropriate to qualitative research' (Silverman 1993: 156).

Triangulation

Ethnographic observation often includes a degree of triangulation in that multiple sources of data collection (e.g. direct participation, observation, informant and respondent interviews, etc.) are used. A study design which relies on interviews as the primary method may benefit from using other sources, such as a survey or a review of case notes or a combination of group and individual interviews. However, as Hammersley and Atkinson have pointed out: 'one should not adopt a naively "optimistic" view that the aggregation of data from different sources will unproblematically add up to produce a more complete picture' (Hammersley and Atkinson 1983: 199). The problem is that different methods do sometimes produce different results and 'rarely does the inaccuracy of one approach to the data complement the accuracies of another' (Fielding and Fielding 1986: 35).

Respondent validation

Once the researcher has drawn tentative results from the data, they may choose to go back to the respondents and refine their findings in the light of their comments. In some research settings this will not be feasible. Fielding and Fielding recognize that the respondent may be able to clarify points and provide additional information about the context of their actions, but 'there is no reason to assume that members have privileged status as commentators on their actions ... such feedback cannot be taken as direct validation or refutation of the observer's inferences. Rather such processes of so-called "validation" should be treated as yet another source of data and insight' (Fielding and Fielding 1986: 43).

Respondent validation of group interviews may be achieved through conducting a small number of individual interviews with members of the focus groups, or running follow-up focus groups with the original participants to discuss the findings (Morgan 1993).

Reporting

Qualitative research will not usually be presented in a manner which adheres rigidly to the structure most commonly used in quantitative research (objective, setting, respondents, methods, results, conclusion), but detail of equivalent significance should be available. The report should include the background to the project; the relationship to the existing research and theory; the methods which were used; how access was achieved; how the observations were made and the sample was chosen; and how the categories and themes were developed and analysed. Qualitative research is predisposed towards the tentative rather than the conclusive, so is more likely to be followed by a discussion than a conclusion.

Reference to existing literature

As with any research, the study report should clarify where the work lies in relation to the existing body of knowledge about the subject. Appropriate reference to the literature enables the reader to assess the originality of the research and the way in which it relates to prior theoretical knowledge.

Methods

The appropriateness of the methods for the type of issues which are being addressed should be clear. It is also important to explain the way in which the researcher presented themselves in the field, the manner in which respondents were recruited to a study and the way in which the analysis was conducted.

Analysis

The procedures for the analysis need to be systematic and described. In most cases a reference to the published analytic procedure which has been used will suffice, although for audiences unfamiliar with qualitative methods a more detailed description of the methods may be considered appropriate.

Presentation of results

In qualitative research the analysis evolves out of the data and this will be reflected in the presentation. Lofland writes that the 'analysis and data should be *interpenetrated* in written reports. That is, analytic passages should not run on for very long without the use of descriptive materials and vice versa. Such *alternation* of description and analysis makes the relation between the two more evident' (Lofland and Lofland 1984: 146).

When reporting a qualitative study it is usual to provide sufficient identifiers for each extract from the data (e.g. a quote from an interview or a selection from fieldnotes) which is used directly in the report in order to demonstrate the extent to which the data are being used. When quoting a respondent it would be usual to include an encoded identifier and whatever other characteristics are pertinent to the category being analysed. This could include any of a number of characteristics, e.g. the number of years a cancer patient had been in remission; or a diagnostic category; or the year a health professional finished their training. Although it is tempting to quote only the more articulate respondents, it is important to avoid excessive selectivity in reporting the data.

In a survey where everyone within a given population has had an equal chance of being selected to participate (the cornerstone of sampling theory) and all respondents have been asked the same questions, in the same manner, it is usually helpful to report responses as frequencies and percentages (relative frequencies). Surveys are designed to recruit sufficient numbers to represent the whole population and trials to identify significant differences between treatment and control groups. The qualitative methods of in-depth interviewing and observation are intended to uncover the range of views and generate theory, which means that data collection will often continue until a saturation point is reached, rather than until the sample is large enough to be considered statistically representative.

In a qualitative study where the sample has not been (and often cannot be) selected to be strictly and numerically representative of the whole population and where the interview technique is flexible and responsive it can be frankly misleading to report relative frequencies. This particularly applies if the questions have not been asked of all respondents, or have not been phrased in the same way, or delivered at the same stage in the interview.

While a reliance on numerical descriptions of qualitative data courts the danger of misleading the reader about the representativeness of the sample, the use of certain 'crude quantitative data' can be useful if one wants to give a flavour of the overall data or to check that the analysis does represent the overall picture. The results may be instructive. Silverman quotes his study of private and NHS clinics in which he had an impression that appointments at the private clinics were longer. Although this was borne out when comparing the overall mean length of appointments, it did not hold for initial appointments which were actually longer (34 compared with 30 minutes) in the NHS setting (Silverman 1993).

Conclusion

Qualitative methods are often used to explore relatively complex issues, producing rich data for thoughtful and scrupulous analysis. It is seen as a strength of the qualitative approach that the insights which are gained sometimes expose unanticipated layers of complexity rather than provide final answers. By concentrating on the most commonly used techniques of qualitative research we have been able to demonstrate the wide range of applications of observational and interview based research in health and health services research. These applications have been illustrated with examples which reveal the variety of topics, sample groups and contexts in which such research is conducted. Some of the aspects of validity and reliability which need to be considered when designing, conducting or evaluating qualitative research have also been discussed.

This chapter has considered two of the components of qualitative research which are frequently and diversely applied in health and health services research. Other methods which draw on observation and interviewing approaches include critical incident technique for focused interviewing (Bradley 1992); case studies (Yin 1994) action research (Webb 1989), rapid appraisal techniques (Ong and Humphris 1994) and discourse analysis (Burman and Parker 1993). We hope that readers will feel inclined to look at fuller reports of some of the studies we have mentioned and, if they wish to conduct a qualitative study themselves, to consult the specialist methodological literature to which we have referred.

References

Atkinson, P. (1995) *Medical Talk and Medical Work*. London: Sage:
Ayres, P.J. (1996) Rationing health care: views from general practice, *Social Science and Medicine*, 42: 7, 1021–5.
Black, N. (1994) Why we need qualitative research, *Journal of Epidemiology and Community Health*, 48: 425–6.
Bowes, A.M. and Meehan Domokos, T. (1996) Pakistani women and maternity care: raising the muted voices, *Sociology of Health and Illness*, 18(1): 45–65.
Bradley, C.P. (1992) Turning anecdotes into data – the critical incident technique, *Family Practice*, 9 (1): 98–103.
Britten, N. (1994) Patients' ideas about medicines: a qualitative study in a general practice population, *British Journal of General Practice*, 44: 465–8.
Britten, N. and Fisher, B. (1993) Qualitative research and general practice [editorial], *British Journal of General Practice*, 43: 270–1.

Britten, N. (1995) Qualitative interviews in medical research, *British Medical Journal*, 311: 251–3.

Brody, H. (1991) Qualitative research in primary care, in P. Norton, M. Stewart, F. Tudiver, M. Bass and E. Dunn (eds) *Primary Care Research: Traditional and Innovative Approaches*. Newbury Park: Sage.

Burman, E. and Parker, I. (1993) *Discourse Analytic Research*. London: Routledge.

Carney, O., McIntosh, J. and Worth, A. (1996) The use of the Nominal Group Technique in research with community nurses, *Journal of Advanced Nursing*, 23: 1024–9.

Daykin, N. (1993) Young women and smoking: towards a sociological account, *Health Promotion International*, 8(2): 95–102.

Dey, I. (1993) *Qualitative Data Analysis: A User Friendly Guide for Social Scientists*. London: Routledge.

Dicker, A. and Armstrong, D. (1995) Patients' views of priority setting in health care: an interview survey in one practice, *British Medical Journal*, 311: 1137–9.

Dowell, J., Huby, G. and Smith, C. (1996) *Scottish Consensus Statement on Qualitative Research in Primary Health Care*. Dundee: Tayside Centre for General Practice.

Fielding, N. (1992) Qualitative interviewing, in N. Gilbert (ed.) *Researching Social Life*. London: Sage.

Fielding, N. and Fielding, J. (1986) *Linking Data, Qualitative Research Methods Series No. 4*, London: Sage.

Fitzpatrick, R. and Boulton, M. (1994) Qualitative methods for assessing health care, *Quality in Health Care*, 3: 107–13.

Fontana, A. and Frey, J.H. (1994) Interviewing. The art of science, in N.K. Denzin and Y.S. Lincoln (eds) *Handbook of Qualitative Research*. Thousand Oaks: Sage.

Frey, J.H. and Fontana, A. (1993) The group interview in social research, in D. Morgan (ed.) *Successful Focus Groups. Advancing the State of the Art*. Newbury Park: Sage.

Glaser, B. and Strauss, A. (1967) *The Discovery of Grounded Theory*. Chicago: Aldine Press.

Goffman, E. (1961) *Asylums*. Harmondsworth: Penguin.

Goffman, E. (1964) *Stigma: Notes on the Management of Spoilt Identity*. Harmondsworth: Penguin.

Gorter, A., Miranda, E., Smith, G.D., Ortelis, P. and Low, N. (1993) How many people actually use condoms? An investigation of motel clients in Managua, *Social Science and Medicine*, 36(12): 1645–7.

Graham, H. (1989) Women and smoking in the United Kingdom: the implications for health promotion, *Health Promotion*, 3(4): 371–82.

Graham, H. (1987) Women's smoking and family health, *Social Science and Medicine*, 25(1): 47–56.

Jones, J. and Hunter, D. (1995) Consensus methods for medical and health services research, *British Medical Journal*, 311: 376–80.

Kelle, U. (ed.) (1995) *Computer-aided Qualitative Data Analysis Theory, Methods and Practice*. London: Sage.

Kelleher, D. (1988) Coming to terms with diabetes: coping strategies and non-compliance, in R. Anderson and M. Bury (eds) *Living with Chronic Illness*. London: Allen & Unwin.

Keen, J. and Packwood, T. (1995) Case study evaluation, *British Medical Journal*, 311: 444–6.

Kitzinger, J. (1995) Introducing focus groups, *British Medical Journal*, 311: 299–302.

Kitzinger, J. (1994) The methodology of focus groups: the importance of interaction between research participants, *Sociology of Health and Illness*, 16(1): 101–21.

Kitzinger, J. (1990) Audience understandings of AIDS media messages: a discussion of methods, *Sociology of Health and Illness*, 12(3): 319–35.

Krueger, R.A. (1994) *Focus Groups. A Practical Guide for Applied Research*. Thousand Oaks: Sage.

Lee, R.L. (1993) *Doing Research on Sensitive Topics*. London: Sage.

Lee, R. and Fielding, N. (1995) User's experiences of qualitative data analysis software, in U. Kelle (ed.) *Computer Aided Qualitative Data Analysis*. London: Sage.

Lenaghan, J., New, B. and Mitchell, E. (1996) Setting priorities: is there a role for citizens' juries?, *British Medical Journal*, 312, 1591–3.

Lofland, J. and Lofland, L.H. (1984) *Analysing Social Settings* (2nd edn). Belmont, CA: Wadsworth.

Marshall, C. and Rossman, G.B. (1995) *Designing Qualitative Research*. Thousand Oaks: Sage.

Mays, N. and Pope, C. (1995) Observational methods in health care settings, *British Medical Journal*, 311: 182–4.

Mays, N. and Pope, C. (1995) Rigour and qualitative research, *British Medical Journal*, 311: 109–12.

Merton, R.K. and Kendall, P.L. (1946) The focused interview, *American Journal of Sociology*, 51: 541–57.

Moore, C.M. (1994) *Group Techniques for Idea Building*. Thousand Oaks: Sage.

Morgan, D.L. and Krueger, R.A. (1993) When to use focus groups and why, in D.L. Morgan (ed.) *Successful Focus Groups. Advancing the State of the Art*. Newbury Park: Sage.

Morgan, D.L. (1988) *Focus Groups as Qualitative Research*. London: Sage.

Morgan, D.L. (1993) Future directions for focus groups, in D.L. Morgan (ed.) *Successful Focus Groups. Advancing the State of the Art*. Newbury Park: Sage.

Murphy, E. and Mattson, B. (1992) Qualitative research and family practice: a marriage made in heaven?, *Family Practice*, 9: 85–91.

O'Brien, K. (1993) Improving survey questionnaires through focus groups, in D.L. Morgan (ed.) *Successful Focus Groups. Advancing the State of the Art*. Newbury Park: Sage.

Ong, B.N. and Humphris, G. (1994) Prioritizing needs with communities: rapid appraisal methodologies in health, in J. Popay and G. Williams (eds) *Researching the People's Health*. London: Routledge.

Oppenheim, A.N. (1992) *Questionnaire Design, Interviewing and Attitude Measurement*. London: Pinter.

Patton, M.Q. (1987) *How to Use Qualitative Methods in Evaluation*. Newbury Park: Sage.

Pope, C. (1991) Trouble in store: some thoughts on the management of waiting lists. *Sociology of Health and Illness*, 13: 193–212.

Pope, C. and Mays, N. (1993) Opening the black box: an encounter in the corridors of health services research, *British Medical Journal*, 306: 315–18.

Pope, C. and Mays, N. (1995) Reaching the parts other methods cannot reach: an introduction to qualitative methods in health and health services research, *British Medical Journal*, 311: 42–5.

Pound, P., Bury, M., Gompertz, P. and Ebrahim, S. (1995a) Stroke survivors' evaluations of their health care, in G. Wilson (ed.) *Community Care. Asking the Users*. London: Chapman and Hall.

Pound, P., Bury, M., Gompertz, P. and Ebrahim, S. (1995b) Stroke patients' views on their admission to hospital, *British Medical Journal*, 311: 18–22.

Pound, P., Bury, M., Gompertz, P. and Ebrahim, S. (1994) Views of survivors of stroke on benefits of physiotherapy, *Quality in Health Care*, 3: 69–74.

Renzetti, C.M. and Lee, R.M. (1992) The problem of researching sensitive topics. An overview and introduction, in *Researching Sensitive Topics*. London: Sage.

Rifkin, S. (1995) The use of qualitative methods, *Social Science and Medicine*, 41(12): 1653–4.

Rosenhan, D.L. (1973) On being sane in insane places, *Science*, CLXXIX: 250–8.

Roth, J. (1963) *Timetables: Structuring the Passage of Time in Hospital Treatment and Other Careers*. Indianapolis: Bobbs Merrill Co.

Silverman, D. (1987) *Communication and Medical Practice*. London: Sage.

Silverman, D. (1993) *Interpreting Qualitative Data*. London: Sage, 1–224.

Strong, P. (1979) *The Ceremonial Order of the Clinic*. London: Routledge & Kegan Paul.

Strong, P. and Robinson, J. (1990) *The NHS Under New Management*. Milton Keynes: Open University Press.

Weaver, A. (1994) Deconstructing dirt and disease: The case of TB, in M. Bloor, P. Taraborrelli (eds) *Qualitative Studies in Health and Medicine*. Aldershot: Avebury.

Webb, C. (1989) Action research: philosophy, methods and personal experiences, *Journal of Advanced Nursing*, 14: 403–10.

Williams, S. and Calnan, M. (1994) Perspectives on prevention: the views of General Practitioners, *Sociology of Health and Illness*, 16(3): 372–93.

Wright, L., Harwood, D. and Coulter, A. (1992) *Health and Lifestyles in the Oxford Region*. Oxford: Health Services Research Unit, University of Oxford.

Yin, R.K. (1994) *Case Study Research, Design and Methods*. London: Sage.

8

Economic evaluation of health care

Katherine Watson

Introduction

This chapter[1] discusses the contribution which economists can make to
health care evaluation. It reviews various approaches adopted in economic
analyses of medical outcomes, and considers how these have evolved during the last twenty years. Particular attention is paid to the significant role
played by the concept of Quality Adjusted Life Years (QALYs) in analyses
of cost-effectiveness. The chapter reviews the methods and problems associated with single-index measures of health-related quality of life, such as
the Rosser index and the EuroQol, and explains how QALYs are constructed. Finally, the chapter introduces some of the recent attempts to
incorporate economic evaluation of medical outcomes into health care
programmes; it also reviews the practical issues raised by such policies,
focusing in particular on the Oregon experiment. Despite the limitations
of existing measures of cost-effectiveness, economic assessments of medical
outcomes must be regarded as a fundamental element of the evaluation of
health care.

Economics and its place in the evaluation of health care

Economic analysis addresses the fundamental problem of how to allocate
scarce resources between competing claims. In the context of the provision
of health services, broadly two questions can be identified which are of
concern to economists: first, what proportion of society's resources should
be spent on health care; and second, how should this sum be distributed
between different types of health care and between individuals? Thus, for

example, at the macroeconomic level a choice might be made to increase public expenditure on health services at the expense of education or defence,
while microeconomic analysis would focus on whether those resources
allocated to health care should be devoted to kidney transplants rather
than palliative care for cancer patients, or whether priority should be given
to treatment of certain groups within society, such as, for example, children,
or parents of young children, at the expense of the elderly.

It follows from the notion of scarcity that the demand for resources
exceeds their supply. If a choice must be made between two competing claims
on scarce resources, then one party will always lose out. Economists refer
to this loss as opportunity cost: by allocating resources in one way rather
than another, the opportunities or benefits from the alternative allocation
are foregone, and therefore represent a cost of the decision actually taken.
When public perception of rationing is as sensitive as it must be when
decisions can have life or death outcomes, then it is not surprising that
considerable controversy can accompany economic evaluation of health care.
Equally, it is the significance of these competing outcomes which indicates
the importance of the potential contribution of economics to health care
evaluation.

Recent public anguish about the case of Jaymee Bowen (Child B), who
died from leukaemia in May 1996, is indicative of this problem. In March
1995 the Court of Appeal endorsed the decision by Cambridge Health
Authority to deny Child B further chemotherapy and a second bone mar-
row transplant. Initially treatment had been withheld on the grounds that
the probability of success was very slight and far outweighed by the trauma
and suffering further intervention entailed. However, in his final judgement, Sir Thomas Bingham argued that the decision could also be justified
on rationing criteria. The cost of the treatment denied amounted to some
£75,000, and, it was argued, given the low prospects for success and the
poor quality of life for Child B, it would be better to spend this sum
meeting the needs of other patients (Klein *et al.* 1996).

Economists might argue that the widespread concern about the denial of
publicly funded treatment for Child B was motivated by emotionally under-
standable considerations regarding the future of a particular sick child, but
was nevertheless based on a defective understanding of opportunity cost.
Media coverage ensured that the public knew of the appalling costs this
decision entailed for Child B and her family, but they could not secure a
similarly vivid conception of the costs facing the alternative patients who
would have suffered had her High Court Appeal been successful.

Given competing claims on scarce resources, some rationing is inevitable. It is preferable, then, that rationing decisions are made in as informed
and systematic a way as possible to ensure that considerations of fairness
and efficiency are not impaired or ignored. Economic evaluation of health
care seeks to identify the costs and benefits of alternative allocations of

scarce health care resources. The framework for analysis is explicit: choices should be made on the basis of efficiency rather than *ad hoc* considerations which could be biased by emotional influences.

This is not to deny the importance of clinical evaluation of alternative therapies, which, for example, by randomized control trial, can identify the range of effective treatments from which a choice must be made. The task of an economist is to compare the costs and consequences of alternative procedures under consideration to determine the most efficient allocation of resources (Drummond *et al.* 1987; Mooney 1992). Economic evaluation makes a vital contribution to a society's aggregate health by ensuring that a constrained budget yields the maximum benefit possible. Recently, Maynard and Bloor have argued this point particularly forcefully, suggesting that if the economic dimension of clinical decisions is ignored, inefficiency, and therefore unethical practice, inevitably prevails. Clinicians are advised to do all for their patients that is demonstrably cost effective, and no more (Maynard and Bloor 1995).

As medical technologies improve and life expectancies increase, it is inevitable that the demand for health care resources also expands. In the UK alone in 1995–96 some £33 billion of public money was spent on health, and total expenditure on health care amounted to approximately 7 per cent of GDP during the early 1990s. Political reluctance to raise taxation to deepen the public purse has ossified across both major parties. The dilemmas raised by scarce resources have become an inevitable feature of the modern National Health Service. Under these circumstances the contribution which economic evaluation can make to enhancing health care provision in our society must be taken seriously.

Methods of economic evaluation

There are four main methods of economic evaluation which seek to compare the costs and consequences of competing procedures: cost-minimization analysis, cost-effectiveness analysis, cost-benefit analysis, and cost-utility analysis. All these approaches consider costs in broadly the same way, but consequences are analysed differently. Cost should always be valued at opportunity cost (i.e. the cost of the next best alternative use for the resources consumed). Typically market prices are assumed to capture these costs effectively (Robinson 1993a).

If health care is being evaluated from the perspective of society as a whole, then costs can be identified under three headings. Direct costs include those incurred in the provision of health services, e.g. the fixed and variable costs of running hospitals and GP surgeries. A second category includes costs borne by patients and their families. This could include expenses incurred as a direct consequence of treatment, as well as indirect costs such as income foregone as a result of being unable to work. The third group of costs includes externalities, i.e. costs which affect those not directly involved in treatment (Robinson 1993a). If, for example, a policy of care in the community were adopted in place of institutional care for psychiatric patients, then, as well as the costs placed on those caring directly for patients' psychiatric needs, externalities might arise, for example, in the form of an enhanced role for social workers or even the police which should also be considered in the economic evaluation of this policy.

Cost-minimization analysis

Cost-minimization analysis can be used to evaluate the costs of alternative therapies which generate exactly the same clinical outcomes. This approach therefore evaluates on the basis of technical efficiency. Clinical effectiveness would be established by randomized control trial, and then the choice between alternative interventions would be determined according to whichever treatment was cheapest. Various studies comparing in-patient treatment of minor conditions requiring surgery with out-patient treatment have been conducted using this approach (see, for example, Russell *et al.* 1977).

Cost-effectiveness analysis

If the clinical outcomes of alternative therapies differ, then the consequences as well as the costs of each procedure need to be considered as part of their economic evaluation. If the effectiveness of the alternative procedures can be expressed in terms of a common unit of measurement such as life years saved or pain-free days gained, then they can be evaluated on the basis of cost-effectiveness, i.e. for each procedure, cost per pain-free day, or cost per life year gained, could be compared. One example of a study applying this method of analysis is that conducted by Ludbrook who examined alternative treatments for chronic renal failure by comparing costs per life year gained (Ludbrook 1981).

Cost-effectiveness analysis is limited by the need to express outcomes in the same units. If this is not possible, because outcomes have more than one dimension, then some more sophisticated evaluation of the benefits derived from a procedure is required.

Cost-benefit analysis

Cost-benefit analysis seeks to place a money valuation on both the costs and benefits of alternative treatments in order to determine the net benefit (i.e. benefits minus costs) accruing from each programme. One advantage with this approach is that it also facilitates comparison between the net benefits gained from a given level of expenditure on health care and those which would follow from the same sum being spent on alternative services, such as education or transport. This method of analysis could therefore be helpful in determining the optimal proportion of GDP to allocate to the health care.

The difficulty of cost-benefit analysis of health care is how to value the benefits accurately. Two approaches have generally been adopted. The first method is derived from human capital theory. This treats health care as an investment in human capital which will yield a return once the individual recovers and returns to work. That return could be valued as a discounted stream of future income.[2]

Unfortunately, this approach is incomplete since it values benefits by reference to productive potential valued at the market rate for that individual. This makes unrealistic assumptions about the labour market being competitive, and omits a personal appraisal of benefits, both direct and indirect. This approach, then, measures benefit in terms of livelihoods rather than lives (McGuire *et al.* 1988). This would imply, for example, that the benefits from treating a highly paid professional would exceed those gained by treating a low paid worker, even if their conditions and post-operative prognoses were identical. It also creates obvious problems in valuing the benefits from treating people who have retired or who are unemployed.

An alternative approach is to value health care interventions by identifying how much people would be willing to pay to secure the benefits from a given treatment or to escape the costs of the related illness. However, this method also has its weaknesses. An individual's valuation of a treatment may be influenced by the framing of questions designed to elicit that valuation. Individuals have also been shown to vary their valuations according to whether they suffer from the illness concerned, and according to their income. These problems may become more acute the more severe the condition under consideration or the larger the valuation attached to treatment. Given this range of responses, the sample of individuals surveyed in the willingness to pay surveys from which benefit valuations are derived should either be identified using stratified random sampling techniques to reflect differences in income and health status, or their responses should be weighted to reflect these characteristics in the population. If the latter option is taken, a further problem is then how to select the appropriate weights for these responses (Robinson 1993c).

Cost-utility analysis

Rather than trying to express benefits as a monetary valuation, benefits could be valued in terms of utility. Utility refers to a subjective assessment of the well-being gained from alternative interventions. This measure therefore takes account of qualitative as well as quantitative medical outcomes.

The most common approach is to adjust the number of life years gained from an intervention by the quality of life enjoyed by those treated. This method allows a more sophisticated appreciation of cost-effectiveness. If, for example, a condition can be treated in two ways which produce different outcomes in terms of mortality and say, subsequent patient mobility, simple cost-effectiveness would be an inappropriate method of economic evaluation to adopt since it could not capture both dimensions, mortality and mobility.[3] If, however, the full implications of impaired mobility could be rated using a quality of life index, these two features of medical outcome could be combined into a single measurement of the benefits from treatment. This would enable evaluation of alternative programmes to be made on the basis of cost per quality-adjusted life year (QALY).

The challenge with this approach is how to assess the multifarious factors which constitute the quality of life. Various clinical profiles have been developed to try to assess qualitative medical outcomes. These include, for example, the Functional Limitations Profile, the Nottingham Health Profile (NHP), and the SF-36 (see Chapter 5 for further details). These assess health status on a range of dimensions such as social interaction, pain, emotional functioning, mobility, etc. However, one of the limitations of multi-dimensional assessments is that comparison of outcomes between different conditions is difficult since different dimensions within the profile may assume varying degrees of significance according to the disease under consideration. While these profiles permit comparison of health status for alternative treatments of the same condition, economic evaluation to determine resource allocation between conditions would be impossible (or, at best, imprecise). In order for economic analysis to be meaningful the quality of life needs to be expressed as a single index which could then be combined with measures of mortality to identify a QALY.

In order to generate a single unit index of life quality three issues must be addressed. First, the relevant dimensions of life quality need to be determined. Second, utility must be measured for each dimension. Finally, valuations of utility for each dimension need to be aggregated (Brooks 1995). The next section considers briefly the four methodological responses most commonly adopted when seeking to measure utility.

Measuring health state utility

In order to incorporate utility measures into economic evaluations of health care we must be able to rank medical outcomes in order of preference and establish the distance between positions on this scale. We need, that is, to be able to say *how much* better one outcome is than another (Mooney 1992). Commonly implemented approaches to this problem are rating scales, magnitude estimation, time trade-off, and the standard gamble.

Some of the technical limitations of these methods are addressed in the section later in this chapter appraising QALYs.

Rating scales

Rating scales require subjects to place conditions on a continuum, say between 0 and 100. These limits of 0 and 100 correspond to the least preferred and most preferred outcomes respectively. If a score of 100 represents perfect health, then a score of 50 would indicate life in that condition would yield only half the utility enjoyed by someone who has no health problems. This methodology, among others, has been used to derive valuations for the EuroQol (Williams 1995).

Magnitude estimation

Magnitude estimation techniques ask respondents to state how many times worse one condition is than another as a ratio. For example, in her work Rosser asked respondents to judge a number of health states in terms of their perceived severity compared to 'no disability, no distress' (the 'reference state'). Subjects were told each health state would last 20 years followed by death. They were then asked whether each health state was better or worse than the reference state and how many times better or worse.

Time trade-off (TTO)

The time trade-off approach was developed in health care evaluation by Torrance (1987). Respondents are asked to identify a trade-off between a shorter life of perfect health and a longer life suffering from a chronic condition. Subjects are asked how many years of perfect health they would be willing to sacrifice in order to be relieved of the condition. A health state is valued by identifying the point at which an individual is indifferent between H years of healthy life and S years of sickness, where H is less than S. The ratio of H to S determines the relevant quality of life score. TTO is one of the methods that has been used to generate valuations for the EuroQol instrument (Williams 1995).

The standard gamble

The standard gamble offers a choice between the certainty of continued life with a chronic condition or a gamble. There are two possible outcomes if the gamble of treatment is accepted: there is a probability p that perfect health will be restored, and probability $(1-p)$ that the patient will die. Respondents are asked to vary p until they are indifferent between taking the treatment gamble and continued suffering of the condition being valued.

The value attributed to p represents the measure of utility attributed to that condition. The lower the score (i.e. the lower the probability of a cure which is regarded by the respondent as equivalent to continued existence in the poor health state) the lower the utility attached to that condition (Torrance 1987).

One of the difficulties with this method is that the risk preferences of subjects may not be constant. It could therefore be difficult to disentangle differences in valuations of various conditions from disparities in degrees of risk aversion. This creates a problem of how to aggregate individual utility ratings over several subjects.

Quality of life measures

Various studies have applied these methods to assess the utilities associated with individual health states. However, two studies are worthy of particular attention, the Rosser index and the EuroQol project.

The Rosser index

Rosser's initial survey of 60 doctors from a range of specialties revealed that the primary criteria used to assess the severity of health states were disability and distress (Rosser 1988). Disability referred to loss of physical and social functioning objectively assessed, whereas distress was classified by subjective evaluation of factors such as pain and psychological condition. Using the information gleaned from this survey and from subsequent discussions and testing with doctors, disability was ultimately classified into eight states ranging from unconsciousness to no disability, and distress was classified into four groups from severe to no distress. Table 8.1 reports Rosser's categories.

These 12 states were combined to generate 29 health states.[4] Thus, for example, state 1A represents a condition of perfect health and no distress, whereas state 7C indicates a patient who is bedridden and in moderate distress. Seventy subjects drawn from six groups including psychiatric and medical patients, experienced doctors, psychiatric and general nurses, and 20 healthy volunteers, were then interviewed to elicit valuations for these 29 health states. Six states (1C, 2D, 5B, 6B, 7B and 7D) were selected as the 'marker states' to represent the full range of conditions. Subjects were initially asked to rank these six states in order of severity. They were told that the patients in these states were all the same age (e.g. young adults) and, in the first instance, that these people would be cured if they were treated, but would remain in these states until another condition intervened if they were ignored.

Table 8.1   Rosser's classification of states of sickness (from Rosser and Kind 1978)

Disability
1 No disability.
2 Slight social disability.
3 Severe social disability and/or slight impairment of performance at work. Able to do all housework except very heavy tasks.
4 Choice of work or performance at work very severely limited. Housewives and old people able to do light housework only, but able to go out shopping.
5 Unable to undertake any paid employment. Unable to continue any education. Old people confined to home except for escorted outings and short walks and unable to do shopping. Housewives only able to perform a few simple tasks.
6 Confined to chair or to wheelchair or able to move around in the home only with support from an assistant.
7 Confined to bed.
8 Unconscious.

Distress
A None
B Mild
C Moderate
D Severe

Subjects were then asked to assess the relative severity of successive pairs of marker states. The ratio 1:x between states was intended to reflect, first, the relative proportions of NHS resources which would be needed to equate the two states and, second, the point at which subjects were indifferent between curing one person in the more severe state and x people in the relatively healthier state.

Once the relationship between marker states had been established, respondents were then asked to evaluate the remaining 23 health states. At a later stage of interviews, the initial assumptions that these conditions could be cured were revised, but this produced little change in the relative values ascribed. Respondents were also asked to add a valuation for death (Rosser and Kind 1978).

Median values of the final scores were subsequently transformed so that a score of zero was attributed to death and perfect health with no distress (state 1A) was scored at 1. These values, which have formed the basis for many QALY assessments, even though the index was not originally designed with this purpose in mind, are reported in Table 8.2. Negative values refer to conditions which are regarded as being worse than death.

Despite the wide application of the Rosser index in QALY estimates, work has continued to revise these evaluations of life quality. These have

Table 8.2   Transformed quality of life values

Disability	Distress			
	A	*B*	*C*	*D*
1	1.000	0.995	0.990	0.967
2	0.990	0.986	0.973	0.932
3	0.980	0.972	0.956	0.912
4	0.964	0.956	0.942	0.870
5	0.946	0.935	0.900	0.700
6	0.875	0.845	0.680	0.000
7	0.677	0.564	0.000	−1.486
8	−1.028			

Notes:
dead = 0 and perfect health = 1
Source: Kind *et al.* (1982)

included, for example, work based on the original Rosser classifications of health states, but tested using different measures of utility assessment such as the time trade-off and standard gamble techniques outlined above (see for example, Gudex *et al.* 1993). Rosser has also been developing a new instrument to measure health-related quality of life, the Index of Health-Related Quality of Life (IHQL) which is based on multi-dimensional classification of health status developed from the original Rosser classification. In the new index distress is subdivided into two categories of physical distress (discomfort) and emotional distress, allowing the description of 175 composite health states. These categories are subdivided further according to seven attributes and then by 44 scales. The IQHL explicitly aims to maintain the ability to present a health state evaluation as a unified aggregate score, but combine with it the advantages of clinical instruments providing profiles of subjective health assessment (Rosser *et al.* 1992).

The EuroQol©

The EuroQol Group was also formed with the intention of developing a measure of health-related quality of life which could be expressed as a single value to facilitate cost-effectiveness analysis, but also retained the benefits of profile assessment. Researchers from a range of disciplines and European countries sought to construct an instrument which could be employed in parallel with the growing bank of tests already available and which could act as a common point of reference permitting the translation of individual scores on existing tests into an index which could be used for international comparisons. A further objective was to design a measure which could be applied relatively easily; the EuroQol therefore had to avoid excessive complexity in describing alternative health states so that it would be possible to complete the evaluation by postal questionnaire rather than via the more expensive interview system which Rosser had used. In addition, the instrument should be concisely, but simply, presented so that when used in studies to elicit health status it would not be contaminated by fatigue or inadequate comprehension (Kind 1996).

The descriptive system which provided the framework for the EuroQol, was derived from several of the existing instruments for health status measurement, including the Rosser index, the Nottingham Health Profile, Sickness Impact Profile, and the Quality of Well Being Scale (see Chapter 5). Ultimately, five dimensions were defined, which were sub-divided into three levels according to whether the dimension represented no problem, a moderate problem, or a severe problem. The five dimensions were mobility, self-care, usual activity, pain and mood.[5] The five dimension, three level classification system generated 243 health states, which were extended to 245 with the addition of death and unconsciousness.

The valuation methodology adopted was largely determined by practical considerations. It was felt that respondents would find it easier to value states using a visual analogue scale than by time trade-off or standard gamble. EuroQol therefore adopted a design represented by a thermometer which ranged from the worst possible state at 0 to the best possible state (perfect health) at 100. Initial valuations of 14 key health states were determined by pilot surveys conducted in Sweden, the Netherlands and the UK. Subjects were asked to rate 16 states presented in boxes around the thermometer scale. Values were determined by drawing a line from the box describing the condition to the relevant point on the thermometer. Consistency was checked by replicating two states – death and one other, hence the determination of values for only 14 states. These 14 states were supposed to represent a wide range of health states and include those which occurred most frequently (EuroQol Group 1990). Subsequently, the York Group on the Measurement and Valuation of Health has extended this methodology and decided to incorporate the time-trade-off method in interviews, as well as ranking and the visual analogue scale, to generate a much larger set of valuations from a sample of approximately 3000 members of the adult population of England, Scotland and Wales. This survey also generated population norms for the EuroQol dimensions (Williams 1995).

The instrument itself asked subjects to tick one of three boxes corresponding to each of the levels for the five dimensions. These could then be converted into a health state with an associated quality of life valuation. For example, the state 32312 would describe a patient who was confined to bed, experiencing some problems with washing and dressing, was unable to perform her usual activities, in no pain and suffering moderate depression.

If this state were valued at say 65, then it would imply that the quality of a life living with this condition should be weighted at 0.65 relative to a life in perfect health. Subjects completing the instrument (rather than the initial valuation surveys) were also asked to indicate on a scale what they considered their current health state to be. From this some measure of the difference between individual perceptions of health status and socially determined valuations could be recognized. This would allow interventions to be evaluated on the basis of community preferences, which might be the most appropriate valuations for determining resource allocations, and individual preferences, which would allow the impact of interventions on the individuals concerned to be assessed (Kind 1996).

Several problems are associated with the EuroQol measure. First, presentational problems have been identified which suggest that when eliciting preferences via post differences in the number of boxes representing the various conditions presented per page, and variations in the length of the thermometer, influence the valuations for some states although interviewing seems to largely overcome this problem. In addition, valuations proved to be vulnerable to the declared purpose for the scale: respondents tended to record higher scores for the more severe conditions if they were told that the index would be used to inform resource allocations than if they were simply told to consider the states as referring to 'people like you' (Kind 1996).

Some respondents also recorded inconsistent ratings. If states differed only to the extent that the level recorded for one dimension was lower in state B than state A, subjects should place B at a lower position on the thermometer than A. In the early work these inconsistencies were found to be particularly problematic when the only dimension to change was pain (Carr-Hill 1992). Inconsistent responses seemed most likely to occur with elderly or poorly educated respondents (Kind 1996), suggesting that the valuations might also be vulnerable to sample selection bias. In addition these kinds of problems may suggest that the EuroQol may not achieve the level of cross-cultural validity initially desired in the pursuit of a standard measure which could be used for international comparisons. However, it should be noted that these inconsistencies are far less common when valuations are generated by interview, which is the methodology adopted in the more recent studies (Williams 1995).

Carr-Hill has also criticized the use of composite health states, rather than a weighted average of scores for the individual dimensions. He suggests that subjects are not likely to regard these components as being of equal significance in determining a health state, but it is difficult to disentangle these influences if valuations are based on composite conditions. Furthermore, the interpretation of some of the key states valued in the plot surveys may be made more difficult if respondents try to relate them to real conditions. The difficulty in comprehending what these states mean may increase the variance in individual valuations (Carr-Hill 1992). Williams (1995) documents some recent work that may overcome these problems. EuroQol researchers have responded to these criticisms by reiterating the importance of their initial objectives and acknowledging that since their work is still in progress, many of these problems have yet to be addressed effectively. The instrument has not been developed to the point where health managers can adopt it uncritically (EuroQol Group 1992), but the importance of the questions raised by this project justify the attempt to improve this index.

Many of the other criticisms levelled at the EuroQol focus on the potential applications for the index, and in particular the weaknesses of cost-utility analysis (see, for example, Gafni and Birch 1993). Before we can evaluate challenges such as these, it is essential that we review the significance of health-related quality of life indicators to cost-utility analysis.

Quality adjusted life years (QALYs)

QALYs are used as a single-index measure of health benefits which can then be applied in cost-effectiveness analysis. Life expectancy estimates (the quantity of life gained by intervention) are weighted by a quality of life quotient. If it is assumed that both quantity and quality of life are relevant parameters for health care appraisal, and these can be captured effectively in health related quality of life indicators, QALYs provide a useful source of information for health care managers seeking to evaluate the efficiency of alternative treatments, and also to prioritize the claim of competing health care projects on scarce resources.

The first problem to be addressed is that reviewed above, namely how to describe and value health-related quality of life. As we have seen, the various measures adopted in cost-utility analysis differ in their dimensions and/or in the valuation methodology. A further issue is to consider whose views should be taken into account in determining the quality of life associated with a condition. Again, empirical studies have varied according to whether a generic index (such as the Rosser index) is applied, or whether specific valuations are gained from patients suffering from the relevant condition, the general public, or from doctors.

Having established the relevant measure of quality of life, these quotients can then be applied to mortality data to determine the benefits from treatment expressed in terms of quality adjusted life years. Thus if the health-related quality of life score for a given condition is 0.8, one year of life in this state would be equivalent to 0.8 QALYs. Similarly, five years of life in a health state which achieved a quality of life score of just 0.5 would be equivalent to 2.5 QALYs. Since an intervention will not necessarily be successful, the QALYs associated with a successful procedure need to be moderated by the probability of success being achieved. If costs were then attached to each intervention, league tables of costs per QALY could be estimated for a range of procedures in order to facilitate economic evaluation.

This process can be illustrated if we consider an example of 100 patients who are the same age and suffer from the same condition (the first part of the example below follows the form outlined by Kind and Gudex 1993). Their initial health status is valued at 0.6 and they have a life expectancy of 20 years. Their condition can either be treated by surgery or by chemotherapy. Surgery has a probability of achieving a complete cure of 90 per cent, but a probability of death of 10 per cent; all the patients receiving chemotherapy survive, but their quality of life is only enhanced to 0.8. Which treatment is the most effective? If 50 patients are treated using each method, the two procedures can be compared as follows:

Surgery

Successful: QALYs are measured as the net gain in QALYs achieved by survivors over and above what they would have enjoyed had they not been treated, i.e.:

$$QALYs = (20 \text{ years} \times 1) - (20 \text{ years} \times 0.6)$$
$$= 20 - 12 = 8 \text{ QALYs per patient}$$

If 90 per cent of patients survive the operation then the total QALYs gained from successful surgery can be identified as:

$$0.9 \ (50) \times 8 = 360 \text{ QALYs}$$

Unsuccessful: QALYs are measured as the net loss of QALYs suffered by casualties of surgery below what they would have enjoyed had they never been treated, i.e.:

$$QALYs = 0 - (20 \text{ years} \times 0.6)$$
$$= -12 \text{ QALYs per casualty}$$

If 10 per cent of patients die during the operation, the net loss of QALYs can be identified as:

$$0.1 \ (50) \times -12 = -60 \text{ QALYs}$$

So, the net effect of surgery on the fifty patients treated in this way is:

$$360 - 60 = 300 \text{ QALYs}$$
$$= 6 \text{ QALYs per patient undergoing surgery.}$$

Chemotherapy

QALYs here are found by the same method:

$= (20 \times 0.8) - (20 \times 0.6)$
$= 16 - 12 = 4$ QALYs per patient
$= 200$ QALYs for all fifty patients treated in this way

Thus the net benefit of receiving surgery rather than chemotherapy can be found by subtracting the total QALYs achieved by the latter treatment from the former, i.e. 100 QALYs.

If we wanted to determine which procedure was the most cost-effective, we could work out the relative costs per QALY. If an operation costs £1000, and drug treatment costs £25 per year for 20 years (i.e. £500 per patient), then the cost per QALY can be estimated for surgery at £166.67 and for drug treatment at £125. On this basis, chemotherapy would be shown to be more cost-effective.

Although QALYs have considerable potential for aiding decisions concerning health resource allocation, they have been subject to significant criticism. First, it has been argued that there are technical limitations in the quality of life indicators from which QALYs have been calculated. The original Rosser index is based on just 70 respondents from six categories, so there is a high probability of small sample error. However, this criticism is not valid for the EuroQol as valuations have been gained from much larger samples, with the largest sample to date being 3,000. The test-retest reliability of these measures is often limited,[6] and the various methodologies adopted to value utilities produce different results (Williams and Kind 1992). Some subjects have displayed difficulty in reporting consistent results using the standard gamble or time trade-off approaches to valuing utilities. Individual perceptions of risk may also differ, so some may prefer less time in a certain but poorer condition, whereas others would take the risk to achieve a higher health state. In addition, if subjects are drawn from different groups, such as patients, doctors, and the healthy public, valuations range quite widely (Slevin *et al.* 1988). This problem could apply with respect to age, gender, ethnic origin and economic status, as well as according to health status. Furthermore, the basic principle of QALYs is that there is a constant proportional trade-off between length of life and health status, so ten years in a health state valued at 0.8 is assumed to be equivalent to eight years of perfect health and five years in the same health state would be equivalent to four years of perfect health. However, there may be a threshold effect where patients are only willing to trade length of life for greater quality once they are guaranteed a certain amount of future life. Certainly it is unlikely that the rate of trade-off will remain constant whatever the duration of life (Loomes and McKenzie 1989).

Other concerns focus on the use of QALYs in league tables. One problem may be that the cost per QALY is subject to how much money has already been invested into a programme. Cost per QALY may vary over time for a number of reasons. First, there may be economies of scale and experience as a new technique becomes adopted more widely resulting in lower costs per QALY. Second, if the patients who are treated first are those for whom the number of QALYs gained are highest per unit of costs, then as more is spent, patients must increasingly be being treated who yield fewer QALYs per unit of expenditure. Both of these influences suggest that league tables would have to be updated at regular intervals if they were to be an effective indicator of relative costs and benefits (Mooney 1994).

Ethical objections have also been levelled at QALYs focusing in particular on their implications for distributive justice and the equality principle. For example, although Harris accepts their contribution in evaluating alternative treatments for the same patient, he suggests that they are completely inappropriate for interpersonal comparison. QALYs are unjust because they do not allow equal access to resources according to need, they distribute according to the benefits gained per unit of cost. Harris maintains that this permits discrimination. He argues, for example, that ageism is an inevitable consequence of the adoption of QALYs, since other things being equal the elderly have a lower life expectancy than the young (Harris 1987). One defence of QALYs against the challenge of ageism (which Harris acknowledges) is that they prefer those with longer rather than shorter life expectancies, irrespective of age. Indeed it has been argued that QALYs are not ageist enough: if it is accepted that the elderly are fortunate to the extent that they have enjoyed a 'good innings' then justice considerations might advocate treating younger patients, even if they had lower life expectancies (Lockwood 1988). Indeed this view seems to be embraced by some health economists who claim that if we wish to equalize lifetime experience of health then those who have had a 'fair innings' should not expect to have as much spent on health improvement as younger people who seem less likely to lead such a healthy life (Williams 1997).

Justice conditions might also be violated by the case of people who suffer from rare conditions which were expensive to treat who would also be disadvantaged by QALYs. This could also create a problem of inefficiency since experimental treatments could be ruled out initially by their relative expense, even if as they were used more widely their cost would fall (Harris 1988). Economists might respond to this challenge by advocating a cost structure which discounts expenditure on research and development and compensates for uncertainties in the success of new treatment methods.

If health-related quality of life is considered to be an important factor to include in economic evaluations of health care, this raises a question as to why (other than for practical reasons) we should fail to take account of other qualitative factors in distributing health resources. QALYs allow treatment to be distributed to those who enjoy better rather than inferior health states, since the QALYs gained by intervention will be greater, other things being equal, in the former case. However, QALYs do not advocate distribution on the basis of incomes, even if the quality of life of the rich were regarded as superior to that of the poor. Broome argues that this latter case is no more unfair than the former (Broome 1988).[7]

Many of the criticisms of QALYs focus on the practical difficulties associated with their construction and whether or not they reflect fully the benefits accruing from health care interventions. These problems have been brought into sharp focus by recent attempts to implement rationing policies in public health care. The next section focuses on the practical applications to which economic evaluation of health care has been directed so far, and considers some of the difficulties this has generated.

Rationing health care: the Oregon Plan

The Oregon Health Plan was developed in response to a growing awareness of the deficiencies in existing methods for rationing of health care within the Medicaid system designed to support health care for the poor. In 1986 the response to a budget shortfall of $35 million had been to drop over 4300 Oregonions from the Medicaid programme. Additional cuts in 1987 were funded in part by cutting the Medicaid programme for major organ transplants. As a result of this decision a 7-year-old child was denied a bone marrow transplant and died before funds could be raised by charitable donation. A huge public outcry ensued and pressure grew to reverse the transplant decision. It was decided that what was required was an explicit framework for determining resource allocation which would not be influenced by *ad hoc* emotional factors. This policy framework was required to prioritize health care claims on the basis of eligibility, cost and benefits. It was also decided that this framework should be socially determined so as to command public support (Kitzhaber and Kemmy 1995).

Oregon decided to extend health coverage to all those eligible under the Medicaid system: rationing was now to be conducted on the basis of what, rather than who, was to be covered. A Health Services Commission was established, consisting of five doctors, a nurse, a social worker and four consumers, and charged with the task of generating a ranked list of health service priorities. The first attempt to prioritize treatments was released in May 1990. This ranked 1600 condition and treatment pairs according to a cost per QALY rating. However, there were practical problems in compiling commensurate costs and quality of life measures for all pairs, and the resulting ranking seemed to defy intuitive support. Appendectomies were rated just below tooth-capping on the grounds that treatment of tooth decay derived relatively little net benefit, but the cost was correspondingly low, and hence many more people could be treated, and more

QALYs per unit cost achieved. Although this was justifiable in terms of cost-effectiveness, it seemed to be ethically unacceptable. The motivation for public concern has been termed 'the rule of rescue': although in terms of cost-effectiveness tooth capping was preferable, most people did not want to see life-saving interventions such as appendectomies denied in order to fund relatively trivial treatments (Hadorn 1991).

The Commission then tried an approach which combined a ranking of a set of categories with rankings of condition-treatment pairs within the relevant category. The categories were determined at public meetings throughout the state and initially included, for example, prevention, quality of life, cost-effectiveness, ability to function, equity, effectiveness of treatment, social impact, numbers benefiting and length of life. The revised priority list was completed in February 1991. This ranked 709 condition-treatment pairs within 17 categories. Within each category rankings were determined by the benefits resulting from treatment and the duration of those benefits. Acute fatal conditions which, if treated resulted in full recovery, were ranked highest. Preventive and maternity care were also ranked very high, while the lowest positions were reserved for treatments of limited or no effect (such as treatment for terminally ill patients). This list was then costed and dispatched to the State legislature. The legislature determined what constituted a basic package to meet fundamental health care needs, and increased the budget (by approximately 25 per cent) to meet those demands. This funded the top 587 items on the list of 709 (Kitzhaber and Kemmy 1995).

Despite the important role played by public consultation in prioritizing Oregon health care programmes, the final rankings owed much to the Health Commissioners' judgements. More than half of the condition-treatment pairs moved at least 25 lines from their original positions, and a quarter were moved more than 100 places. President Bush rejected the plan due to lobbying from disabled groups, and, ironically, given the origins of the plan, all evaluations based on quality of life indicators were required to be eliminated from the list. Two items were challenged in particular: denial of liver transplants for those suffering cirrhosis due to alcoholism (rank 609) was challenged on the grounds that alcoholism was a disability, and rejection of life support for very low birth weight (i.e. less than 500g) babies (rank 708) was considered a potential violation of child protection laws. Yet another revised list presented 688 items of which 568 were funded and changed subsequently to a final list of 696 items of which 565 were funded. The plan was finally implemented for a pilot run of five years in February 1994 (Honigsbaum et al. 1995).

Various criticisms have been levelled at the Oregon experiment. First, it has been regarded as a rather impracticable process for determining priorities, requiring expensive collection of information on costs and benefits. In addition, the public accountability exercise proved to be of limited influence in practice. Many of the final judgements came from the health commissioners, and a clear self-selection bias emerged in the members of the public who did become involved, with health workers comprising most of the audience at public meetings. A further problem is associated with implementation and monitoring of the cut-off points in the rankings of health care interventions. For example, it may be the case that in the course of treating a condition endorsed in the Oregon Plan, other medical needs are identified, which lie below the line, but which could perhaps be treated in tandem with the original 'acceptable' complaint. Above all, the criticism of these kinds of schemes is that they lack the flexibility to cope with regional and cultural diversity within national communities. Nevertheless, despite the criticisms, Oregon has become an important, if flawed, flagship for those seeking to formalize health care rationing.

One example of this influence of Oregon is the recent history of health care policy in the Netherlands. Since 1985, the Dutch government has been trying to modify its health care system largely in response to growing concern about how to meet the needs of an ageing population. In 1987 the Dekker Committee proposed a scheme of compulsory universal health insurance which offered 85 per cent (later raised to 95 per cent) of the health services previously provided. In 1990, the Dunning Committee was established to determine health care priorities which could be met given budget constraints, following the guidelines established in Oregon (Honigsbaum *et al.* 1995).

Similar discussions at a more preliminary level have taken place in the UK. The 1995 House of Commons health committee report on priority setting in the NHS advocated policy being determined by the health needs of local populations, and stated explicitly that public opinion should be canvassed on these matters (Bowling 1996). The imperfections in existing systems for resource allocation have been recognized and, despite the evident practical design and implementation difficulties, pressure is growing to devise new publicly accountable schemes for the rationing of health care.

Conclusions

The significance of economics for the evaluation of health care has become increasingly evident during the last twenty years. Health economics is still an emerging discipline, but there has been considerable progress in the conceptual and analytical contributions it has made to health care analysis. This is apparent in the huge literature on the subject, and in the proliferation of instruments for quality of life appraisal intended for incorporation in cost-effectiveness studies. It is clear that rationing is not a recent development within the National Health Service, but hitherto the devices employed, and the medical outcomes which ensued, were only subjected to limited public scrutiny. As concerns about constraints on the national budget for health care have intensified, there has been a proportionate growth in the desire to address questions of efficiency and equity in health care delivery. Despite the limitations of existing approaches to economic evaluation, it is essential that these measures continue to be debated and improved. It is no longer acceptable for the public, the government and health care professionals to ignore their responsibilities for resource allocation. Delivery of an effective health care system therefore requires an appreciation of the economic principles which underpin its operation.

Notes

1 I am grateful to Matthew Clayton, Crispin Jenkinson and Alan Williams for their help with this chapter.
2 Considerable debate has taken place and continues concerning whether or not it is appropriate to discount the benefits from health care. This decision is important since discounting will reduce the relative attraction of procedures producing long term benefits such as those which provide a lifetime cure for chronic childhood illnesses. Clearly, then, studies applying a zero rate of discount will tend to value interventions such as neonatal care more highly. Traditionally most studies argued that future benefits would be valued less than immediate benefits and hence discounting was appropriate. Evidence for a positive rate of time preference was presented in the form of the smoking and drinking habits of many adults who clearly weight present pleasures more than future sickness. A further argument applied generally in cost-benefit analysis is that benefits accruing immediately could be invested to yield future income which should therefore be discounted. Dissenters from this view have suggested that health cannot be invested to produce a future flow of health, so discounting is meaningless in this context (Robinson 1993b: 794–5). (See also Broome 1988: 69–71 for an interesting alternative conception of discounting which there is insufficient space to consider here.)
3 An example here might be how to evaluate two treatments for a leg bone tumour. Let us imagine that intervention A entails amputation yielding a relatively high probability of survival with impaired mobility (and the associated implications for psychological, social and economic well-being), and treatment B relies on chemotherapy which has an inferior outcome in terms of mortality but leaves the patient with almost perfect mobility. The costs of the treatments also differ. Which programme should be implemented?
4 Unconsciousness clearly creates no distress for the patient, thereby eliminating three cells from the matrix.
5 Initially, a sixth dimension – social relationships – was included, but this was found to play only a limited role in determining health state valuations. In more recent EuroQol classifications this dimension was subsumed into the category covering usual activities which encompassed work, study, domestic and leisure activities.
6 This is one of the criticisms which the multi-dimensional EuroQol index aimed to address.

7 There might even be an economic reason for treating the rich rather than the poor if their net addition to economic wealth is greater. Their survival might enhance resources more than the survival of the poor. Questions of distributive justice could be addressed by progressive taxation.

References

Bowling, A. (1996) Health care rationing, the public debate, *British Medical Journal*, 312: 670–4.

Brooks, R.G. (1995) *Health Status Measurement. A Perspective on Change*. London: Macmillan.

Broome, J. (1988) Good, fairness and QALYs, in M. Bell and S. Mendus (eds) *Philosophy and Medical Welfare*. Cambridge: Cambridge University Press.

Carr-Hill, R.A. (1992) A second opinion. Health related quality of life measurement – Euro style, *Health Policy*, 20: 321–8.

Drummond, M.F., Stoddart, G.L. and Torrance, G.W. (1987) *Methods for the Economic Evaluation of Health Care Programmes*. Oxford: Oxford University Press.

EuroQol Group (1990) EuroQol – a new facility for the measurement of health related quality of life, *Health Policy*, 16: 199–208.

EuroQol Group (1992) EuroQol – a reply and reminder, *Health Policy*, 20: 329–32.

Gafni, A. and Birch, S. (1993) Searching for a common currency: critical appraisal of the scientific basis underlying European harmonisation of the measurement of health related quality of life (EuroQol), *Health Policy*, 23: 219–28.

Gudex, C., Kind, P., van Dalen, H., Durand, M., Morris, J. and Williams, A. (1993) *Comparing Scaling Methods for Health State Valuations – Rosser Revisited*, working paper no. 107, York: Centre for Health Economics, University of York.

Hadorn, D.C. (1991) Setting health care priorities in Oregon, *Journal of the American Medical Association*, 265: 2218–25.

Harris, J. (1987) QALYfying the value of life, *Journal of Medical Ethics*, 13: 117–23.

Harris, J. (1988) More and better justice, in M. Bell and S. Mendus (eds) *Philosophy and Medical Welfare*. Cambridge: Cambridge University Press.

Honigsbaum, F., Calthorp, J., Ham, C. and Holmström, S. (1995) *Priority Setting Processes for Health Care*. Oxford: Radcliffe Medical Press.

Kind, P. (1996) The EuroQol instrument: an index of health-related quality of life, in B. Spilker (ed.) *Quality of Life and Pharmoeconomics in Clinical Trials* (2nd edn). Philadelphia: Lippincott-Raven.

Kind, P. and Gudex, C. (1993) The role of QALYs in assessing priorities between health-care interventions, in M.F. Drummond and A. Maynard (eds) *Purchasing and Providing Cost-effective Health Care*. London: Longman.

Kind, P., Rosser, R. and Williams, A. (1982) Valuation of Quality of Life: Some Psychometric Evidence, in M.W. Jones-Lee (ed.) *The Value of Life and Safety*. Amsterdam: North-Holland Publishing Company.

Kitzhaber, J. and Kemmy, A.M. (1995) On the Oregon trail, *British Medical Bulletin*, 51: 808–18.

Klein, R., Day, P. and Redmayne, S. (1996) *Managing Scarcity*. Buckingham: Open University Press.

Lockwood, M. (1988) Quality of life and resource allocation, in M. Bell and S. Mendus (eds) *Philosophy and Medical Welfare*. Cambridge: Cambridge University Press.

Loomes, G. and McKenzie, L. (1989) The use of QALYs in health care decision making, *Social Science and Medicine*, 28: 299–308.

Ludbrook, A. (1981) A cost-effectiveness analysis of the treatment of chronic renal failure, *Applied Economics*, 13: 337–50.

McGuire, A., Henderson, J. and Mooney, G. (1988) *The Economics of Health Care. An Introductory Text*. London: Routledge.

Maynard, A. and Bloor, L. (1995) Help or hindrance? The role of economics in rationing health care, *British Medical Bulletin*, 51: 854–68.

Mooney, G. (1992) *Economics, Medicine and Health Care* (2nd edn). London: Harvester Wheatsheaf.

Mooney, G. (1994) *Key Issues in Health Economics*. London: Harvester Wheatsheaf.

Robinson, R. (1993a) Economic evaluation and health care. Costs and cost-minimisation analysis, *British Medical Journal*, 307: 726–8.

Robinson, R. (1993b) Economic evaluation and health care. Cost-effectiveness analysis, *British Medical Journal*, 307: 793–5.

Robinson, R. (1993c) Economic evaluation and health care. Cost-benefit analysis, *British Medical Journal*, 307: 924–6.

Rosser, R. (1988) A health index and output measure, in S.R. Walker and R.M. Rosser (eds) *Quality of Life: Assessment and Application*. Lancaster: MTP Press Ltd.

Rosser, R. and Kind, P. (1978) A scale of valuations of states of illness. Is there a social consensus? *International Journal of Epidemiology*, 7: 247–58.

Rosser, R., Cottee, M., Rabin, R. and Selai, C. (1992) Index of health-related quality of life, in A. Hopkins (ed.) *Measures of the Quality of Life and the Uses to Which Such Measures May be Put*. London: Royal College of Physicians of London.

Russell, I.T., Devlin, H.B., Fell, M., Glass, N.J. and Newell, D.T. (1977) Day case surgery for hernias and haemorrhoids: a clinical, social and economic evaluation, *Lancet*, i: 844–7.

Slevin, M.L., Plant, H., Lynch, D., Drinkwater, J. and Gregory W.M. (1988) Who should measure quality of life, the doctor or the patient? *British Journal of Cancer*, 57: 109–12.

Torrance, G.W. (1987) Utility approach to measuring health-related quality of life, *Journal of Chronic Diseases*, 40: 593–603.

Williams, A. (1995) *The Measurement and Valuation of Health: A Chronicle*. York: Centre for Health Economics.

Williams, A. (1997) Intergenerational equity: an exploration of the 'fair innings' argument. *Health Economics*, 6: 117–132.

Williams, A. and Kind, P. (1992) The present state of play about QALYs, in A. Hopkins (ed.) *Measures of the Quality of Life and the Uses to Which Such Measures May be Put*. London: Royal College of Physicians of London.

9

Evaluating screening programmes: theory and practice

Sarah Stewart-Brown

Introduction

This chapter defines screening and distinguishes it from other similar activities. The classic criteria for evaluating screening programmes are presented and the aims of screening programmes described. The research methodologies appropriate for establishing these criteria are defined and discussed. The chapter goes on to look at the gap between what should be done in theory and what has been done in practice. This gap is large and means that the benefits of many current screening programmes cannot be defined. Screening programmes are proliferating and the need for rigorous evaluation has never been greater. The basic principles of screening are set out in Figure 9.1.

Definition of screening

The theoretical basis of screening programmes was first drawn together in a monograph published by the World Health Organization in 1968 (Wilson and Junger 1968). In this monograph screening was defined as: 'the presumptive identification of unrecognised disease or defect by the application of examinations or other procedures which can be applied rapidly'. This definition, wordy as it is, remains the one which is most commonly quoted because it covers all the important points about screening. The first is that the tests used in screening programmes are not diagnostic. They sort people into two groups: those at low risk of having a disease and those at high risk. The low risk group will always contain some people who have the disease and the high risk group some that do

The disease
- the disease must pose an important public health problem
- the natural history of the disease should be understood
- it should have a latent or pre-symptomatic phase
- the disease process should be reversible or more amenable to intervention in its latent or pre-symptomatic phase

The screening test
- there must be a suitable test which is safe, acceptable, valid, reliable, sensitive, specific and not costly
- there must be adequate facilities available to make a diagnosis in those found to be at high risk

The treatment
- an effective intervention must be available
- there must be adequate service provision to treat those found to have the disease
- there must be an agreed policy on whom to offer the treatment or intervention

Figure 9.1   Principles of screening (adapted from Wilson and Junger 1968)

not. Working out how well a programme performs this sorting function is therefore a cornerstone of the process of evaluation. The second point encompassed in this definition is that screening programmes aim to identify diseases or health problems which have not been 'recognized'. This excludes activities which may be described as 'screening' like healthy lifestyle checks in primary care. It does not require a screening test to recognize that someone smokes or takes no exercise. It is important to question people about their lifestyles to ensure that everyone who smokes or takes no exercise knows how this may affect their health and that they also know what other people have found helpful in trying to change their behaviour. Although this may be carried out as part of a package of interventions which includes true screening tests, such as serum cholesterol or blood pressure measurement (Imperial Cancer Research Fund Oxcheck Study Group 1995; Family Heart Study Group 1994) it is not 'screening' and the principles of evaluation need to be considered with a slightly different emphasis.

The WHO definition does not specify whether it is the person with the problem or their health professionals to whom the disease should be 'unrecognizable'. In some programmes for example breast cancer screening and the new-born screening programme for phenylketonuria (Powell 1984) neither patient, parent nor health professionals can 'recognize' whether the disease is present without applying a technology dependent test. Sometimes health professionals are able to recognize a problem that may not be obvious to an individual or their carers without the aid of any tests. Talipes equinovarius (clubfoot) in new-born babies and delayed language development in pre-school children are good examples (Hall 1989). In neither of these circumstances is it necessary for the health professional to apply a test to recognize the problem. They are able to do this because, unlike parents, they know what they are looking for and understand the significance of the observation.

Screening versus case finding

In screening programmes people are sent invitations to attend for a specific test or check. This may not be necessary if people attend their GP surgery or clinic for other reasons. If the test does not require a special technology and consultation rates in the relevant age group are high 'opportunistic case finding' may be a more appropriate way to identify people with a problem. Common examples are blood pressure measurement in general practice consultations and urine analysis in ante-natal clinics. These tests can also be carried out as part of screening programmes in which everyone is invited (called) to have the test. Case finding is an intervention and needs to be evaluated but the principles of evaluation are slightly different from those for screening. However, the onus on health professionals, to make sure that people who have a problem will benefit from being 'found' is just as great and possibly more often ignored than it is with screening.

Screening versus enhancing 'spontaneous presentation'

Sometimes with appropriate education and support people can be enabled to recognize problems themselves and bring them forward at a stage when they can be prevented or treated. The promotion of self-examination for breast cancer is an example of this. The child health surveillance programme provides other examples. Parents can recognize sensori-neural deafness in their children, but do not always act on their concerns. Health visitors asking parents whether they think their babies can hear, can increase the early identification of sensori-neural deafness (Hitchings and Haggard 1983). The hearing check list which is now routinely offered to parents with parent-held records is intended to serve this function. The assumption is often made that these methods are cost free and are harmless. Although they are undoubtedly much cheaper than screening programmes, some of the costs may be hidden. There are costs to the individual in terms of time and worry and if the method is ineffective there may be a problem of false reassurance (see below). These programmes are in need of rigorous evaluation like any other intervention. Breast self-examination has to date only been evaluated with case-control studies. These show favourable tumour staging and survival in those practising the technique, but the studies are all potentially biased (see below). The necessary rigorous evaluations are now being carried out in Russia and China (Austoker 1994a).

Aims of screening

Defining the outcomes

Evaluations of health interventions need to start from a clear statement of the aim of the intervention. This is just as true for screening programmes as it is for treatments. However, defining the aims of some established programmes can be remarkably difficult. Even for cancer-screening programmes where the aim seems obvious (prevention of premature death) the situation may be more complex. If, for example, a study showed a one-year survival advantage, at the expense of a two-year reduction in quality of life there would be room for discussion about the benefits.

Health gain

In theory screening programmes like all other interventions should aim for an overall health gain using the WHO definition of health: a state of complete physical, psychological and social well-being (WHO 1947). The concept of health is, however, still being debated and defined. Most doctors operate under a slightly different definition of health than most sociologists and screening programme evaluations have tended to define health in terms of the more limited medical model. Methods of measuring health outcomes according to the WHO definition have only recently been developed (see Chapter 5) and have rarely been used in screening programme evaluations.

Secondary prevention

Screening is usually carried out with the aim of secondary prevention: identifying a disease or disease process at a stage where the process can be reversed. This is the case for cancer-screening programmes where the primary aim is eradication of the cancer and prevention of death from the disease.

Primary prevention

Screening programmes may also aim to prevent disease by identifying and reversing a risk factor for that disease. This is the aim of coronary heart disease prevention programmes which include screening for serum cholesterol and hypertension. As the aim is to prevent the clinical manifestation of CHD these programmes have primary prevention as their goal.

Other programmes such as glaucoma screening (Wormald 1995) aim to prevent disability by reversing or controlling the development of a disease. These programmes therefore aim at primary prevention of disability but secondary prevention of the disease process.

Tertiary prevention

Some of the child health screening programmes (Hall 1989) aim only for tertiary prevention: the amelioration of disability. Sensori-neural deafness cannot be treated but the provision of hearing aids, family support and special education make a major impact on the extent to which the individual is disabled by his/her hearing loss. This screening programme is justified on the grounds that the impact of these interventions is greater, the earlier the hearing loss is detected in a child's life. Although this is a firmly held belief the supporting research evidence is poor.

Population benefit

Some screening programmes are not designed primarily to benefit the screened individuals at all. Hepatitis B testing for health professionals and chest X-rays for teachers are both intended to protect other people. Before treatment became available screening for HIV status was undertaken solely in an attempt to limit the spread of the disease.

Efficiency

Screening programmes should aim to achieve their effect on health as efficiently as possible. Efficiency is a measure of how well a programme achieves a given objective using a given amount of resources. The differences between the concepts of efficiency and effectiveness and between cost-effectiveness and cost-benefit analysis are complex (see Chapter 8 and also Cairns and Shackley 1994). The efficiency or cost effectiveness of screening programmes can be manipulated in a number of ways.

Targeting

Restricting the offer of screening to people who are at high risk of a disease enables more cases to be detected for every person screened. All screening programmes are to some extent targeted in that they are restricted to people of a certain age or sex. Decisions as to whether to target may be easy. Screening men for breast and cervical cancer is not likely to be fruitful; nor is screening people who do not have diabetes for diabetic retinopathy. The decision about whether to offer breast cancer screening to women under the age of 50 years or screening foetuses for Down's syndrome in women under 40 years is very much more complex but is central to establishing costs and benefits.

Changing the cut-off point

When the screening programme aims to detect a risk factor for a disease for example serum cholesterol, the risk factor may be continuously distributed in the population. In this situation the efficiency of the programme can be controlled by manipulating the cut-off point defining screen positive cases. The higher the level is set the fewer people will be sorted wrongly into the at risk groups, but the more will be sorted wrongly into the not at risk group. The optimum solution can be defined mathematically (Mant and Fowler 1990).

Methods of evaluating screening programmes

The WHO monograph on which definitions of screening are based (Wilson and Junger 1968) also provides the best description of the principles on which screening programmes should be established. They are usually grouped into principles relating to the disease, those relating to the screening test and programme, and those relating to treatment. Most of these are self-explanatory, but the first is more complex because it combines measures of disease prevalence with those of disease impact. Life-threatening rare diseases may be worth screening for when commoner diseases which cause minor problems are not. The most important requirement is that the health problems caused by the disease are well defined and that the prevalence of the problem is known.

Almost all epidemiological methods have been applied in studies attempting to establish whether screening programmes fulfil these criteria.

Observational studies

Relatively simple observational studies are sufficient to evaluate some of the measures of performance of the screening test, those which measure how well screening programmes perform their sorting function. In the simplest study design a defined representative population is offered screening and the screen positive cases are followed up through to the end of their investigations. This type of study can measure the positive predictive value (the proportion of screen positive cases who turn out to have the disease), the false positive rate (the proportion of screen positive cases who turn out not to have the disease[1]) and the programme yield (the number

	disease	no disease	total
screen positive	a	b	a + b
screen negative	c	d	c + d
total	a + c	b + d	a + b + c + d

positive predictive value = a/(a + b)

false positive rate b/(a + b)

false negative rate = c/(c + d)

sensitivity = a/(a + c)

specificity = d/(b + d)

programme yield = a/(a + b + c + d)

Figure 9.2 Calculation of false negative/positive rates, positive predictive value, sensitivity, specificity and programme yield

of true positive cases divided by the number of people screened). The manner in which these are calculated is shown in Figure 9.2.

This type of study not altogether surprisingly is the commonest type of methodology used to evaluate screening programmes in the published literature. These studies are also able to provide a crude evaluation of the acceptability of the test by measuring the uptake rate (the proportion of those invited for screening who attend). They can demonstrate that it is possible to identify people with a condition or problem with a screening test and provide an estimate of the NHS resources which would be required to investigate screen positive people.

More sophisticated observational studies are required to evaluate the other three important parameters of the performance of screening tests which depend for their calculation on an accurate knowledge of the number of false negative cases. These are the false negative rate, the sensitivity and the specificity. The false negative rate is the proportion of cases that are incorrectly identified as not having the disease. Sensitivity is the proportion of truly diseased persons in the screened population who are identified as diseased by the screening test while specificity is the number of truly non-diseased people who are correctly identified by the screening test.

In these studies the whole cohort of people who were screened, screen negative as well as screen positive cases need to be followed up. Because screen negative cases are very much more numerous than positive cases this addition adds disproportionately to the expense of the research and there are some short cuts which are frequently used. Studies of screening programmes for life threatening diseases often use death registration information to identify cohort members who have died in this country and UK nationals who have died abroad. This data is available from the NHS register at relatively low cost. The death certificate gives the certifying doctor's opinion as to cause of death (the consequence of the condition being screened for or another disease) which is not as accurate as autopsy evidence, but allows an estimate to be made of the number of cases of the disease which were missed in screening.

Studies of cancer screening programmes can make use of the regional cancer registries to identify false negative cases. Some regions also run registries of people with genetic disorders which present in childhood. These allow the performance of screening programmes like those for Down's syndrome to be monitored at local level. Studies which use registry data as their outcome are only as good as the register. Running an accurate register is a time consuming, meticulous and therefore expensive task. Many registers are run on the enthusiasm and energy of one individual. The cancer registries have established funding but their quality varies from one region to another.

Studies of screening programmes for non-fatal, non-malignant conditions in defined geographical areas may assume that all cases will eventually present to the local hospital. These studies use hospital case notes to determine the outcome in people who were screened and in those who did not attend. People who develop the disease being screened for, who move away from the locality will be missed in this study design, which will therefore always tend to underestimate the number of false negatives.

Most of the study designs described above are subject to a greater or lesser degree to bias from under-ascertainment (i.e. under-estimating the number of false negatives) and are likely, therefore, to over-estimate sensitivity and specificity. At best they can only provide a measure of the efficiency of the screening programme in sorting people who have the disease from those who do not. In the absence of studies of the effectiveness of treatment and the health impact of the disease they cannot begin to answer the question of whether screening is worthwhile.

Evaluations based on observational or cohort study designs also over-estimate the value of screening because they do not take into account the effect of spontaneous presentation in the absence of screening. Some investigators have resolved this problem by investigating a comparable control cohort (Bolger *et al.* 1991). This could be a cohort of people in a neighbouring district which is similar in all ways except that no screening programme is in place. 'Controlled' studies of this sort provide a more accurate estimate of the additional benefit of screening but are subject to bias due to unidentified differences between control and intervention districts. They can also allow an estimate of the combined effect of screening and treatment to be made: for example a comparison of total mortality and disease specific mortality in screened and unscreened cohorts. Due to the possibility of bias in studies of this sort the results will be less accurate than those gained from a properly conducted randomized controlled trial, but they can be gained at considerably lower costs.

Case control studies

Studies looking at the screening history of people with and without a condition can and have been used to provide a combined measure of the effectiveness of screening and treatment (Sasco *et al*. 1986). They are very much less expensive and complicated to carry out than randomized controlled trials (see below) but are inevitably subject to attender bias (described below) which can have a substantial impact on the estimate of efficacy (Connor *et al*. 1991). There are a number of other methodological problems with assessing the protective value of screening programmes using this method (Knox 1991; Hosek *et al*. 1996). Such studies can also only be undertaken in communities where screening is widely available. If screening is only available to a minority group the chances of either a case or a control being screened may be too low to establish whether a benefit exists. Case control study evidence is unlikely ever to be a sufficient basis for establishing a new screening programme but this methodology may have a continuing place in the monitoring of established programmes.

The randomized controlled trial

The randomized controlled trial has been claimed as the optimum study design for assessing the effectiveness of any intervention (Cochrane 1972). It can be argued that RCT evidence of the effectiveness of treatment for a condition is an absolute pre-requisite for establishing a screening programme for that condition (see below), but this method has been used less often to establish the other essential criteria for screening.

An RCT of an entire screening programme requires people to be randomly allocated to screened or not screened groups, screen positive cases to be investigated and treated if they have the disease, and all members of both groups to be followed up to the point where any disease which might have been present at the time of screening is fully manifest and the outcome of treatment can be measured. Because very large numbers of people need to be screened to identify diseased people, RCTs of screening programmes need to be very large indeed to achieve adequate statistical power (see Chapter 2). The need for large numbers of study participants for a long period of follow up make such trials a formidable and expensive undertaking.

Providing screening on the basis of random selection of participants can be problematic as well as expensive. Because such a large number of people need to be involved knowledge of the existence of the screening programme and its potential benefits becomes widespread. If the community is not adequately informed about the current state of knowledge and the need for the trial, people in the control group may seek screening privately. To overcome this problem some trials have randomly allocated communities to be screened or not screened. This reduces 'contamination' of the control group but also reduces the power of the randomization process to control for bias and may result in the need for an even larger study.

Partly because of the difficulties of the conducting such trials and partly because it is only recently that the importance of RCT evidence has become widely appreciated the number of screening programmes which have been evaluated in this way is very small. The breast cancer screening programme is one notable exception (Austoker 1994a). The method has also been applied to ultrasound screening for aortic aneurysm (Scott *et al.* 1995) and to ultrasound screening in pregnancy to prevent placental insufficiency (Duff 1993).

RCTs are undoubtedly the method of choice for evaluation but even these studies may be subject to design flaws and give conflicting results (Austoker 1994a). Using the RCT methodology does not resolve the problem of selecting the appropriate outcome measures so that the full impact on health can be measured. No RCTs of screening programmes have yet incorporated patient perceived health outcomes (see below).

The RCT has been used to evaluate component parts of the screening programmes. Some studies use as their outcome the number of cases of the disease identified in control and screening arms. For diseases where the effectiveness of treatment is in no doubt this study design is adequate. Such studies can assess the additional value of the screening programme against spontaneous presentation of disease and against measures designed to increase public awareness of disease. Information from studies like these can be combined with studies of treatment effect to give an overall measure of the benefits of the programme (see below).

RCTs have also been used to evaluate different ways of inviting people for screening looking at the effect on uptake rates (Pierce *et al.* 1989). Others have looked at different ways of explaining the programme and gaining consent. The latter measure knowledge and anxiety levels as an outcome (Marteau *et al.* 1993).

The combined approach

An assessment of the effectiveness of screening can be gained from combining the results of different types of study: studies of the effectiveness of the screening programme in finding people and studies of the effectiveness of treatment in reversing the disease process or preventing disability. Combining studies like this can give a false picture of the overall. The effectiveness of screening is calculated from data collected on the population of people who turn up for screening and the treatment effect is calculated from data on people who present for treatment. Because people who turn up for screening are different from those who do not (Jones *et al.* 1993) the assumption that the treatment effect is the same in this population as it is in the non-attender population is not likely to be valid. It is reasonable to suppose that treatment might be more effective in a group of people found by screening than in those who present spontaneously at a later stage of the disease; if this was the case the combined approach would under-estimate the effect of screening. It may, however, also over-estimate it, if the adverse effects of treatment outweigh the benefits in those in an early stage of disease.

In spite of these problems the combined approach probably offers the most realistic methodology for measuring the effectiveness of screening programmes in current practice (Thompson 1996).

Health economic studies

Screening programmes can be subject to both cost-effectiveness and cost-benefit studies (these terms are explained in detail in Chapter 8). Cost-effectiveness studies provide evidence on whether screening is the best way to use a limited resource to achieve a defined outcome. For example, is it better to screen people for hypertension or to undertake opportunistic case finding? This type of study can provide measures of both cost per case detected and cost per case cured or life saved. When more knowledge is available about the health outcomes of disease this method could be used to compare the health gain which could be achieved for a given amount of money by screening with that from other types of intervention.

Cost-benefit studies aim to translate the health gain from an intervention into a monetary cost and to compare this with the amount of money spent on the intervention. The results of these analyses are dictated by the assumptions made about the monetary value of different disease states. Health economic studies should take into account not only the health gain attributable to screening in people who are found to have the disease but also any of the dis-benefits or health losses attributable to the programme. These have only recently begun to receive the research effort they warrant (see below).

Issues in the evaluation of screening programmes

The effectiveness of treatment

The requirement that an effective treatment be available is arguably the most important of the criteria which need to be established before a screening programme is put into place. Implicit in the invitation to attend for screening is the assumption that those who are found to have a problem will benefit from being found. For many current screening programmes the research evidence to support such an assumption is lacking.

If good studies of the natural history of a condition have been carried out it is possible to establish that treatment affords some benefit from observational studies of treatment impact, but without this, the latter studies cannot distinguish treatment effect from spontaneous improvement or resolution. Some of the screening programmes undertaken as part of child health surveillance were started on the basis of evidence from observational studies of treatment impact in the absence of evidence on the natural history of the condition (congenital dislocation of the hip, undescended testes, amblyopia), but the problem is not confined to screening for non-fatal conditions. The national cervical cancer screening programme is built on an inadequate knowledge of the natural history of cervical dysplasia. It is certain that most cases of dysplasia do not progress to cancer, but precise knowledge of the risk of progression for different degrees of dyplasia is not available. It can be estimated that around 15,000 women are told they need repeat smears and 5000 receive further investigation, many with treatment, for a disease that would have affected only 200 of them in the absence of screening programmes. At present both the number needing repeat investigation and the number referred for further investigation and treatment is rising. This is probably because pathologists are diagnosing more minor abnormalities as significant (Raffle et al. 1995). This very expensive programme for a relatively rare condition is a good example of the consequences of failing to properly evaluate screening programmes before their introduction.

Screening programmes for lung cancer set up in the 1960s and subsequently discontinued in the UK, demonstrate other pitfalls of introducing screening without evidence of treatment benefit (Fontana 1984). Proponents of the programme believed that if they caught the disease early enough there was bound to be something that they could do to help. Case-control studies of these programmes demonstrated that people whose cancers were diagnosed by screening had a survival advantage. This proved to be the equivalent of the time it would have taken for the tumour to present clinically, a phenomenon known as lead time bias. All that the screening programme achieved was to let people know that they had a fatal disease a year earlier than they would have done otherwise. A recent RCT of lung cancer screening in Czechoslovakia has demonstrated this phenomenon (Kubik and Haerting 1990). Lung cancer cases identified by screening were more likely to have resectable tumours and had longer survival time from diagnosis but there was no difference in average age at death between patients in screened and unscreened groups.

In today's world, evidence of treatment benefit from several well-conducted, adequately powered RCTs should be an essential pre-requisite for establishing a screening programme. It could be argued that it is a waste of public money to fund research into screening until a clearly effective treatment has been identified. However, calls are now being made to establish screening programmes for prostate cancer in the absence of trials which show effective treatment for localized disease (Austoker 1994b).

The extent of disability attributable to the condition being screened for

The importance of establishing that a medical condition causes some disability or health problem before embarking on screening seems hardly worth stating. It might be imagined that this was an essential pre-requisite even for embarking on treatment in people presenting spontaneously but this is not universally the case. Most health authorities run screening programmes to detect amblyopia (loss of vision in one eye detectable with a visual acuity chart). The impact of unilateral poor vision on the lives of either children or adults has however never been established. The assumption is made that it must be a problem on the grounds that 'God gave us two eyes for a purpose'. Yet there are adults with severe amblyopia who do not know they have got it and do not appreciate that they have a problem. The research evidence that amblyopia causes a problem in children or young adults is at the level of a weak association; none of the criteria for establishing causality have been fulfilled (Beaglehole 1993). This is one of the screening programmes for which there is also no evidence of treatment benefit. However, even if it had been shown that patching the good eye (the standard treatment for amblyopia) did improve visual acuity the evidence on disability is arguably inadequate to embark on this potentially distressing treatment regime let alone to offer screening (Snowdon and Stewart-Brown 1997). Measuring the outcome of trials of treatment and screening programmes using patient perceived health outcomes would help to prevent this sort of occurrence.

The Down's syndrome screening programme raises some particular ethical issues related to disability which can never be answered in RCTs and do not seem to have been addressed elsewhere. This screening programme is carried out to identify and abort affected foetuses. The ethics of this programme seem clear to the medical profession and health economists but extreme variation in opinion of parents has been documented (Elkins 1986). People with Down's syndrome all have some degree of learning disability and some have severe physical anomalies as well. On average children and adults with this condition need more care and support from their parents and society than people who are not so afflicted but they do not need more care than children and adults with physical disorders like cystic fibrosis whose doctors and parents choose to keep them alive with intensive technological support. It may be that learning disability is regarded as less acceptable to society than physical disability, but if it is, this should be made explicit. Given the difficult ethical dilemmas involved it is particularly important that women and their partners undergoing screening for Down's syndrome understand what they are being offered and what the risks and benefits are. This at least allows them to decide whether they could provide what their child would need. Qualitative research on what women do know and understand about this programme makes it clear that there is a big gap between theory and practice (Marteau *et al.* 1988).

Adverse effects of screening

Most studies of screening programmes have concentrated exclusively on identifying the benefits which the screening brings to those who are identified as having the disease. Very large numbers of people are screened to find people with the disease and any adverse effects on people who do not have the disease could be important in public health terms.

Screening is a relative newcomer to health care provision. It is likely to have had some impact on the way people think about health and disease. Public misconceptions about the purpose of screening programmes and the accuracy of tests have been demonstrated in Australia (Cockburn 1995), but other plausible hypotheses have not yet been investigated. If for example the existence of screening programmes made people more likely to believe that the maintenance of good health could be achieved by regular visits to their doctor for screening and check ups they might be less likely to believe that their own behaviour could have an important impact. Changes in health-related lifestyles (reductions in smoking, increases in exercise participation) would have an impact on the public health which outweigh advantages to be gained from screening, so a small impact on health behaviour could have a major effect in a cost benefit analysis. These potential generalized effects of screening warrant more research than they currently get.

A number of research reports have now been published which suggest that there are real adverse effects on specific groups. Screening programme evaluations which do not look for such effects will inevitably over-estimate the health gain attributable to these programmes. Adverse effects may be found in the following groups of people.

False positive cases

People who have no disease but are sorted by the screening programme into the high risk group suffer dis-benefits without any benefits. At minimum this group suffers the nuisance and waste of time in attending for further investigation and treatment, but more definite adverse health effects have also been shown. Research on three very different screening programmes – prenatal testing for Down's syndrome (Marteau *et al.* 1988b), screening for congenital hypothyroidism (Tymstra 1986) and breast cancer screening (Cockburn *et al.* 1994) has shown that people in this false positive group develop high levels of anxiety which do not resolve immediately even when subsequent testing shows no signs of disease. Probably the most serious dis-benefit to false positive cases in a current screening programme occurs in the Down's syndrome screening programme (Tabor *et al.* 1986). Women who fall into a high risk category after screening with biochemical tests (alpha-foetoprotein or the triple test) are offered a diagnostic amniocentesis. These women suffer a one in 100 risk of spontaneous abortion. In some reported programmes the risk of terminating a normal pregnancy is greater than the chances of identifying a Down's foetus.

False negatives

Anecdotal evidence suggests that parents of deaf children who pass a hearing screening test are less likely to take notice of any concerns they may have about the child's hearing (Hall 1989). For these families participation in a screening programme will have the effect of increasing the time before treatment can be offered and in this way increasing the disability. The same has been claimed of false negative cases on cervical cancer screening. Women who have recently had a negative cervical smear may take no notice of symptoms like post menopausal bleeding which would otherwise have worried them sufficiently to take them to the doctor. These potential adverse effects need documenting more systematically.

True negatives

The adverse effects for true negative cases are usually considered to be outweighed by the reassurance to be gained from a true negative result, but this may not always be the case. One study in general practice has suggested that people who attend heart disease screening programmes are a psychologically healthy group, but that they suffer raised anxiety levels for up to three months even after receiving a negative result (Stoate 1989). Other plausible adverse effects have been proposed (Tymstra and Bielman 1987) but not adequately sought. It is possible, for example, that people who have had their cholesterol measured and are found not to be in the high risk group for heart disease are more resistant to public information about healthy eating than people who have not been screened. It is equally possible that people who have had a negative cancer screening test feel more confident about continuing to smoke. The potential that participation in a screening programme with a negative result has to influence health related behaviour has been suggested by one study in which women who had previously examined their breasts were less likely to do so after a negative biopsy (Haefner *et al.* 1989).

True positive cases

On balance the potential advantages for people who are identified by screening as having a problem which can be treated should far outweigh any disadvantages, but this does not obviate the need to look for disadvantages. An American study showed that people who were found to be hypertensive in a workplace screening programme had increased sickness absence, increased anxiety and reduced self-perceived health status following detection (Haynes *et al.* 1978; Johnstone 1984). These effects were observed whether or not the person received treatment. If they were not treated there would of course have been no benefits from screening even though they were in theory true positive cases. On the other hand, if the hypertension had been partly caused by work stress this might be a good thing. If, however, it resulted in termination of employment it might not.

Several studies of the effectiveness of cholesterol screening in preventing death from coronary heart disease have shown a paradoxical effect of screening: heart disease deaths were reduced but there appeared to be a small increase in total mortality (Muldoon *et al.* 1990). It has been suggested that men who knew that they were at increased risk of dying from heart disease might be more inclined to take other risks.

Non-attenders

People who are not invited to attend and those who are invited, but do not do so may suffer harm through reduction in other services as a consequence of providing resources for the screening programme. The opportunity costs of investing in screening programmes are potentially widespread. When public spending is constrained as it is in this country at present, the introduction of the breast cancer screening programme must have had an impact on resources available to the NHS and possibly other public services, for example education and housing.

Ethical considerations in screening programmes

The ethics of screening programmes have received far less attention than the ethics of other medical activities, like research, which affect a smaller proportion of the population and where the potential for harm is arguably much less (Skrabanek 1990). There can be no doubt that the ethical basis of screening differs from that of the treatment services. In the latter people take a problem to a health professional asking for their help. For the health professional to do their best to help is likely to be considered ethical unless their lack of knowledge is so great that it breaches professional standards. In an invitation for screening there is an implicit assumption that participation is going to be beneficial. Programmes for which benefit cannot be demonstrated may be considered to be unethical.

Screening programmes make work for health professionals which in turn makes them feel valued and useful. As a general rule, therefore, there is likely to be a bias among health professionals in favour of providing rather than not providing such services. In contrast primary preventive programmes like provision of safe water, good housing and healthy food reduce work for heath professionals. Although unlikely to be more than a minor component of decision making, this bias may account for the current proliferation of screening programmes and the lack of rigour with which many of them have been evaluated.

Conclusions

Many screening programmes currently provided by the NHS have not been adequately evaluated and it is impossible to demonstrate on the basis of current research that they achieve health gain. Evaluation of programmes which are already running is more difficult than evaluating new programmes. There is an urgent need to ensure all future programmes are properly evaluated before being introduced into practice. When the public are invited to participate in screening programmes for which the evidence of benefit is weak then they should be offered honest information about likely costs and benefits.

Note

1 The false positive rate is defined differently in different textbooks. Here it is defined in the way it is most commonly used by clinicians. This is equivalent to '1- positive predictive value'. The alternative definition is the equivalent to '1-specificity'.

References

Austoker, J. (1994a) Screening and self-examination for breast cancer, *British Medical Journal*, 309: 168–74.

Austoker, J. (1994b) Screening for ovarian, prostatic and testicular cancers, *British Medical Journal*, 309: 315–20.

Beaglehole, R., Boital, R. and Kjellstrom, T. (1993) *Basic Epidemiology*. Geneva: World Health Organization.

Bolger, P.G., Stewart-Brown, S.L., Newcombe, E. and Starbuck, A. (1991) Vision screening in pre-school children: comparison of orthoptists and clinical medical officers as primary screeners, *British Medical Journal*, 303: 1291–4.

Cairns, J.A. and Shackley, P. (1994) Assessing value for money in medical screening, *Journal of Medical Screening*, 1: 9–44.

Cochrane, A. (1972). *Effectiveness and Efficiency: Random Reflections on Health Services*. London: Nuffield Provincial Hospitals Trust.

Cockburn, J., Redman, S., Hill, D. and Henry, E. (1995) Public understanding of medical screening, *British Medical Journal*, 2: 224–7.

Cockburn, J., Staples, M., Hurley, S. and de Luise, T. (1994) Psychological costs of screening mammography, *British Medical Journal*, 1: 7–12.

Connor, R.J., Prorok, P.C. and Weed, D.L. (1991). The case control design and the efficacy of cancer screening, *Journal of Clinical Epidemiology*, 44: 1215–21.

Duff, G.B. (1993) A randomised controlled trial in a hospital population of ultrasound measurement screening for the small for dates baby, *Australian and New Zealand Journal of Obstetrics and Gynaecology*, 33: 374–8.

Elkins, T.E., Stovall, T.G., Wilroy, S. and Dacus, J.V. (1986) Attitudes of mothers of children with Down's syndrome concerning amniocentesis, abortion and prenatal genetic counselling techniques, *British Journal of Obstetrics and Gynaecology*, 68: 181–4.

Family Heart Study Group (1994) Randomised controlled trial evaluating cardiovascular screening and intervention in general practice: principal results of British Family Heart Study, *British Medical Journal*, 308: 313–20.

Fontana, R.S. (1984) Early detection of lung cancer: the Mayo lung cancer project. In Screening for Cancer: General Principles, in P.C. Provok and A.B. Miller (eds) *Evaluation of Screening for Cancer, IUAC Technological Report Series*, 78: 107–22, Geneva.

Haefner, D.P., Marshall, H.B., Janz, N.K. and Rutt, W.M. (1989) Impact of a negative biopsy on subsequent breast self examination practice, *Patient Education and Counseling*, 14: 137–46.

Hall, D.M.B. (1996) *Health for all Children*. Oxford: Oxford University Press.

Hall, D.M.B. (1989) *Health for all Children: A Programme for Child Health Surveillance*. Oxford: Oxford University Press.

Haynes, R.B., Sackett, D.L., Taylor, D.W., Gibson, E.S. and Johnson, A.L. (1978) Increased absenteeism from work after detection and labelling of hypertensive patients, *New England Journal of Medicine*, 299: 741–4.

Hitchings, V. and Haggard, M.P. (1983) Incorporation of parents' suspicions in screening infants, *British Journal of Audiology*, 17: 71–5.

Hosek, R.S., Flanders, W.D. and Sasco, A.J. (1996) Bias in case control studies of screening effectiveness, *American Journal of Epidemiology*, 143: 193–201.

Imperial Cancer Research Fund Oxcheck Study Group (1995). Effectiveness of health checks conducted by nurses in primary care: final results of the OXCHECK study, *British Medical Journal*, 310: 1099–104.

Johnstone, M.E., Gibson, S., Wayne, T.C., Haynes, R.B., Taylor, G.A., Sicurella, J. and Sackett, D.L. (1984) Effects of labelling on income work and social function among hypertensive employees, *Journal of Chronic Diseases*, 37: 417–23.

Jones, A., Cronin, P.A. and Bowen, M. (1993) Comparison of risk factors for coronary heart disease among attenders and non attenders at a screening programme, *British Journal of General Practice*, 43: 375–7.

Knox, G. (1991) Case-control studies of screening procedures, *Public Health*, 105: 55–61.

Kubik, A. and Haerting, J. (1990) Survival and mortality in a randomized study of lung cancer detection, *Neoplasma*, 37(4): 467–75.

Mant, D. and Fowler, G. (1990) Mass screening: theory and ethics, *British Medical Journal*, 300: 916–18.

Marteau, T.M., Kidd, J., Michie, S., Cook, R., Johnston, M. and Shaw, R.W. (1993) Anxiety knowledge and satisfaction in women receiving false positive results on routine prenatal screening: a randomised controlled trial, *Journal of Obstetrics and Gynaecology*, 14: 185–96.

Marteau, T.M., Kidd, J., Cook, R., Johnston, M., Michie, S., Shaw, R.W. and Slack, J. (1988) Screening for Down's syndrome, *British Medical Journal*, 297: 1469.

Muldoon, M.F., Manuck, S.B. and Mathew, K.A. (1990) Lowering cholesterol concentrations and mortality: a quantitative review of primary prevention trials, *British Medical Journal*, 301: 309–14.

Powell, R.M. (1984) Medical screening and surveillance, in G. Lindsay (ed.) *Screening for Children with Special Needs*. London: Croom Helm.

Pierce, M., Lundy, S., Palanismay, A., Winning, S. and King, J. (1989) Prospective randomised controlled trial of methods of call and recall for cervical cytology screening, *British Medical Journal*, 299: 106–2.

Raffle, A.E., Alden, B. and Mackenzie, E.F. (1995) Detection rates for abnormal cervical smears. What are we screening for?, *Lancet*, 345: 1469–73.

Sasco, A.J., Day, N.E. and Walter, S.D. (1986) Case control studies for evaluating screening, *Journal of Chronic Diseases*, 39: 399–405.

Scott, R.A., Wilson, N.M., Ashton, H.A. and Kay, D.N. (1995) Influence of screening on the incidence of ruptured aortic aneurysm. 5 year results of a randomised controlled study, *British Journal of Surgery*, 82: 1066–70.

Skrabanek, P. (1990) Why is preventive medicine exempted from ethical constraints?, *Journal of Medical Ethics*, 16: 187–90.

Snowdon, S. and Stewart-Brown, S. (1997) *Preschool Vision Screening: A Systematic Review of the Evidence of Effectiveness*. Oxford: Health Services Research Unit, University of Oxford.

Stoate, H.G. (1989) Can health screening damage your health?, *Journal of the Royal College of General Practitioners*, 38: 193–5.

Tabor, A., Philip, J., Madsen, M., Bang, J., Obel, E.B. and Norgaard-Pedersen, B. (1986) Randomised controlled trial of genetic amniocentesis in 4606 low-risk women. *Lancet*, 1(8493): 1287–93.

Thompson, J.R. (1996) *On the Assessment of the Effectiveness of Screening with Application to Pre-School Vision Screening*. Department of Ophthalmology, University of Leicester (internal report).

Tymstra, T. (1986) False positive results in screening tests: experiences of parents of children screened for congenital hypothyroidism, *Family Practice*, 3: 92–6.

Tymstra, T. and Bielman, B. (1987) The psychosocial impact of mass screening for disease, *Family Practice*, 4: 287–90.

Wilson, J.M.G. and Junger, G. (1968) *Principles and Practice of Screening for Disease*, Public Health Papers: 34. Geneva: World Health Organization.

World Health Organization (WHO) (1947) The constitution of the World Health Organization, *WHO Chronicle*, 1: 13.

Wormald, R. (1995) Glaucoma screening, *Journal of Medical Screening*, 2: 109–14.

10

Systematic reviews and meta-analysis

Tim Lancaster, Sasha Shepperd and Chris Silagy

Introduction

Whether planning a research evaluation, or looking for guidance on clinical or policy decisions, it is important to have access to a reliable summary of existing evidence bearing on the issue. Secondary sources, such as review articles and textbooks, are often the most convenient way of accessing the evidence, and it is important that they are not misleading (Mulrow 1987). It is surprising, therefore, that only quite recently has greater attention been given to the science of summarizing research in medicine. Mulrow (1987) showed that most review articles published in major medical journals in the 1980s did not use valid scientific methods. It was rare for them to address focused questions, or describe explicitly the methods by which reviewed studies were identified and summarized. In most there was no way of judging whether adequate attempts had been made to control bias in the selection of studies for review, or to account for random error (the play of chance). In other words, the central scientific principles of primary evaluative research were being ignored when research was synthesized.

There is increasing evidence that this informal approach to research synthesis has been both wasteful and misleading. For example, Antman and colleagues (Antman *et al.* 1992; Lau *et al.* 1992) used systematic methods to identify and summarize evidence about the value of treatments for myocardial infarction. Using the technique of cumulative meta-analysis, in which each new study alters the summary estimate of effectiveness, they went on to show that textbooks and review articles had been failing to recommend treatments of proven value for myocardial infarction (most notably thrombolysis) many years after research had shown their benefit.

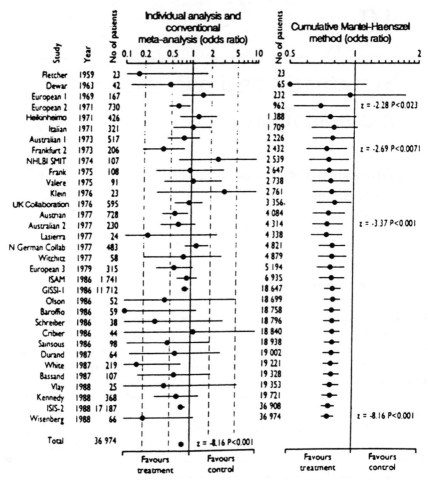

Figure 10.1 Conventional and cumulative meta-analysis of 33 trials of intravenous streptokinase for acute myocardial infarction (Lau *et al.* 1992)

Figure 10.1 shows the results of a cumulative meta-analysis, which gives odds ratios and 95 per cent confidence limits. The left side of the figure shows that treatment was favourable in 25 of the 33 trials (although statistically significant in only six of them). The overall pooled estimate of treatment was significantly in favour of treatment, as is shown on the right hand side of the figure. This systematic review indicated that intravenous streptokinase could have been shown to be a life saving treatment decades prior to its general promotion in medical practice. On the other hand, treatments of no value (for example, prophylactic treatment of arrhythmias) continued to be recommended when there was strong evidence that they were ineffective. Antman and colleagues concluded that a more systematic

---

Problem formulation
• Is the question (of the review) clearly focused?

Study identification
• Is the search for relevant studies thorough?

Study selection
• Are the inclusion criteria appropriate?

Appraisal of studies
• Is the validity of included studies adequately assessed?

Data collection
• Is missing information collected from investigators?

Data synthesis
• How sensitive are the results to changes in the way the review was done?

Interpretation of results
• Do the conclusions follow from the evidence that is reviewed?
• Are recommendations linked to the strength of the evidence?
• Are judgements about preferences explicit?
• If there is no evidence of effect is caution taken not to interpret this as evidence of no effect?
• Are subgroup analyses interpreted cautiously?

Figure 10.2   Checklist for assessing a systematic review (from Oxman 1994)

approach to the summarization of clinical research could have saved thousands of lives (Antman *et al.* 1992; Lau *et al.* 1992).

Although areas of uncertainty and controversy still exist, a number of principles have now been suggested for the better conduct of reviews (Oxman 1994). Figure 10.2 outlines a checklist recommended by Oxman to assess the quality of papers claiming to be systematic reviews of areas of the medical literature (Oxman 1994). Reviews conducted according to these principles are known as systematic reviews, or overviews. Meta-analysis, which may or may not be part of a systematic review, refers to the quantitative synthesis of different studies using specialized statistical techniques. A particular advantage of meta-analysis is that, by increasing the sample size, it can increase the power of existing research to determine the presence or absence of moderate, but clinically significant effects. The techniques of meta-analysis are most well accepted as a method of combining data from randomized trials of medical treatment. They are, however, increasingly applied to observational data, particularly for studying the aetiology of disease. For example, a recent collaborative meta-analysis explored the relationship between use of hormonal contraception and breast cancer, using data from 54 epidemiological studies (Collaborative Group on Hormonal Factors in Breast Cancer 1996).

The number of published meta-analyses is increasing all the time, and the movement to make reviews more scientifically valid has been given considerable impetus by the formation of the Cochrane Collaboration. The aim of this international collaborative effort is to facilitate the preparation, maintenance and dissemination of systematic reviews in all fields of health care (Chalmers *et al.* 1992; Chalmers and Haynes 1994). Already a number of systematic reviews have been published under its auspices. It is therefore increasingly important for those involved in the evaluation of health care to understand the principles underlying systematic reviews. They will need to know them in order to make judgements about the validity of the reviews they read, and in order to prepare proposals for and reports of the primary research they undertake. Whether data are experimental or observational, and whether or not meta-analysis is used, reviews should be approached in the same way as primary research with pre-specified objectives and a formal written protocol. Those who set out to do research without first preparing a formal review of the existing evidence are likely to find it increasingly difficult to get their work funded or published.

Setting objectives

Like any scientific inquiry, reviews should set out to answer a question. A review that sets out to give a narrative account of a disease, or even a whole speciality ('cardiology update') is far less likely to provide clinically useful information than one whose aim is to address a clearly focused objective, or hypothesis. Most questions in medical research can be articulated in four parts (Richardson *et al.* 1995):

1 a patient or problem;
2 an intervention or exposure;
3 the clinical outcomes of interest;
4 a comparison intervention or exposure, when relevant.

For example, we were interested in evaluating methods for helping people stop smoking. Since a wide range of such interventions has been suggested, we decided to undertake a series of reviews of individual interventions. For each review, a general question was formulated. For example, in patients who smoke cigarettes (problem), does nicotine replacement therapy (intervention) lead to greater abstinence from cigarettes (outcome) than conventional care alone (comparison)?

It seemed to make sense to group together different forms of nicotine replacement (gum, transdermal patch, inhaler, nasal spray) because they share a common physiological mechanism. However, we were also interested in whether there were differences in the effectiveness of the different preparations. Other issues also seemed clinically important, such as the

1 The use of NRT is more effective than placebo or 'no NRT' intervention in promoting smoking cessation.
2 4 mg nicotine gum is more effective than 2 mg nicotine gum.
3 The provision of high-intensity support, in addition to the use of NRT, is more effective in producing abstinence than addition of low-intensity support programmes.
4 The effectiveness of the nicotine patch is greater with longer duration of use, with weaning rather than abrupt withdrawal, and with 24-hour patches than with 16-hour patches.
5 NRT is more effective when offered to smokers who are motivated to quit and will, therefore, be more effective in clinical settings which selectively recruit motivated smokers.
6 Increasing the delivery of nicotine replacement by raising the dose of nicotine patch therapy or combining different forms of NRT is more effective than conventional dose monotherapy.

Figure 10.3 Hypotheses to be tested in reviewing the effectiveness of nicotine replacement therapy (NRT)

appropriate level of support for patients using nicotine replacement therapy, or whether nicotine replacement therapy was as effective with general practice patients as with motivated volunteers. We therefore defined a number of specific objectives for the review (Figure 10.3).

Inclusion criteria

In primary research, we expect there to be a clear statement of the methods of the study, and the way in which the subjects were recruited for the research. We use this information to judge whether the results are valid and whether they are applicable to our own setting. We can then avoid wasting reading time on inadequate or irrelevant studies. For example, many clinicians would not bother to read a report of a beneficial new treatment, if the investigators had not allocated the treatment randomly to both the intervention group and a control group (i.e. if they had not undertaken a randomized controlled trial; this methodology is discussed in Chapter 2). The likelihood of a biased result is too high to ensure valid results. Similarly, a general practitioner concerned with helping her patients to stop smoking, might choose to discard a valid study showing that intensive behavioural interventions promoted smoking cessation among motivated volunteers, if she considered that the intervention was too complex to use in a primary care setting.

The same standards should apply to review articles. There should be a clear statement of the criteria by which studies were selected for inclusion in the review. This should include a description of the types of study design

Types of intervention:
- All randomized controlled comparisons of nicotine replacement therapy (including nicotine chewing gum, transdermal nicotine patches, nicotine nasal spray, and nicotine inhalers) versus placebo or no nicotine replacement therapy control.
- Randomized trials of different doses of nicotine replacement therapy were also included.
- In some analyses we categorized the trials into 2 groups depending on the level of additional support provided (low or high). Low-intensity additional support was regarded as part of the provision of routine care. If the duration of time spent with the smoker (including assessment for the trial) exceeded 30 minutes at the initial consultation or the number of further assessment and re-enforcement visits exceeded 2, the level of additional support was categorized as high.

Types of patients:
Smokers of either gender were included irrespective of the setting from which they were recruited and/or their initial level of nicotine dependency. Studies that randomized therapists, rather than smokers, to offer NRT or a control were included providing that the specific aim of the study was to examine the effect of NRT on smoking cessation. Trials that randomized physicians or other therapists to receive an educational intervention, which included encouraging their patients to use NRT, were not included but are being handled as part of a separate review.

Types of outcome measures:
- We confined the review to a comparison of the effects of NRT versus control on smoking cessation, rather than withdrawal symptoms. Trials in which follow-up was of short duration (less than 6 months), or which did not include measurement of smoking cessation, were also excluded.
- In each study the strictest available criteria to define abstinence were used. For example, in studies where biochemical validation of cessation was available, only those participants who met the criteria for biochemically confirmed abstinence were regarded as abstinent. Wherever possible a sustained cessation rate, rather than point prevalence, was used. In trials where patients were lost to follow-up they were regarded as continuing smokers.

Figure 10.4 Inclusion criteria for systematic review of the effectiveness of nicotine replacement therapy

to be considered in the review (methodological criteria). It should also include content criteria – a description of the types of participants, interventions and outcomes that will be considered. The practical value of the review will depend on using good judgement at this stage. Figure 10.4 shows an example of the inclusion criteria that we specified when reviewing the effectiveness of nicotine replacement therapy for helping people to stop smoking (Silagy *et al.* 1996).

Identifying relevant studies

Having decided the inclusion criteria, the next step is to determine an explicit strategy for identifying as many of the relevant studies as possible. Many traditional review articles include no statement of how studies were identified and included. Such an approach may lead to biased conclusions: authors may selectively cite studies that support their own views, or have been previously prominently cited. For example, Ravsnkov showed that studies (Ravnskov 1992) of the effect of cholesterol lowering on heart disease were far more likely to be cited in reviews if they had positive results than if the results were negative. Other biases in selecting research may result from exclusion of studies in journals that are not easily accessible, especially when they are not published in English. Selective publication represents another threat to the validity of research synthesis. Dickersin and colleagues showed that clinical trials yielding positive results were far more likely to be published than those with negative results – apparently because negative studies were less likely to be written up and submitted for publication (Dickersin et al. 1987). The suppression of negative studies, either through failure to cite or to publish, clearly poses a significant threat to the validity of the conclusions of research synthesis.

How can such bias be reduced? All reviews should include a clear description of the strategy used to identify studies. Although there may be practical difficulties in tracking down every relevant study, this strategy should aim to be as comprehensive as possible. At a minimum, it should include a search of relevant electronic databases stating the search terms used. However, it is important to be aware of the limitations of electronic databases. For example, the most widely used medical database, Medline, indexes only a proportion of the available biomedical literature, and important journals may be missed altogether if this is the sole source. Even when journals are available on Medline, it is easy to miss relevant studies. The efficiency of the search can be enhanced by using sensitive search strategies. Even so, a significant proportion of relevant studies will not be retrieved (usually because of the way they were indexed as they entered the database) (Dickersin et al. 1994; Adams et al. 1994).

Other methods for identifying studies are therefore important to supplement an electronic search strategy. These might include searching reference lists of papers identified by electronic searching, hand searching specialist journals, and consulting experts in the field. Valuable information may also be found in 'grey literature', for example as abstracts in conference proceedings, or may even be unpublished. The issue of whether to include unpublished data is controversial. Concern over publication bias has to be weighed against the difficulties in ensuring the quality of unpublished data. Prospective registration of trials in progress may ultimately provide a solution to this difficult problem (Dickersin 1992).

- A computerized literature search on 7 electronic databases (MEDLINE, CAN-CERLIT, PSYCH ABSTRACTS, DISSERTATION ABSTRACTS, HEALTH PLANNING & ADMINISTRATION SOCIAL SCISEARCH, and SMOKING & HEALTH), using the terms (1) SMOKING and (2) SMOKING CESSATION in combination with RANDOMIZED CONTROLLED TRIAL or PROSPECTIVE or RANDOM ALLOCATION or DOUBLE-BLIND METHOD.
- Scrutiny of published reviews, reference lists from clinical trials, conference abstracts (from primary-care meetings and the World Conferences on Tobacco and Health), smoking and health bulletins, and the bibliography on smoking and health.
- Hand searching of two specialist journals.
- Correspondence with pharmaceutical companies to identify unpublished studies.

Figure 10.5 Methods for searching for randomized trials in smoking cessation

Resources may not be available to use all of the available methods. The most important principle is that there is a description of what was done, so that the reader can judge how reliable the search is likely to have been. Figure 10.5 shows an example of the search strategy we used for our review of nicotine replacement therapy.

No gold standard exists to determine whether a search has truly been comprehensive. A description of the strategy used will at least allow the user of the review to decide whether reasonable attempts have been made to track down the evidence in an unbiased fashion.

Data extraction

Having identified the population of studies that will form the data of the review, the next step is to reduce bias in data extraction. Standardized data extraction forms, and systems for entering data and checking for errors, are as important in preparing systematic reviews as they are in primary research. Individuals reading papers may make transcriptional or interpretative errors in reading papers. Thomas Chalmers and colleagues suggested that data extraction should be blinded, and occur in duplicate (Chalmers *et al.* 1987). They suggested a system of differential photocopying. In this method, the methods and results sections of the papers under review are separately copied, and examined by different reviewers. Those assessing the methods are blind to the results, and vice versa. Both are blind to the names and affiliations of the authors.

Not many reviewers have the resources to adopt such a rigorous approach to data extraction. However, it is important that attempts are made to make the extraction of data as reproducible as possible. In our reviews of interventions to promote smoking cessation, two individuals extract data for each review. Disagreements are resolved by discussion or by referral to a third party. Ideally, the results of the review should include a description (and statistical test) of the degree of agreement between the different reviewers.

In the majority of published meta-analyses, tabulated data is extracted from published reports for pooling. A few, however, have attempted to collect individual patient data through cooperation with the investigators on the original studies (Antiplatelet Trialists' Collaboration, 1994). Stewart and Parmar (1993) studied trials of chemotherapy for ovarian cancer. They showed that meta-analyses based on published data over-estimated the effects of treatment in comparison to an analysis based on individual patient data from the same studies (Stewart and Parmar 1993). Publication bias, patient exclusion, length of follow-up, and method of analysis all contributed to this observed difference. They recommended meta-analysis of updated individual patient data as the least biased method of addressing questions not resolved by individual clinical trials. The drawback of this approach is that it is extremely labour-intensive, requiring a major investment of time and money over a number of years. In the foreseeable future, it is likely that such an approach will be possible for a relatively small number of important health problems.

Assessing the validity of studies included in the review

A priori, it seems obvious that studies with strong methodology should be accorded greater weight in a review than studies of poorer quality. An assessment of the validity of the studies included in a review has been recommended as an essential step in the review process (Mulrow 1987; Oxman 1994). It has, however, proved more difficult to determine which aspects of quality are most important. A number of quality scores for clinical trials have been proposed (Chalmers *et al.* 1981; Emerson *et al.* 1990), but it has been difficult to show that these scores are useful for detecting differences in the results obtained. Only one dimension of trial quality has been show empirically to affect the reported effects of treatment. Schulz and colleagues showed that trials that did not contain an adequate description of allocation concealment systematically over-estimated the effects of treatment in comparison to those which did report an adequate method (Schulz *et al.* 1995).

It is therefore unclear how differences in quality should affect the conclusions of a review. The options are to exclude studies that do not meet quality criteria, to weight the statistical analyses by a quality score (Detsky *et al.* 1992), or to perform a 'sensitivity analysis'. In sensitivity analysis, the summary estimate is computed with and without the studies of poorer quality to determine whether their exclusion affects the robustness of the conclusions. At present, sensitivity analysis based on the quality of allocation concealment is probably the strategy with the best evidence to support its validity.

Methods for synthesizing the results of a review

Having identified and assembled data from the individual studies that are the subject of a review, it is important to have some method for synthesizing the results and arriving at an overall conclusion. In traditional review articles, this process is rarely quantitative, and often apparently intuitive.

There are a number of problems with such an approach. First, because it is not explicit, its reproducibility is difficult to determine. It is, of course, perfectly reasonable for individual reviewers to come to different conclusions about the same set of evidence. It is, however, quite unreasonable for the consumer of the review to have no idea of how those judgements were reached. A common error is to use a semi-quantitative 'vote counting' approach in which the reviewer compares the number of 'positive' studies with the number of 'negative' studies (Oxman 1993). With such an approach, a study may be counted as 'positive' in one review and 'negative' in another, depending on how the results are interpreted by the reviewers. There is also a tendency to overlook small but clinically important effects when counting votes, particularly when counting studies with statistically 'nonsignificant' results as 'negative', and to give equal weight to studies of different size and quality.

Increasingly, therefore, systematic reviews include statistical methods to analyse and summarize data. If used appropriately, such methods (meta-analysis) can provide a powerful tool for deriving meaningful conclusions from the data. In evaluating treatment, for example, individual randomized trials may produce false positive or false negative results, usually because of limited sample size. By increasing the sample size, meta-analysis can be particularly useful in detecting moderate, but clinically important, differences between groups, and may be able to address subgroup analyses for which individual trials lacked power. For example, investigators who had run clinical trials of warfarin to prevent stroke in non-rheumatic atrial fibrillation, performed a collaborative meta-analysis of their data (Anon 1994). Although each of the trials was consistent in showing a reduction in risk of stroke with warfarin, individual trials had been too small to determine whether treatment efficacy varied by clinical or demographic characteristics. By combining their data, they were able to answer a number of important questions. For example, they showed clearly that the benefits of treatment were seen equally in women and men and in patients with and without diabetes and hypertension. They were also able to identify a set of clinical characteristics that identified a very low risk of stroke. Further trials to explore these important issues were not feasible because the strong evidence that warfarin was effective rendered further trials including an untreated control unethical. The meta-analysis therefore represented the only chance to answer a number of clinically relevant questions.

Much of the information about the direction of the overall effect can be obtained by visual inspection of the estimated treatment effects and their confidence intervals for each study (Spector and Thompson 1991). There are a number of available statistical methods for obtaining a combined estimate of effect. Their shared characteristic is that they weight the summary estimate according to the inverse of the variance. In other words, larger studies will, in general, contribute more to the summary estimate than smaller studies. The most commonly used methods are the so called 'fixed effect' and 'random effects' method. The fixed effect model is based on the assumption that each study is contributing a different estimate of a single, uniform effect and differences arise by random variation alone. In Peto's method for the fixed effect model (Yusuf et al. 1985), the observed number of events in the treated group is compared with that expected if the treatment had no effect in each study. If the sum of the observed numbers differ systematically from the expected numbers, then there is evidence of an effect of treatment. The overall estimate is expressed as an odds ratio (odds ratio of 1 = no effect). This estimate is usually given with its confidence interval, which indicates the precision of the estimate.

An important issue to consider in meta-analysis is whether there is heterogeneity among the studies reviewed. Heterogeneity refers to differences in results that are greater than can be explained by the play of chance. If differences are not due to chance, then there must be some true difference between the studies. This may reflect differences in quality – that is studies are measuring the same underlying effect, but some are more reliable than others. It may also, reflect true differences between the studies, either in the nature of the intervention, the participants, or the way the outcomes were measured. A frequent complaint about meta-analyses is that they combine 'apples and oranges' (Eysenck 1994, 1995). Eysenck (1994) quotes the example of a meta-analysis of the benefits of psychotherapy (Smith et al. 1980) Eysenck noted that the studies included in the meta-analysis used a range of different methods of psychotherapy (psychodynamic therapy, behaviour therapy, etc.), and consequently that the pooling of data made no sense and the results of the meta-analysis were invalid. Clearly, deciding when to pool data requires judgement. When analysing trials of nicotine replacement therapy we first looked at the pooled estimates for different forms of this treatment. The odds ratios for abstinence from smoking (relative to controls who did not receive the intervention) ranged from 1.65 (with nicotine gum) to 3.05 (with inhaled nicotine). For transdermal patch and nasal spray the odds ratio for abstinence were 1.97 and 2.45 respectively. However, there was no significant difference in the effectiveness of the four types of treatment and no obvious heterogeneity. We therefore considered it reasonable to calculate an overall estimate of the effectiveness of treatments for nicotine replacement. When the abstinence rates for all trials were pooled, according to the longest duration follow up available, 18 per cent of smokers allocated to some form of treatment for nicotine replacement had successfully quit compared with 10 per cent in the control group. This represented a 77 per cent increase in the odds of abstinence with nicotine replacement therapy (95 per cent confidence intervals: 63–92 per cent).

Although there are formal statistical tests for heterogeneity, significant heterogeneity is often obvious from examining visual plots of the results of the different studies. If results are going in opposite directions, with little or no overlap of the confidence intervals around the point estimate, heterogeneity is probably present. There is considerable uncertainty about how best to deal with heterogeneity when it is detected. One suggested approach is to discard the fixed effects model, which assumes no hetero- geneity, and compute a summary statistic using the random effects model (DerSimonian and Laird 1986). This method takes into account between study variance and within study variance (and therefore does not assume a single uniform effect). It usually leads to wider confidence intervals around the summary estimate. A more conservative approach is simply to aban- don any attempt at computing a summary estimate in the presence of significant heterogeneity.

Others argue that heterogeneity should be explored, since it may indic- ate important clinical differences between studies that can yield useful insights (Thompson 1994). The objection to this approach is that interpre- tation is 'post-hoc' (inspired by looking at the data). Such interpretation is therefore prone to the problems inherent in retrospective sub-group analysis (Oxman and Guyatt 1992). If this approach is adopted, it should probably be considered 'hypothesis generating' rather than 'hypothesis testing' (Oxman 1993).

Generally, each study is summarized using a measure of association that represents the within-study comparison of the treatment (exposed) and control groups. In this way patients in each study are only compared with patients in the same study. Occasionally a meta-analysis is published in which an 'effect size' is calculated for each study group based on the dif- ference in outcomes before and after treatment, and groups from different studies are directly compared with each other. The power of randomization is completely lost with this approach, and the data have been reduced to the equivalent of much weaker before-after studies (Oxman 1993).

Since publication bias is such an important threat to the validity of meta- analysis, it may be appropriate to attempt to account for possible bias in the analysis. One method is to do a calculation of the number of unpub- lished studies that would need to exist in the 'file drawer' to overturn the conclusions of the review. Obviously, if this number is very large, it increases our confidence in those conclusions. Another method is to plot the observed effect sizes of the individual sizes against their sample size. This should produce a plot resembling an inverted funnel, with individual studies scattering in a roughly symmetrical fashion around the true underlying value. Gaps in the funnel plot may indicate missing unpublished studies (Egger and Smith 1995).

Conclusions

This chapter has stressed the importance of applying scientific principles to the synthesis of research findings. Although the face validity of this approach is now widely accepted, it is obviously important to determine whether the extra effort involved in this process does indeed lead to more reliable results. It is difficult to be certain that the conclusions of systematic reviews and meta-analysis are closer to the truth, because there is no clear gold standard. Perhaps the closest we have to a gold standard, however, is the 'mega-trial', in which the findings of meta-analysis can be compared to the results of studies enrolling many patients, and following a single protocol. There is increasing evidence that meta-analysis can yield similar results to 'mega-trial'. The most prominent example of this was the use of thrombolytic therapy for myocardial infarction where a large trial (ISIS-2 (Second International Study of Infarct Survival) Collaborative Group 1988) found similar reductions in mortality to those suggested by meta-analysis.

However, a more recent example has given cause for concern about the reliability of meta-analysis. Meta-analysis of trials of intravenous magnesium to prevent death in acute myocardial infarction suggested that this treatment was beneficial. In a very large clinical trial, however, this treatment had no effect (ISIS-4 (Fourth International Study of Infarct Survival) Collaborative Group 1995). Egger and Davey Smith used a funnel plot to suggest that publication bias was the explanation for this discrepancy (Egger and Smith 1995). Meta-analysis may be most suspect when it is based on many small trials, particularly where there is a high likelihood of publication bias.

There is obviously a danger that the use of formal methods for assembling reviews may confer an authority to their conclusions that is not always justified. Those conducting reviews should, of course, be cautious about the conclusions they draw from their work. Meta-analysis, like all research studies, should be viewed with a critical eye. All findings should be provisional and subject to revision as new research is published. It is important to remember that the alternative of informal narrative reviews, frequently driven by expert opinion, is just as likely to be over-interpreted, and the validity of their conclusions far more difficult to judge.

References

Adams, C.E., Power, A., Frederick, K. and Lefebvre, C. (1994) An investigation of the adequacy of MEDLINE searches for randomized controlled trials (RCTs) of the effects of mental health care, *Psychological Medicine*, 24: 741–8.

Anon (1994) Risk factors for stroke and efficacy of antithrombotic therapy in atrial fibrillation. Analysis of pooled data from five randomized controlled trials, *Archives of Internal Medicine*, 154: 1449–57.

Antiplatelet Trialists' Collaboration (1994) Collaborative overview of randomised trials of antiplatelet therapy – I: Prevention of death, myocardial infarction, and stroke by prolonged antiplatelet therapy in various categories of patients, *British Medical Journal*, 308: 81–106.

Antman, E.M., Lau, J., Kupelnick, B., Mosteller, F. and Chalmers, T.C. (1992) A comparison of results of meta-analyses of randomized control trials and recommendations of clinical experts. Treatments for myocardial infarction, *Journal of the American Medical Association*, 268: 240–8.

Chalmers, I., Dickersin, K. and Chalmers, T.C. (1992) Getting to grips with Archie Cochrane's agenda, *British Medical Journal*, 305: 786–8.

Chalmers, I. and Haynes, B. (1994) Reporting, updating, and correcting systematic reviews of the effects of health care, *British Medical Journal*, 309: 862–5.

Chalmers, T.C., Smith, H., Jr., Blackburn, B., Silverman, B., Schroeder, B., Reitman, D. and Ambroz, A. (1981) A method for assessing the quality of a randomized control trial, *Controlled Clinical Trials*, 2: 31–49.

Chalmers, T.C., Levin, H., Sacks, H.S., Reitman, D., Berrier, J. and Nagalingam, R. (1987) Meta-analysis of clinical trials as a scientific discipline. I: Control of bias and comparison with large cooperative trials, *Statistics in Medicine*, 6: 315–28.

Collaborative Group on Hormonal Factors in Breast Cancer (1996) Breast cancer and hormonal contraception: collaborative reanalysis of individual data on 53297 women with breast cancer and 100239 women without breast cancer from 54 epidemiological studies. *Lancet*, 347: 1713–27.

DerSimonian, R. and Laird, N. (1986) Meta-analysis in clinical trials, *Controlled Clinical Trials*, 7: 177–88.

Detsky, A.S., Naylor, C.D., O'Rourke, K., McGeer, A.J. and L'Abbe, K.A. (1992) Incorporating variations in the quality of individual randomized trials into meta-analysis, *Journal of Clinical Epidemiology*, 45: 255–65.

Dickersin, K., Chan, S., Chalmers, T.C., Sacks, H.S. and Smith, H., Jr. (1987) Publication bias and clinical trials, *Controlled Clinical Trials*, 8: 343–53.

Dickersin, K. (1992) Why register clinical trials? – revisited, *Control Clinical Trials*, 13: 170–7.

Dickersin, K., Scherer, R. and Lefebvre, C. (1994) Identifying relevant studies for systematic reviews, *British Medical Journal*, 309: 1286–91.

Egger, M. and Smith, G.D. (1995) Misleading meta-analysis, *British Medical Journal*, 310: 52–754.

Emerson, J.D., Burdick, E., Hoaglin, D.C., Mosteller, F. and Chalmers, T.C. (1990) An empirical study of the possible relation of treatment differences to quality scores in controlled randomized clinical trials, *Control Clinical Trials*, 11: 339–52.

Eysenck, H.J. (1994) Meta-analysis and its problems, *British Medical Journal*, 309: 789–92.

Eysenck, H.J. (1995) Meta-analysis or best evidence synthesis?, *Journal of Evaluation in Clinical Practice*, 1: 29–38.

ISIS-2 (Second International Study of Infarct Survival) Collaborative Group (1988) Randomised trial of intravenous streptokinase, oral aspirin, both, or neither among 17,187 cases of suspected acute myocardial infarction: ISIS-2, *Lancet*, 2: 349–60.

ISIS-4 (Fourth International Study of Infarct Survival) Collaborative Group (1995) ISIS-4: a randomised factorial trial assessing early oral captopril, oral mononitrate, and intravenous magnesium sulphate in 58,050 patients with suspected acute myocardial infarction, *Lancet*, 345: 669–85.

Lau, J., Antman, E.M., Jimenez Silva, J., Kupelnick, B., Mosteller, F. and Chalmers, T.C. (1992) Cumulative meta-analysis of therapeutic trials for myocardial infarction, *New England Journal of Medicine*, 327: 248–54.

Mulrow, C.D. (1987) The medical review article: state of the science, *Annals of Internal Medicine*, 106: 485–8.

Oxman, A.D. (1993) Meta-statistics: Help or hindrance?, *ACP Journal Club*, 118: A-13.

Oxman, A.D. (1994) Checklists for review articles, *British Medical Journal*, 309: 648–51.

Oxman, A.D. and Guyatt, G.H. (1992) A consumer's guide to subgroup analyses, *Annals of Internal Medicine*, 116: 78–84.

Ravnskov, U. (1992) Cholesterol lowering trials in coronary heart disease: frequency of citation and outcome, *British Medical Journal*, 305: 15–19.

Richardson, W.S., Nishikawa, J., Wilson, M.C. and Hayward, R.S. (1995) The well-built clinical question: a key to evidence-based decisions, *ACP Journal Club*, 123: A-12.

Schulz, K.F., Chalmers, I., Hayes, R.J. and Altman, D.G. (1995) Empirical evidence of bias. Dimensions of methodological quality associated with estimates of treatment effects in controlled trials, *Journal of the American Medical Association*, 273: 408–12.

Silagy, C., Mant, D., Fowler, G.H. and Lancaster, T. (1996) The effectiveness of nicotine replacement in smoking cessation, in T. Lancaster, C. Silagy and D. Fullerton (eds) *The Cochrane Library: Tobacco Module of the Cochrane Database of Systematic Reviews, 1996* [updated 4 June 1996]. London: BMJ.

Smith, M., Glass, G. and Miller, T. (1980) *The Benefits of Psychoanalysis*. Baltimore: The Johns Hopkins University Press.

Spector, T.D. and Thompson, S.G. (1991) The potential and limitations of meta-analysis, *Journal of Epidemiology and Community Health*, 45: 89–92.

Stewart, L.A. and Parmar, M.K. (1993) Meta-analysis of the literature or of individual patient data: is there a difference?, *Lancet*, 341: 418–22.

Thompson, S.G. (1994) Why sources of heterogeneity in meta-analysis should be investigated, *British Medical Journal*, 309: 1351–5.

Yusuf, S., Peto, R., Lewis, J., Collins, R. and Sleight, P. (1985) Beta blockade during and after myocardial infarction: an overview of the randomized trials, *Progress in Cardiovascular Disease*, 27: 335–71.

Index

MEASURING HEALTH (2nd edition)
A REVIEW OF QUALITY OF LIFE MEASUREMENT SCALES
Ann Bowling

Reviews of the first edition:

... a useful reference for the increasing number of clinicians who are interested in measuring the effect of their care for patients.

British Journal of General Practice

The book could serve well as an introductory resource for students beginning to investigate research topics in the field of health measurement.

Women and Health

... a useful text, written in a clear style and providing a nice balance of practical information and theoretical background. It is well embellished with concrete examples.

European Journal of Public Health

The coverage of the literature on each scale is thorough and up-to-date, and the organization of the material is clear and logical.

Sociology

This thoroughly revised and updated version of the bestselling book, *Measuring Health*, offers a comprehensive guide to measures of health and functioning, including psychological well-being, emotional well-being, social networks and support. The new edition includes a number of recently developed scales like the increasingly popular Short Form-36 Health Status Questionnaire. Complete with index and list of scale distributors, *Measuring Health* is an essential reference resource for health professionals.

Features:
• Well-known author of two best-selling texts
• Fully revised and updated edition
• New edition has an index and list of scale distributors
• Includes most recently developed and increasingly popular scales.

Contents
The conceptualization of functioning, health and quality of life – Theory of measurement – The measurement of functional ability – Broader measure of health status – Measure of psychological well-being – Measuring social networks and social support – Measure of life satisfaction and morale – Appendix – References – Index.

176pp   0 335 19754 X (Paperback)   0 335 19755 8 (Hardback)

MEASURING DISEASE

Ann Bowling

This book is intended to supplement the author's previous work *Measuring Health: A Review of Quality of Life Measurement Scales*. In assessing the outcomes of disease and treatments, measurement scales must be relevant to their specific effects. Generic health related quality of life, or health status, scales will need to be supplemented with, or replaced by, disease specific items and scales.

Some specialities, particularly in psychiatry and cancer, have made considerable progress in the development of disease specific scales of quality of life. Others still use batteries of single domain and generic measures in the assessment of quality of life. There is now considerable interest in measures which go beyond one dimensional assessments, and which are also highly sensitive to specific disease and treatment effects.

This book reviews disease specific measures of quality of life and, where appropriate, pertinent symptom and single domain scales which are still sometimes used to supplement them. It is intended as a source book for health services researchers, health care professionals, and others who are involved in the measurement of outcome of therapies in relation to broader health status and quality of life.

Contents
Preface – Health-related quality of life: a discussion of the concept, its use and measurement – Cancers – Psychiatric conditions and psychological morbidity – Respiratory conditions – Neurological conditions – Rheumatological conditions – Cardiovascular diseases – Other disease- and condition-specific scales – Comments on measurement issues and sources of information – Appendix: a selection of useful scale distributors and addresses – References – Index.

400pp   0 335 19225 4 (paperback)

EVALUATING HEALTH SERVICES' EFFECTIVENESS
A GUIDE FOR HEALTH PROFESSIONALS, SERVICE MANAGERS AND
POLICY MAKERS

A.S. St Leger, H. Schnieden and J.P. Walsworth-Bell

Resources can never keep pace with the demand for more and better health services.
Health service clinicians, managers and policy makers must make increasingly difficult choices among many options, seeking not only economy and efficiency but
benefit to individual patients and to the community.

This book is aimed at all those involved in planning, carrying out and acting upon
evaluations of health services' effectiveness. It provides an essential and comprehensive guide to the theory, practice and interpretation of evaluation. Throughout
this book, the reader is provided with practical tips, case studies and discussions
of advantages and disadvantages of particular techniques or procedures. While the
authors have based the book on their experiences as practising public health
physicians in the British National Health Service, it is applicable to any kind of
health service – nationalized or private.

> Many books are available on how to conduct research, but there are precious
> few on how to get research translated into policy. This is one of the few and
> I highly recommend it.
>
> (*Nursing Times*)
>
> ... the book should be read by all trainees in health service management and
> public health – and by those who actually look after patients.
>
> (*The Lancet*)

Contents
*Preface – An overview of evaluation – Key concepts and the setting of objectives
– Planning and executing health service evaluation – Using routinely gathered data
to assist in evaluation – Some basic economic concepts and their uses – Descriptive,
testimony, case studies and case-control studies – Intervention studies – Assessing
patient satisfaction – The evaluation of disease prevention services – Technology
assessment – Important methodological issues – making evaluation work – Appendix
A: obtaining data – Appendix B: template for a checklist for the evaluation of
innovatory proposals – References – Further reading.*

224pp   0 335 09356 6 (Paperback)